LOCAL INITIATIVES IN RELOCATION

THE STATE AND NGOs AS PARTNERS?

Local Initiatives in Relocation
The State and NGOs as Partners?
From Research to Action

Maartje van Eerd

IDPAD

MANOHAR
2008

The study was conducted with financial support of the Indo-Dutch Programme on Alternatives in Development (IDPAD)—A Joint Programme on Development Research of the Indian Council of Social Science Research (ICSSR), New Delhi and Science for Global Development (WOTRO), The Hague

First published 2008

ISBN 81-7304-734-0

Published by

Ajay Kumar Jain for
Manohar Publishers & Distributors
4753/23 Ansari Road, Daryaganj
New Delhi 110 002

Typeset at

Digigrafics
New Delhi 110 049

Printed at

Lordson Publishers Pvt. Ltd.
Delhi 110 007

For Kiki and Lotje

Contents

Tables

Illustrations

Preface

This book is about the urban poor in Chennai who were forcefully relocated to the outskirts of the city in the early 1990s. Relocation projects resulting from infrastructural developments in city centres have affected millions of people in India's urban areas. People who were relocated have to restart their lives almost from scratch, although formal housing programmes are sometimes offered to them. The relocatees in Chennai used to live in the city centre, but due to infrastructural development, they were moved to a 'relocation project' at the border of the city. This dissertation describes and analyses the initiatives these relocated slum and pavement dwellers have taken up in order to organize their lives. The initiatives selected for this research are in the areas of housing, access to basic facilities, social security, and all other collective activities. The study also takes a look at the initiatives the government and the NGOs have undertaken to develop the area and improve conditions. The focus of this study is to investigate whether these initiatives can be bettered.

This study originated in an Indo-Dutch Programme on Alternatives in Development (IDPAD) project,[1] a collaboration between the Madras Institute of Development Studies in Chennai (MIDS), India, where my colleague Ajit Menon was working, and Leiden University, where I was employed. Ajit was responsible for a rural study, whereas my study took place in an urban site. When the project was complete, I received a scholarship from the research institute Amsterdam Research Institute for Global Issues and Development Studies (AGIDS) of the Universiteit van Amsterdam and from the Research School CNWS Asian, African and Amerindian Studies of Leiden University to turn my urban part of the study into a Ph.D. thesis.

I have long had special interest in urban poverty and urban development issues, specifically in India. While studying Human Geography, I did my fieldwork in Bangalore in 1994. The topic of that study was gender and labour market fragmentation in the informal recycling sector. I studied the influence of gender on the division of work in wholesale enterprises. I continued to focus on waste collection and recycling even after completing my study, and joined WASTE in Gouda, the Netherlands. I now did a study on occupational health aspects related to waste collection and recycling with a specific case study on India, for which I carried out fieldwork in Delhi, Kolkata and Bangalore. After writing two working documents for WASTE, I was asked to do the IDPAD study, which for me was a great opportunity.

What attracted me most in this study was the central role it attributed to the initiatives, priorities and expectations of poor people themselves. Also, equally important to me was that it tried to analyse whether and how NGOs and the government succeed in addressing the needs of the urban poor, and find ways in which policies and programmes more effectively improve the lives of their people. This study combines theoretical research with applied research, which, while it was still an IDPAD-funded project, tried to give specific recommendations as to how to improve the matching between the government and the NGOs on the one hand and local initiatives on the other.

This study focuses on local initiatives and government and NGO programmes in order to investigate whether these can be matched. Its central question is formulated as follows: can local initiatives and forms of collective organization of the urban poor be matched with the implementation of formal development programmes. If so, how can this be done more effectively? This academic problem has led me to raise the following, more specific, questions: what are the initiatives and forms of collective organization of the urban poor; how do poor urban households perceive policy and implementation with regard to their habitat, and what are their expectations in this respect; what policies have the government and NGOs developed and implemented with regard to relocated urban poor; and finally, whether current initiatives of collective action and government and NGO programmes are accountable, effective, and appropriate.

As the study focuses on government policies and local initiatives, one of the criteria for selecting the study area was that it had to be a site where a policy had recently been implemented, or was still in progress. Chennai, the capital of Tamil Nadu, was selected to be the city where the research would take place as numerous programmes are implemented there. Velacheri was selected to be the specific study area.

The relocation site at Velacheri, called Ambedkar Nagar, used to be part of a tank, located 15 km from the Chennai city centre. It was handed over to the Tamil Nadu Slum Clearance Board (TNSCB) in 1989 which planned the relocation scheme. The development of the site and the construction of shelter units were carried out in phases over a period of four years between 1989 and 1993 and a total of 2,640 households from different localities in Chennai were relocated here.

In order to capture the local initiatives undertaken by the inhabitants of Ambedkar Nagar, to access the policies and programmes undertaken by the government and the NGOs, and to investigate the priorities and expectations of the local community in Ambedkar Nagar, I made use of a variety of research techniques, both quantitative and qualitative, ranging from a rapid urban appraisal, an elaborate household survey which, among other aspects, gave insight into the existence of local initiatives and collective action; case studies on local (collective) initiatives such as chit funds, temple festivals, water provision, housing; and the local slum organization. Furthermore, participatory observation techniques were used, data was collected on government and NGO policies, informal conversations held, and library research undertaken.

Organization of the Book

This book consists of seven chapters organized in the following order: theoretical background, research framework and methodology, empirical findings, and finally conclusions and areas for further research.

Chapter 1 provides an insight into the theoretical concepts that are relevant to this study. It discusses approaches to poverty in general, the livelihood strategies of the poor, and their perceptions of and expectations from the State and the NGOs. It also presents an overview of housing and urban development policies and the role of NGOs. Lastly, it discusses the changing role of the government throughout the last decade and gives insight into emerging trends.

Chapter 2 presents the research framework and methodological procedures used in this study. First, the academic problem and the different research questions and their operationalization are discussed. The scheme of actors and agencies and their relationships is presented and the study area is described, after which the major concepts are made operational. The different research methodologies that were used to gather the data are then presented, after which the limitations and strengths of this study are discussed.

Chapters 3 to 6 discuss the data. Data was collected through different means, as discussed in detail in Chapter 2, including library research, the use of questionnaires, case study research and group discussions.

Chapter 3 presents an overview of the government programmes on relocation and housing, employment, basic services, and social security. In order to get an overview of policy implementation areas, existing gaps and the urban poor's eligibility for programmes, it describes the policies as implemented at the Central, state, and corporate levels. The role of NGOs is also discussed.

Chapter 4 focuses on the relocation project and its inhabitants. It describes the project outline, household characteristics of the inhabitants, and the ways in which the inhabitants of the area obtained land and shelter. Other issues related to housing in the relocation site are also presented.

Chapter 5 describes the role of the government in the provision of employment, basic services, and social security. The initiatives the inhabitants themselves take up in these fields and the role of the NGOs present in the area are likewise examined.

Chapter 6 discusses what is known as local initiatives and local knowledge. A theoretical introduction to the concept of local or grassroots initiatives is followed by case studies describing: chit funds, water distribution, and temple festivals. These case studies are introduced through an overview of relevant theory. Furthermore, the functioning of temples and of a mosque, and the position of local leaders in the area are described.

Chapter 7 presents theoretical and empirical conclusions. Based on the study findings, new areas for research are also suggested.

NOTE

1. IDPAD promotes social science research that is of relevance to development in India and is jointly implemented by the Indian Council for Social Science Research (ICSSR), New Delhi and the Netherlands Foundation for the Advancement of Tropical Research (WOTRO) in The Hague. Our project was part of the fourth phase (project 4.1.7) of IDPAD.

Acknowledgements

The list of people who have made this study and this publication possible is long and countless and I am afraid that I will commit an injustice by omitting someone. However I would like to thank those who played a crucial role.

First of all I am very grateful to the inhabitants of the relocation site Ambedkar Nagar. Talking and listening to them without being able to do something substantial for them while seeing them struggle daily with poverty and difficult circumstances made me at times feel a bit of a voyeur, and I am most grateful to those who were willing to share their thoughts and opinions with me, who provided me with valuable information, and with whom we also had some good laughs from time to time!

I would also like to thank Vijayalakshmi Damodaran, who assisted me in Ambedkar Nagar, and with whom I also had many nice conversations about cultural and personal matters on our many trips up and down to Ambedkar Nagar.

Many thanks are also due to my partner in the IDPAD project Ajit Menon and his wife Uma, who became good friends of Mark and myself. Furthermore, at the Madras Institute of Development Studies I would like to thank Prof. Paul Appasamy, Prof. Nagaraj, Prof. Vaidyanathan, and from the TNSCB; Mrs Vijanthi, Mr Vengadasami, Mr Zafrullah and Mr Rajendran. Also, I would like to thank Mr Menezes and Mr Dattatri for their help and good advice. Thanks also go to Amitabh Kundu of Jawaharlal Nehru University in Delhi whose work has inspired me and I was much honoured that he was willing to be part of the review committee.

In the Netherlands my first word of thanks goes to my promotors Dirk Kolff and Isa Baud. Dirk was my supervisor once I started with the IDPAD project and he convinced me to turn the project report into a dissertation and I am very grateful for his belief in me. Isa has provided me the opportunities to pursue my long term interest for doing research in India. Under her guidance

I started doing research during my Masters, and a lot of research activities have followed since then. This book is a major result of that. I have learned a lot from her.

I would like to thank the following persons who have helped me with my work in one way or the other: Joop de Wit and Hanne de Bruin in particular, and Maarten Bavinck, Dorine Chalifoux, Darlene Hughes, Marijk Huysman (whose lecture on female waste pickers in India was the start of all of this), Darshan Kumari, Carina Mulié, and Edy Mulié of I/O Graph, and Sjoerd de Vos. Also I would like to say thanks to my colleagues at the Institute for Housing and Urban Development Studies (IHS) who have read and commented the proofs, Claudio in particular, and those who helped and advised me in one way or the other.

I would like to express my sincere thanks to the institutes that enabled my research: Amsterdam Research Institute for Global Issues and Development Studies (AGIDS) at the University of Amsterdam and the Research School CNWS of Leiden University. Furthermore, I am very grateful to Indo-Dutch Programme on Alternatives in Development (IDPAD), and Stichting Jo Kolk Studiefonds and Stichting Fonds Doctor Catharine van Tussenbroek for their financial support.

I am especially grateful to ICSSR and IDPAD, and Sanchitta Dutta and Cora Govers in particular, for financing this publication. Thank you all.

I dedicate this book to my daughters Kiki and Lotje, who were both born during the writing of the dissertation.

Maartje van Eerd

Amsterdam
December 2006

Abbreviations

AIADMK	All India Anna Dravida Munnetra Kazhagam, major political party in Tamil Nadu founded by M.G. Ramachandran after splitting from the DMK in 1972; Anna here is short form of Annadurai, the founder of the DMK.
AMPNS	Ambedkar Makkal Podhu Nala Sangam
ASIS	Accelerated Slum Improvement Scheme
BOT	Build-Operate-Transfer
CBO	Community-Based Organization
CCMC	Chennai City Municipal Corporation
CDO	Community Development Officer
CDW	Community Development Wing
CMDA	Chennai Metropolitan Development Authority
CMNMS	Chief Minister's Noon Meal Scheme
CMWSSB	Chennai Metropolitan Water Supply and Sewerage Board
CPI	Consumer Price Index
DMK	Dravida Munnetra Kazhagam, 'association for the emancipation of Dravidians'; a regionalist party created in 1949 by C.N. Annadurai
EIS	Environmental Improvement of Slums
EIUS	Environmental Improvement of Urban Slums
GEMS	George Educational Medical and Charitable Society
HUDCO	Housing and Urban Development Corporation Ltd.
ICDS	Integrated Child Development Scheme
ICSSR	Indian Council for Social Science Research
IDPAD	Indo-Dutch Programme on Alternatives in Development
IDSMT	Integrated Development of Small and Medium Towns

IMF	International Monetary Fund
IRDP	Integrated Rural Development Programme
JJRS	Jhuggi-Jhompri Removal Scheme
MGR	M.G. Ramachandran, popular leader of the AIADMK party
MIDS	Madras Institute of Development Studies
MOUD	Ministry of Urban Development
MRTS	Mass Rapid Transport System
MUDP	Madras Urban Development Programme
NGO	Non-Governmental Organization
NHP	National Housing Policy
NOAPS	National Old Age Pension Scheme
NOC	No Objection Certificate
NRY	Nehru Rozgar Yojana
NSSO	National Sample Survey Organization
PC unit	Public Convenience unit
PCO	Public Call Office
PDS	Public Distribution System
PHA	Public Housing Agency
PPPs	Private-Public Partnerships
PWD	Public Works Department
SEPUP	Self-Employment Programme for the Urban Poor
SHASU	Scheme of Employment through Housing and Shelter Upgradation
SIP	Slum Improvement Programme
SJSRY	Swarna Jayanti Shahari Rozgar Yojana
SPARC	Society for the Promotion of Area Resource Centres
SRP	Slum Reconstruction Programme
S&S	Sites and Services scheme
SUME	Scheme for Urban Micro Enterprises
SUP	Slum Upgradation Programme
SUWE	Scheme of Urban Wage Employment
TINP	Tamil Nadu Integrated Nutrition Programme
TNHB	Tamil Nadu Housing Board
TNSCB	Tamil Nadu Slum Clearance Board
TNUDP	Tamil Nadu Urban Development Project
UBS	Urban Basic Services

UBSP	Urban Basic Services for the Poor
UNCED	United Nations Conference on Environment and Development
UNCHS	United Nations Centre for Human Settlements
UNDP	United Nations Development Programme
UNEP	United Nations Environment Programme
USEP	Urban Self-Employment Programme
UWEP	Urban Wage Employment Programme
WOTRO	The Netherlands Foundation for the Advancement of Tropical Research

Glossary

Abhishekam	Bathing the image of god with water and other prescribed articles
Adi	Fourth month of the Tamil calender, mid-July to mid-August
Aiyappan	Son of the god Siva and the goddess Mohini
Amavasya	Day of the new moon, particularly celebrated in the months of Adi, Purattaci and Tai in honour of the ancestors
	Ambedkar Makkal Podhu Nala Sangam Ambedkar people's social welfare association, local slum organisation in Ambedkar Nagar
Arrack	Locally brewed spirit
Asafoetida	Resin of the root of the *Ferula asafoetida* used as a spice
Atta	Wheat flour
Autorickshaw	Small three-wheeled motorized passenger vehicle
Balwadi	Creche for children in the age of 3-5 years
Beedie	Small, hand-rolled cigarette
Betel-nut	Round hard nut, also called areca-nut
Bindi	Auspicious mark worn on the forehead by women, except by widows. Traditionally it is black for young girls and red for married women. Symbolically it represents the 'eye of Sakti', the eye of destruction which Sakti, the divine female principal, will give to Siva
Bonda	Ball-shaped, deep-fried snack made of potato, lentils and spices
Brinjal	Eggplant

Buttermilk	The liquid left after butter has been churned from milk or cream
Camphor	A volatile aromatic crystalline compound obtained from the wood and bark of the camphor tree
Chittirai	First month of the Tamil calender, mid-April to mid-June
Chittiraipournami	Full moon day in the month Chittirai, a day dedicated to Chitragupta, the accountant of Yama Dharmaraja, the god of death
Cowdung cakes	Cakes made of cowdung used as fuel by the poor
Crore	One crore is 10,000,000
Curd	Yoghurt made of full milk
Cycle-rickshaw	Small three-wheeled passenger cycle
Dal	Pulse; dish made of lentils and, amongst others, garlic, ginger, cumin seeds and turmeric
Dandumariyamman, Mutalamman, Periyapalaiyattar, Sengeniyamman, Kaliyamman and Selliyamman	Other forms of the goddess Mariyamman
Deepavali	Diwali: by far the most favourite festival in India when houses are decorated, lamps are lit and firecrackers are burned
Dhoti	A loincloth worn by men
Dosa	A type of pancake made of a paste of fermented rice and lentils
Drumstick	A type of vegetable
Fish cart	Four-wheeled cart used to carry and display all sorts of articles for sale, from fish to jackfruit to snacks, kitchenware, bangles, etc.
Gruel	Porridge made of boiled rice
Gurukkal	Priest (but not a Brahmin priest)

Hotel	Local restaurant
Idli	Steamed cake made of rice and lentils
Indira Panchayat	In theory meaning the elected council of the Indira group; in practice the local leaders of the Indira group refer to themselves as the Indira Panchayat
Jaggery	Unrefined brown sugar
Jeeragam	Cumin seeds
Kali	Malevolent form of Siva's bride Parvati, personification of death and destruction
Karaham	A jar filled with water, covered with margosa leaves and used in processions where it represents Mariyamman
Kanji	Millet and *ragi* gruel: a staple dish, usually taken to the workers in the field at midday
Kumkum powder	Vermillion powder, used amongst others for putting *bindis*
Kanniyamman	Another form of the goddess Mariyamman
Karu Mariyamman	Black Mariyamman, another form of the goddess Mariyamman. Karu means black, so it might represent the goddess of black clouds, which means rain
Lakh	One lakh is 100,000
Margazhi	Ninth month of the Tamil calender, mid-December to mid-January
Mariyamman	A major goddess for the Scheduled Castes in Tamil Nadu. As this is the spoken form, this is the way it has been spelled throughout the dissertation.
Marundu kuzhambu	Medicinal curry for a young mother who has just delivered her baby, which is said to 'heat up' the body and kill all the infections
Mattupongal	The second day of the Pongal festival where the cows are honoured, decorated and fed (see also Pongal)

Mohini	A female form of the god Vishnu
Muneeswaran	Name of a village god
Murugan	Second son of Siva and a popular deity in south India, especially Tamil Nadu. God of masculine beauty, youth, war and the mountains; he rides a peacock
Nagar panchayat	Town council
Naga Shakti Karu Mariyamman Festival	Festival in honour of 'Black Mariyamman' who possess the power of a cobra
Neem leaf	Leaves from the Neem tree which are used for many purposes including as a base for Ayurvedic medicines, antiseptic soap, moth-balls, tooth paste, and to put on the skin against inflammation
Paisa	A hundredth of a rupee
Pan	Betel-leaf stuffed with lime, betel-nuts and other spices, and tobaccos, according to desire
Panchayat	Elected village council
Panguni uttiram	This festival occurs in Panguni, the twelfth month of the Tamil calender (mid-March to mid-April). The cold season, which prevailed during the preceding two months of Tai and Masi, is supposed to turn into summer from this day
Parvati	Siva's wife
Patta	Land title
Pickles	Preparation of uncooked vegetables like carrots, lemons, mangoes, and eggplant. The preservatives used are oil and salt. There are two varieties: spicy pickles, and sweet pickles
Pongal	A dish made out of rice boiled in milk, oil, lentils and spices; harvest festival, where, on the second day, oxen and cows are given pongal (see also Mattupongal)
Pooja	The act of prayer and making offerings to a divinity, marked by a more or less elaborate ritual

Poramboku	Common land, neither the state nor a private person owns it
Pournami	Full-moon day
Pujari	Priest, never a Brahmin
Ragi	*Eluesine coracana*, a cereal common in south India
Rasam	Dish made from water, tamarind, tomatoes, chillies, coriander, cumin seeds, curry leaves and asafoetida. Believed to be good for digestion
Saivaites	Followers of the god Siva
Samosa	A triangular north-Indian snack made of dough and spiced potato stuffing
Sangam	Association
Sarasvati pooja	An important all-India festival dedicated to the goddess Sarasvati, goddess of knowledge and education
Siva	God of destruction. One of the three main gods of Hinduism beside Vishnu and Brahma
Tai	Tenth month of the Tamil calender, mid-January to mid-February
Tata	Tata is a car manufacturer and a major industrial house
Thallu	Dividend in chit fund procedure
Thandal	Local moneylender
Tiffin	A light midday meal. The box to carry this midday meal in is also referred to as tiffin (box)
Tricycle	Three-wheeled cycle used to carry loads
Turmeric	Yellow spice made of a root
Vada	Deep-fried south-Indian snack made from a base of lentils and spices
Vaishnavites	Followers of Vishnu
Venkateswara	Another name of Vishnu, who dwells in the temple on the top of the Venkata Hills in Tirupathi in southern Andhra Pradesh
Vinayagar	Another name of the god Ganesa (Ganesha)

Vishnu	God of protection. One of the three main gods of Hinduism beside Siva and Brahma
Water women	Women who are responsible for water distribution in Ambedkar Nagar

1

The Urban Poor, the State, and the NGOs

For many decades, housing and urban development policies were formulated and implemented in a top-down manner, without taking into account the perceptions and expectations of their target groups. This resulted in many programmes not reaching the expected population groups, or such projects being utilized by poor households in 'perverse' ways.

'Relevant and sustainable policy-making requires local voices to be heard. Local perceptions and priorities must be listened to and addressed, and participation by beneficiaries at the different levels of policy-making and implementation needs to be ensured' (Chambers, 1998). Incorporating the perceptions and expectations of target groups could make urban housing and development policies more successful in reaching their beneficiaries. Also, at the local level, there often is a multitude of associations (Mitlin, 2001; Moser, 1996, 1998; Eckstein, 1990; Baud, 2000), and matching these local initiatives with government and NGO policies could be beneficial for all actors involved.

It was decided that the study should be undertaken in a relocation site where government (and NGO) policy is ubiquitous. Given that many relocation projects have taken place in Chennai, the state capital of Tamil Nadu, the city was selected for the research.

The central goal of this study is to investigate whether local initiatives and collective organization of the urban poor can be successfully matched with the implementation of formal development programmes. It therefore focuses on initiatives the inhabitants of the relocation site develop in order to improve their lives in the areas of housing, employment, access to urban services, and social security. The initiatives the government, the corporation, and the NGOs undertake in the areas discussed above have been studied in order to investigate whether these initiatives can be better matched.

This chapter will provide insight into the theoretical concepts and discussions of urban poverty, the way households organize around livelihood strategies, and the contribution of self-help, collective action and social movements. The perceptions and expectations of the urban poor are contrasted with the debates on housing and urban development policies, and the role of NGOs. Lastly, the issue of the potential matching of government policies with collective action is discussed.

1.1 Urban Poverty

Since the last decade the debate about the measurement of poverty has lead to the development of two polarized approaches to the issue. First is the conventional approach that identifies income and consumption as the best indicators of poverty.[1] Income poverty is evaluated by measuring income at the household level. Therefore it cannot reveal such inequalities as those based on gender. Income poverty can be measured through use of the poverty line—the critical cut-off in income or consumption below which an individual or household is classified as being poor. Three points need emphasizing with regard to the use of income as an indicator of urban poverty. The first is that a concept of poverty based on income fails to pay sufficient attention to the social and health dimensions of poverty, as well as other forms of deprivation associated with poverty. The second point of critique is that it fails to involve the poor in determining what should be done to reduce poverty; like how people respond to rising prices when, as a reaction, more women and children join the workforce, families break up for work, stress and violence increase, the support system erodes; in other words pressure on the assets grows. The third point is that equating poverty with income level can obscure the underlying causes and miss the extent to which households face other forms of deprivation by adopting strategies to keep their incomes above the poverty line.[2] The most straightforward way to measure income poverty is to calculate the percentage of the population with income or consumption levels below the poverty line—the headcount ratio. However, this method fails to reflect the fact that among poor people there may be wide differences in income levels, with some people located just below the poverty line and others experiencing far greater shortfalls. Another point of critique on the usage of the poverty line as formulated by Chambers (1995b), is that single poverty lines that divide the population into poor and non-poor are often the most inaccurate because they simplify and standardize what is complex and varied.[3] Other poverty measures take into account the distance of poor people from the poverty line (poverty gap), the degree of income inequality among poor people (squared poverty gap) and expenditure.

The newer, alternative approach acknowledges that poverty is not merely due to lack of income and employment but rather due to a combination of factors. It is multidimensional and is not only encompassed by low levels of income and consumption, but also low achievements in education and health, as well as vulnerability and exposure to risks and voicelessness and powerlessness.[4] Besides, in the conventional method of measuring poverty the poor are labelled as poor by outsiders and not according to their own standards.[5] This understanding has led to a new approach, namely the participatory approach which uses multiple, subjective indicators of poverty status that emerge out of the experience of the poor collected through participatory techniques.[6] New concepts in the poverty debate include vulnerabilities and capabilities, with policies focusing on assets and entitlements. Capturing the multidimensional aspects of changing socio-economic well-being in poor communities requires identification of both levels of poverty and types of vulnerability, which are not the same.[7] Because poverty measures are generally fixed in time, poverty is essentially a static concept. In contrast, vulnerability is more dynamic and better captures change processes as people move in and out of poverty.[8] Vulnerabilities in the urban areas are:

a. *Urban environmental and health risks*: This includes problems like pollution, and water and food contamination.
b. *Vulnerability arising from commercial exchange:* In general, cities are characterized by a greater degree of commercialization than rural areas and often the urban poor need to pay for basic items such as water. Furthermore, they live in illegal settlements, which makes them vulnerable to eviction. Also, many of them work in the informal sector without any security or are unemployed and face increasing education fees.
c. *Social diversity, fragmentation and crime:* Community and inter-household mechanisms of trust can be weakened by greater social and economic heterogeneity, associated with wider distributional ranges of incomes, opportunities, and access to infrastructure, services, and political influence in the urban areas. Furthermore drug and alcohol abuse, AIDS, domestic violence, female depression and family breakdown, while not exclusive to urban areas, have all been associated with urban poverty.
d. *Vulnerability arising from intervention of the State and police:* While government policies can have an important positive impact on poverty alleviation, many poor people experience the State in negative ways—as an oppressive bureaucracy which attempts to regulate their activities without understanding their needs,[9] or as corrupt policemen demanding money in order to turn a blind eye to illicit income-generating activities rather than as servants of the public.[10]

Analysing vulnerability involves identifying not only the threat but also the resilience, or responsiveness, in exploiting opportunities, and in resisting or recovering from the negative effects of a changing environment. The means of resistance are the assets and entitlements that individuals, households, or communities can mobilize and manage in the face of hardship. Vulnerability is therefore closely linked to asset ownership. The more assets people have, the less vulnerable they are. Conversely, the greater the erosion of people's assets, the greater their insecurity.[11] The major assets (or capital as De Haan[12] calls it) the urban poor have and try to use as effectively as possible are:

a. *Human assets or capital:* Labour, health, skills, experience, knowledge, creativity, inventiveness, and household relations.
b. *Natural assets or capital:*[13] Land, water, and energy.
c. *Productive assets or physical capital:* Housing, tools, and machinery.
d. *Financial assets or capital:* Money, loans or credit.
e. *Social assets or capital:* Reciprocity within communities and between households based on trust deriving from social ties. The extent to which a community can be considered an asset that reduces vulnerability or increases opportunities depends on its stock of social capital.[14]

McLeod (2001) has defined two more assets:

f. *Institutional, or political assets/capital:* This includes organized forms, relationships and processes specifically developed by the poor to increase their capacity to escape from poverty. This concept incorporates relationships that facilitate access to, and influence on, the structures and procedures that constitute the external policy and regulatory environment in which organizations of the urban poor operate. In effect this form of asset constitutes the political base for the organizational influence of the urban poor. Votes are another political asset of the poor.
g. *Knowledge assets or capital:* The institutional knowledge created by the poor is a form of capital that has a significant role to play in the negotiation of partnerships and in the formation of collaborative arrangements with the State and with formal financial institutions. The production and collation of information by the poor about the informal settlements where they live provides a basic example. A more complex example is provided by the capacity of the urban poor to share learning and experience locally, nationally, and internationally through exchanges and dialogue, a capacity that has been enhanced by the use of new information technologies that allow almost immediate sharing of information. It is this asset

base that also constitutes the anchor for the development of the institutional (political) capital discussed above.[15]

1.1.1 LIVELIHOOD STRATEGIES[16]

Households aim at a livelihood that has high resilience and low sensitivity to shocks and stress.[17] Livelihood strategies are the combination of survival strategies that households use and which focus on increasing the assets across the following domains:

1. Livelihood and employment.
2. Health and well-being.
3. Habitat and environment.
4. Social networks and political power.[18]

Each of the realms covers a continuum of different themes. Livelihood and employment strategies can range from self-provisioning through work in the family micro-enterprise, subcontracted piecework or disguised wage work to wage employment.[19] Health and well-being covers issues of education, health, safety and personal/family services.[20] Habitat and environment encompasses housing and land tenure, obtaining water and fuel, solid waste disposal, community infrastructure and outdoor pollution. The social networks range from neighbourliness and reciprocal assistance to community organizations, extra-community NGO linkages to social movements and political mobilization.[21] The relative importance given to each of the four realms can change over time and when the situation in the household changes. The way households allocate their assets or capitals through a process of household decision-making to different realms of urban life has been studied extensively, both in urban as in rural contexts under the headings of 'survival strategies', 'livelihood strategies', and more recently, 'sustainable livelihoods'.[22] Studying livelihood strategies is studying 'the way in which people make themselves a living using their capabilities and their tangible and intangible assets'.[23]

There are many reasons why the urban poor allocate their assets in the different realms of life. The livelihood approach is most often limited to the household.[24] McLeod (2001) recently pointed out that the level of institutions established by the urban poor for valuing, developing, applying and leveraging their asset base offers a more adequate consideration of their resource base for the development process. Analysing the way the poor deploy their social capital should then be widened to the analysis of capitals created in collective action.[25]

1.1.2 SELF-HELP, COLLECTIVE ACTION, AND SOCIAL MOVEMENTS

Households are actively engaged in many types and scales of association, the key ones of which include the household itself, the extended family, neighbours and neighbourhoods, religious associations, and patron-client relations. A wide array of studies reveals the many ways through which social relationships create communal systems of exchange based not on market relations but on principles of reciprocity and redistribution, which are embedded in the dynamics of culture and cultural change.[26] Examples are neighbours watching over each other's children, borrowing of small amounts of money and household goods. Among smaller clusters of households, cooperation can include pooling money to form rotating credit arrangements that allow households periodically to obtain larger sums of money than they could on their own.[27] This is also called self-help, which is defined as 'any voluntary action undertaken by an individual or a group of persons, which aims at the satisfaction of individual or collective needs or aspirations'. The distinctive feature of a self-help initiative or activity is the substantial contribution made from the individual's or group's own resources in terms of labour, capital, land and/or entrepreneurial skills. A self-help organization is a membership organization, which implies that its risks, costs and benefits are shared among its members on an equitable basis and that its leadership and/or manager is liable to be called to account by the membership for his/her deeds.[28] A critical note should be placed here as the term 'membership organization' implies these are based on formal arrangements whereas in many cases self-help organizations are very informal. Therefore, instead of speaking of a self-help organization, the term self-help group is preferred, as it emphasizes the informal character. It is also debatable whether, as suggested by Verhagen, the risks and benefits of joining such an organization or group, are shared by all. The research will address this issue.

Mitlin (2001) has analysed numerous case studies of local organizations, which in these studies are also known as grassroots organizations, residents' associations, community organizations, self-help groups and so on, in low-income urban settlements. According to her, these studies suggest that in many settlements there may be a multitude of local associations and that the presence of some form of grassroots organization is the norm rather than the exception. Among the more common factors instigating and then supporting grassroots organizations, as she concludes from the literature, are kinship, ethnicity, trade union involvement, city-based federations, NGOs, religious organizations, political parties, and the private sector. She found that groups could be catalysed by need to secure land, resist eviction, provide themselves with water, manage savings and credit, and a host of other functions.[29] Religious aspirations are not mentioned in these studies but they most probably also play a role. Eckstein (1990) underlines that collective action by poor households in urban areas is widespread, especially in organizing shelter, basic services, employment and security, and occurs without government assistance.[30] She states that it is most likely to occur and achieve goals in settings in which people have a sharpened sense of shared destiny.[31] Desai (1995) has stated that groups with a consciousness of common purpose are likely to form organizations.[32] And according to Baud (2000), under certain conditions, collective action can include a wider variety of views and interests when partners identify strong common interests, promoting a collective identity beyond local divisions; this happens in particular cases where the whole community is threatened from outside.[33] The World Bank report 'Can Anyone Hear Us' also found that informal networks and associations of poor people are common both in rural and urban communities and that in the absence of State resources, they are funded by the poor themselves as critical for their survival.[34] Dia mentions that what he calls 'indigenous institutions' are 'anchored in local culture and values can count on the sound pillars of legitimacy, accountability and self-enforcement. They have a strong hold on people's commitment, dedication and sense of identity'.[35]

Even though different authors have given many examples of collective action, there are also many constraints that hinder the development of collective action. Some of these constraints are social stratification. In contrast to older studies on collective action which emphasize the homogeneous character of communities, current approaches recognize that people have multiple identities, and identify with more than one community.[36] Communities are not necessarily harmonious as there are numerous social divisions and conflicting interests—between men and women, young and old, leaders and inhabitants.[37] De Wit (1989; 1993) found that in the slums he studied in Chennai,[38] the organizations were unable to unite the slum dwellers on a horizontal class-basis. According to him this is due to the persistence of vertical clientelist relations.[39] Other constraints include dependence on the market for much of the household consumption, which demands involvement in the search for wage work, thereby eroding reciprocal and redistributive relations, and the insecurity of land and other resources.[40] Poor people themselves also recognize the limits of their networks as many of these do not transcend community boundaries and rarely enter the political domain. Furthermore, the World Bank report 'Can Anyone Hear Us' found that there are important differences between men's and women's networks. Men are more embedded in formal patron-client relations, whereas women lacking access to formal systems invest heavily in social relations with other women both for social solidarity and for informal sharing of limited resources.[41]

Mitlin (2001) states: 'we need to recognize that the impact of grassroots organizations on poverty may not always be positive. Grassroots organizations do not necessarily assist in the reduction of urban poverty and vulnerability nor in the consolidation of social capital.' The nature of relationships in the grassroots organizations, together with the low levels of participation suggest that they may be limited in their capacity to reduce symptoms of urban poverty (such as the exclusion from access to basic services) as well as to address some of the more structural causes that result in a lack of empowerment and powerlessness.[42] Given that grassroots organizations do not always make decisions according to consensus, or to principles of democratic and equity-oriented decision-making[43] it is debatable whether they always represent the local community, or whether they represent only a minority. Devas et al. (2001) mention that many grassroots organizations even act to reinforce patterns of inequality and social exclusion, and that these organizations are often dominated by men, particularly men of higher status and/or higher income.[44] Another negative aspect of grassroots organizations Dia (1996) mentions is that they are often inflexible to changes.[45]

Much has been written on the so-called collective action. Della Porte and Diani (1999) identify four dominant perspectives in the analysis of collective movements: collective behaviour; resource mobilization; political process; and new social movements.[46] The perspective of collective behaviour defined collective action as behaviour concerned with change. The perspective of resource mobilization analyses collective movements as an extension of the conventional forms of political action in which the actors engage in a rational way, where movements are part of the normal political process. In the political process perspective, a rational view of collective action is also found; however, this approach pays more systematic attention to the political and institutional environment in which social movements operate.[47] The last perspective is the new social movements perspective. New social movements cut across class lines, work with high levels of autonomy from the State, and have at times achieved significant global impact. This in contrast to the 'traditional' social movements, which draw on wide constituencies, but essentially develop conflicts along the lines of social class. New social movements, however, encompass protest across social classes, lobbying and pressurizing government agencies over development and social issues, and tend to be organized on an ad-hoc basis.[48] In other words, while the objective of social movements—perhaps more aptly called 'political movements'—is the capture of State power, new social movements are issue-based and often content to influence policy or resolve specific circumstances. Urban social movements in the developing world tend to be formed around basic issues of survival and struggles to gain access to the basics of collective action, and less around broader issues such as State power and the basic underlying economic structures.[49] Furthermore, Olson (1965) argued that although individuals have a common interest in a collective good, each has a separate, individual interest of contributing as little as possible and often nothing to group formation and collective good attainment. They enjoy the benefit and let others pay the cost. These tendencies dominate in large populations.

Sometimes 'grassroots organizations' are referred to as new social movements.[50] Ghosh (1995) defines these 'grassroots organizations' as 'movements involving people at the local level, asserting democratic rights and ideals, initiating self-help programmes, fighting injustice, making authorities yield to their demands, and in the process, emerging as a political force in the area'.[51] Examples include the women's liberation movements, the ecological protest groups, the peace and civil rights movement, community organizations, and regional separatist movements.

Schuurman and van Naerssen (1989) do not make the distinction between new social movements and traditional social movements and have a more practical approach towards collective action of the poor in developing countries. According to them, urban social movements have as their basic aim the improvement of the quality of individual and collective consumption within marginalized local spaces. In many cities in the third world, the urban poor unite with the aim of improving their physical environment and neighbourhood organizations try to influence urban policy in order to obtain land rights and access to infrastructural services. When they organize themselves in broad-based associations, the possibility for an urban social movement arises. Schuurman and van Naerssen define an urban social movement as 'a social organization with a territorial-based identity, which strives for emancipation by way of collective action'.[52] The adjective 'new' is used to indicate that these movements are not organized along traditional lines, like for instance social class, and that they have their own rules concerning the international organization and decision-making process, carrying grassroots participation high in their banner.[53] On the part of deprived city-dwellers striving for structural change in power relations and/or dominant values, urban social movements are movements of collective action and organization and they are different from political parties as they stress non-institutional means. Of crucial importance to the success of collective action for the poor is how resources (or assets) such as time, money, organizational and other skills can be mobilized by the movement. But it has been pointed out that deprived groups are 'barely able to spontaneously organize and sustain collective action for the development of a (social) movement because they lack these resources and/or skills' and therefore participation by a supporting elite is a necessary resource.[54]

This study will focus on the impact of relocation on the life of the urban poor and the ways in which they respond to this relocation. I will analyse both the capital the urban poor have, and how poor individuals and households deploy their capital, as well as what capital is created and used by collective action while the relocated people are surviving in their new living environment. I will study the way in which they allocate their assets in the four realms of urban life mentioned by Douglass and Zoghlin (1994).[55] These realms are highly interlinked as relocation affects not only habitat and environment but, as will be discussed later in this study, also work, livelihood, health, well-being, and social networks.

1.2 Perceptions and Expectations of the Poor

According to Chambers (1998), 'relevant and sustainable policy making requires local voices to be heard'. He states that local perceptions and priorities must be listened to and addressed, and participation by 'beneficiaries' needs to be ensured early and meaningfully in decision-making at policy, programme and project levels.[56] As discussed before, in the last decade a new understanding about urban poverty has developed, where the poor themselves, through the use of participatory methods, have been involved in defining poverty. This new concept implies that poverty is not defined solely in terms of income or consumption but also encompasses deprivation and insecurity. Secondly, any attempt to place monetary values on these aspects of personal, household and social deprivation involves so many arbitrary assumptions that they are likely to be meaningless. Thirdly, those defined as poor in consumption terms may not include all deprived and vulnerable households and individuals.[57] The information collected from the poor themselves provides policy makers with useful information on priorities of the poor, ways of addressing, framing or presenting anti-poverty programmes so that they are more effective, as well as intervention strategies that represent ways of helping the poor escape poverty.[58]

Responses of the urban poor on relocation and development policies can be studied by analysing individual and collective initiatives of asset building, which is one aspect of this study. Another, more direct way, which is also used in this study is by discussing local priorities and perceptions on relocation and development in general as formulated by the poor themselves, in order to identify the ways in which these policies can be adjusted better to the priorities and expectations of the poor, in order to build up their assets. Apart from the World Bank 'Voices of the Poor' study, which will be discussed below, not many so-called 'perception studies' have been undertaken on priorities and opinions of the poor on development issues like housing, relocation and basic services. A literature review of consultations with the poor is also provided.

'Voices of the Poor' is a World Bank project (2000) undertaken for the *World Development Report 2000/01* on poverty and development. The purpose of the study was to enable a wide range of poor people in diverse countries and conditions to share their views in such a way that they could inform and contribute to the concepts and contents of the *World Development Report 2000/01*. The major conclusions linking to this study are:

1. The poor view well-being holistically, including both material and psychological dimensions.

2. Insecurity has increased, violence is on the rise, and the poor feel they have been bypassed by new economic opportunities.
3. Gender inequity is widespread, domestic violence is pervasive, and gender relations are stressed.
4. The poor want government institutions to be more accountable to them, and corruption emerges as a key poverty issue.
5. NGOs are seen as important but many of them are unaccountable to the poor.
6. The poor rely on informal networks and local institutions to survive.[59]

One important aspect related to this study as mentioned by the poor themselves in the World Bank report is their exclusion from participation in decision-making and an unequal sharing of benefits from government programmes, as well as from those of NGOs. Organizations of the poor are therefore critically important if the poor are to influence decision-making at the local, national, or global levels.[60] The obstacle in organizing themselves is, according to the poor themselves, social fragmentation within their communities.[61]

For the 'Voices of the Poor' study, country-specific documents have been made. The study on India was conducted in 1999 in Bihar, the poorest state in India, and Andhra Pradesh, a state with better-organized government and NGO programme to eradicate poverty. It included two urban sites, two semi-urban sites, and six rural sites. The main findings and conclusions relevant for this study are:

1. The poor have their own mechanism for surviving extreme crises and supports extended to them by government have mostly brought about short-term relief.
2. Homogeneity along class lines appears to be the rallying factor of community dynamics.
3. Government support for elevating the status of the poor has been concentrated in the area of infrastructure provision, but maintenance of government services remains poor. Besides, the poor hardly have any role in the maintenance

of those services, or any inclination to contribute to their maintenance.

4. Disillusionment with the *status quo* appeared to be a prominent state of mind for the poor, driven by high levels of livelihood insecurity.
5. The role of local collectives like self-help groups, committees and panchayats is very important in improving the quality of life of the poor.

An overall conclusion was that there is a need for reforms in the way development services are managed. 'Enhancing the participation of the poor in determining priorities for interventions and facilitating accumulation of more social capital towards maintenance of services and institutions can have significant bearings on the lives of the poor. The greatest bearings have been the increases in self-esteem and confidence levels of the poor in their struggle for survival.'[62]

When asked about the role of the state and the way the poor experience the State, many declared it ineffective, irrelevant, and corrupt. While they appreciated the importance of government-provided services, corruption was experienced by the poor in every sphere of life. They also perceived as problematic the lack of information, as well as the institutional practices which reflect gender norms, and make it difficult for women and girls to get access to State-provided services. This is due to the fact that many government programmes target the head of household, thereby limiting access by women.

Moore et al. (1998) performed a literature survey on poor people's perceptions of poverty, and one of the conclusions was that not much information was available. Even so, there is a fairly standard core of correlates of poverty that are mentioned regularly by poor rural agrarian populations. These include lack of assets (land, housing, equipment); nature of other income sources (wage employment); living standards (food intake, children not attending school); and demographic/labour variables (large number of children, sickness).[63] Another conclusion was that narrow (material) poverty is far from being the only or the dominant problem for poor rural and urban Asians; there are many other issues at hand. For this study, the issues of importance that are raised about the non-material causes and dimensions of deprivation in Asia are: insecurity and uncertainty about future livelihoods that arises in relation to labour markets, etc., and poor access to government, education, health, credit and other public services.[64] Furthermore, there are causes that arise directly from patterns of social relationships which include: the oppressiveness of public officials, including the police and the urban authorities that threaten to evict people from residential properties to which they have no secure rights; gender inequality; lack of physical security; and poor people's stress on respect and self-respect.[65]

The Bangladesh Human Development Report (1998) has, among others, looked at the perceptions of needs of the poor and grouped them into four main requirements: household food security—quantity, and for slightly better-off households also quality, of food; access to services ranging from health care to credit, safe drinking water, sanitation, infrastructure and assistance from NGOs; asset creation (which covers a wide range of issues but the main priority is housing); and security of assets (the need for justice as many poor do not know their rights and when they do, they do not have the money or social standing to gain access to justice).[66]

Sanyal and Mukhija (2001) have described a case in Mumbai, India, where different stakeholders were involved in housing delivery and where the NGO SPARC (Society for the Promotion of Area Resource Centres) became involved in conflicts between the other stakeholders including private actors, government agencies, and even community groups. One of the findings of the case study showed how perceptions on the design of a relocation scheme for the poor were interpreted without consultation of those households, leading to misconceptions and conflict.

1.3 Housing and Urban Development Policies

The housing problems of particularly the urban poor have long been ignored and many national plans of developing countries failed to mention housing until the 1960s. Housing was also seen as an unproductive economic activity that would only drain national resources and provide no returns. The initial reaction in the 1950s and 1960s, when governments started to realize the emerging problems of slum and squatter colonies was one of removal and reconstruction. In both cases, it meant demolition of the 'unfit' huts and construction of 'proper' houses elsewhere.[67] This approach had limited success and resulted in the relocation of large numbers of urban residents to urban fringe areas or to other regions of the country.[68] Following a more positive view of Turner and Mangin, from the 1970s onwards, self-help became accepted in State-aided sites-and-services and related *in situ* slum upgrading schemes. They argued that the poor were just as rational as the middle- and upper-income classes in terms of their responses to a situation, but that the squatter shack, which had been viewed by Oscar Lewis as an evidence of social malaise, was in fact a rational step on the way to self-improvement. Turner argued strongly that if the poor could be given security of tenure for a plot of land in a favourable location, then through progressive improvement, a squatter shack would be transformed into a respectable house and would represent the savings of the particular family.[69] Besides, it was obviously more efficient to improve existing settlements and provide them with infrastructure than to produce new ones from scratch, and to supply serviced land for self-help housing than to merely watch uncontrolled slum proliferation. Among various international organizations, the World Bank promoted the use of aided self-help in low-income housing. This marked another phase; a period of mixed success and failure due to, amongst other reasons, the fact that many slum upgrading and sites-and-services programmes of the 1970s and 1980s did not take the land issues into consideration. So many of the improved settlements were and still are technically illegal. Besides, many sites-and-services schemes were carried out in remote areas where only the people without any choice agreed to live.[70]

In the years 1986-96 (and beyond) a fundamental review of housing and urban policy was started. Until 1986, there existed a project-by-project approach to housing and urban policy; after 1986, there was a change to housing policy and urban sector economic and social development and self-help became a part of a more complex package of policies in land development, finance and economic development. In 1989, the UNCHS published the 'new agenda', which for housing contained some important redirection, and the World Bank converted the ideas into a practical programme. Whereas in the early 1980s World Bank housing policies had been based upon neo-liberalist user-pay principles, by 1990 many international organizations accepted some targeted subsidies in housing for the poorest people. The opinion on the role of the government also changed. Enablement was understood to mean retaining government responsibilities for the performance of the housing sector, but not directly providing it. Provision was the responsibility of the market, NGOs, CBOs and household self-help; but government would have important roles in policy making, in providing some housing-related resources, and in undertaking institutionally loaded reform. It was underlined that housing was much wider and deeper than only shelter. The United Nations Conference on Environment and Development (UNCED) in Rio de Janeiro in 1992, also known as the 'Earth Summit', and the Agenda 21 of the conference stated that all countries needed to address their urban development needs with explicit consideration of the environment. Another important aspect of the evolution of urban and housing policies was the re-elevation of poverty in the agenda of issues. Over the last few years there has been increasing concern with infrastructure, in particular water supply, sewerage disposal and drainage, as many of the cities in developing countries are enormously undersupplied.[71] Housing is no longer seen as an isolated matter and therefore an integrated approach is stressed on, in order to develop sustainable settlements with sufficient infrastructure and services. Also, there is a growing concern with the poor state of public transport, the lack of sufficient means of transportation in terms of quantity and quality, and the rapidly increasing use of private motorized vehicles, which have resulted in chaotic traffic situations. Urban sprawl has produced massive traffic movements daily, and the largely uncontrolled utilization of heavily polluting vehicles contributes to substantial air pollution.[72] But the question remains whether this concern for urban development has actually resulted in the creation of successful approaches.

Relocation[73]

When settlements are for instance located on the borders of rivers, or on tracks needed for the construction of infrastructure, relocation seems unavoidable. Forced displacement results from the need to build infrastructure for new industries, irrigation, transportation, highways, power generation, or for urban developments such as hospitals, schools and airports. During the last two decades of the previous century, the magnitude of forced population displacements caused by development programmes was to the order of 10 million people each year, or over some 200 million people globally over that period.[74] This study will be limited to urban relocation. Cernea (1993b) has listed the following major causes for urban relocation:

1. *Urban economic growth:* Cities are becoming engines of national growth at a pace faster than anticipated earlier. Industrial manufacturing and service activities that benefit from the economics of agglomeration increase massively and diversify. Relocation is used to make room for new industrial estates, transportation corridors, economic ancillary activities, or for other infrastructural equipment entailed by economic growth and population agglomeration.
2. *Environmental improvements:* The anarchic spatial and demographic expansion of urban settlements has far outgrown the capacities for supplying drinking water and energy, for waste disposal and sewerage, for sanitation, etc., leading to snowballing deterioration of the environment. Relocation, temporary or permanent, is caused by the need to make room for structural and infrastructural equipment for environmental services, health facilities, water supply systems, and others, and to insert them into already densely inhabited downtown or residential areas.
3. *Slum upgrading:* Social policies aimed at poverty alleviation and quality of life improvement arrive at a point where they must address slum conditions head on, and change them. Sometimes, slum areas can rarely be upgraded without population movement.

4. *Non-urban programmes:* Certain non-urban development projects infringe upon existing urban settlements, requiring their integral or partial relocation.[75]

Over the last two decades, the State rationale for, and approaches to, slum relocation has changed repeatedly. In the 1940s and 1950s, the policy that prevailed relied on a negative rationale: slum and squatter settlements are an eyesore to the larger community, which justified and rationalized eviction. In fact, governments often did not hesitate to resort to brutal means to evict the inhabitants. The second trend, essentially developed during the 1960s, put forth a broader approach towards urban planning and management, arguing less that the slum and squatter dwellers had no rights and more that they occupied potentially valuable land or that their settlement blocked desired changes in the planning of the city. It became more common for public agencies to make provisions for relocation when they proposed to remove a squatter community. During the 1970s and 1980s, the gradual move away from indiscriminate slum displacements and towards reducing the number of displaces continued with the introduction of the so-called 'urban renewal' programmes. This meant that in some instances the policy of total relocation was abandoned in favour of slum improvement/squatter upgrading approaches, with only partial relocation in order to lower population density. Government agencies shifted gradually from a role of 'providers' and producers of finished dwellings to a role of 'enablers'. This consisted, on the one hand, of using site-and-services approaches to support those relocated to peripheral areas, and on the other hand using urban renewal approaches to support on-site improvements for the remaining dwellers.[76] The major impoverishment risks related to displacement as recognized in several studies on relocation are:[77]

1. *Landlessness:* Unless the land basis of people's productive systems is reconstructed elsewhere, or replaced with steady income-generating employment, landlessness sets in and the affected families become impoverished.
2. *Joblessness:* Many of the urban poor are located in inner city slums as opportunities to earn a living are more promising and the proximity to sources of livelihood is

essential for survival of the poor in the city.[78] Therefore, when they are relocated it often means loss of jobs because, as already mentioned, income earning possibilities in many relocation sites are scarce, especially for women.

3. *Homelessness:* Loss of a family's individual home and loss of a group's cultural space tend to result in alienation and status-deprivation. For refugees, 'homelessness' and 'placelessness' are intrinsic by definition.
4. *Marginalization:* This occurs when families lose economic power and spiral on a 'downward mobility' path. Middle-income farm households do not become landless, they become small landholders; small shopkeepers and craftsmen downsize and slip below poverty thresholds. Many individuals cannot use their earlier acquired skills at the new location; human capital is lost or rendered inactive or obsolete. Besides, the cost of living can be higher in the relocation sites when compared to the city centre as was observed in a relocation site in Bangalore. Furthermore, those who lack legal titles to their shelters and house plots are often regarded as ineligible for compensation or alternative housing. Tenants are also ineligible for these even though they may not be able to find equally affordable tenancy arrangements elsewhere. Economic marginalization is often accompanied by social and psychological marginalization, as expressed in a drop in social status, in resettlers' loss of confidence in society and in themselves, a feeling of injustice, and deepened vulnerability. The coercive character of displacement and the victimization of resettlers tend to depreciate the resettlers' self-image, and host communities often perceive them as a socially degrading stigma.
5. *Food insecurity and a decline in health:* Forced uprooting increases the risk that people will fall into temporary or chronic undernourishment, defined as calorie protein intake levels below the minimum necessary for normal growth and work. Other effects resulting from displacement-caused social stress are insecurity, psychological trauma, and the outbreak of relocation-related illnesses, particularly parasitic and vector-born diseases, as unsafe water supply and

poor sewerage systems increase vulnerability to epidemics and chronic diarrhoeas, dysentery, etc.

6. *Loss of access to common property and services:* For poor people, particularly for the landless and assetless, loss of access to the common property assets that belonged to the relocated communities (pastures, forested lands, water bodies, etc.) results in significant deterioration in income and livelihood levels. Typically, governments do not compensate losses of common property assets. These losses are compounded by loss of access to common public services such as schools. Also, the distance from market and education facilities is a major burden on women and children in particular.
7. *Social disarticulation:* Forced displacement tears apart the existing social fabric. It disperses and fragments communities, dismantles patterns of social organization and interpersonal ties; and scatters kinship groups. Life-sustaining informal networks of reciprocal help, local voluntary associations, and self-organized mutual service are disrupted. This is a net loss of valuable 'social capital' that compounds the loss of natural, physical, and human capital. The social capital lost through social disarticulation is typically unperceived and uncompensated by the programmes causing it, and this real loss has long-term consequences.
8. *Risks to host populations:* Host populations are a major actor with a stake in good resettlement, particularly in the case of mass displacements by either development programmes or conflicts.

Relocation to the places far away from the cities is not accepted by the 'beneficiaries' and has to be forced on them at high economic, social, and political costs. Moreover, it is not sustainable as many of the affected families return to the city, often to their original site.[79] A UNCHS report (1991) lists few general characteristics of relocation sites in many cities in the developing world:

1. Many relocation sites were placed in bad-quality areas, as good-quality land was very scarce, and therefore expensive.

A number of relocation sites were found to be prone to flooding because the land was low-lying.

2. Most relocation sites were placed in remote locations, varying from a couple to several dozens of kilometres from the inner city.
3. In most relocation projects, few opportunities for obtaining an income were provided or existed nearby.

The main conclusion of the UNCHS report was that relocation was 'almost always a disruptive experience causing considerable social and economic hardship for the poor of the inner city'. This reality caused the World Bank in 1988 to adopt the following policy guidelines in projects that they finance: that 'whenever feasible, involuntary resettlement must be avoided or minimized, and alternative development solutions must be explored'.[80] But where it is unavoidable, the report mentions that sufficient resources including the assistance of NGOs and community-based organizations must be used to ensure that the urban poor do not suffer from the process. Besides, in those cases it is vital that sufficient protection and support be built in to ensure that people can improve their lives through the process, rather than suffer over often-extended periods.[81] How it is determined whether and when it is feasible to relocate and who will decide what is sufficient is not elaborated upon.

Another important aspect is the way in which the target group is being informed about the relocation. In heavily politicized societies people are vulnerable to unscrupulous slum leaders; this vulnerability is sometimes reinforced when the news concerning relocation is not communicated in a direct way but via the representatives of the community.[82] Furthermore, all groups affected by the relocation should be allowed to participate in all stages of the project (design, implementation and monitoring).[83]

1.4 The Role of NGOs

Throughout the 1970s and 1980s, development professionals began to acknowledge the contribution of NGOs, with particular emphasis on the ability of the organizations to work directly with the poor and with grassroots organizations.[84] The 1980s and 1990s were characterized by a reduction of the role of the State in virtually every area (as described later in this chapter). In general, the ideology was that the private sector should take over State functions wherever possible, moving from a State allocation system to one based on markets. At the same time, short-term recession extended into longer-term economic difficulties for many countries.[85] NGOs grew in scale. Participation was welcomed as a new opportunity for cost recovery. Rather overshadowed by these economic factors was the continuing recognition of the need for greater participation of the poor themselves in development projects, in order to achieve greater local ownership.[86]

There are many types of NGOs. They can be defined as 'groups and institutions that are entirely or largely independent of government and characterized primarily by humanitarian or cooperative, rather than commercial objectives'.[87] They differ enormously in size, geographical spread or scale of operations, orientation, ideology, ownership, objectives, strategy, financial resources, relations with their beneficiaries and the government and in activities as well.[88] In most countries, there are dozens of NGOs involved in urban projects; in many there are hundreds. In regard to cities, three roles have been identified for NGOs:

1. Enablers (i.e. community developers, organizers or consultants) alongside community-based organizations.
2. Mediators between the people and authorities controlling access to resources, goods and services.
3. Advisers to comment on policy changes and to increase local access to resources and greater freedom to use them in locally determined ways.[89]

NGOs have emerged as critical intermediary institutions supporting citizens' organizations in obtaining access to resources and in negotiating with local government and other State institutions. In some cases, they may also negotiate with the private sector on behalf of the citizens. Many NGOs have developed innovative ways to support disadvantaged groups. Some of the most important research on urban problems and potential solutions in developing countries has been undertaken by NGOs (like for instance the Centre for Science and Environment in New Delhi). The work of NGOs is sometimes controversial. It often centres on demands for social change, perhaps inevitably if a major part of NGOs' work involves demanding a fairer price deal for low-income or disadvantaged groups. Many NGOs whose main work is implementing projects have been criticized for their lack of accountability. At an international level, NGOs campaign and lobby to influence governments and international organizations.[90]

Devas et al. (2001) mention that despite the high expectations of NGOs, they have not been a major significance in poverty reduction due to four reasons:

1. Some NGOs are simply business ventures with no real interest in serving the poor.
2. NGO programmes are almost universally small and in most cases without any clear strategies for multiplication.
3. Opportunities for policy change may be passed by because of poor link between operational activities and advocacy. Hence, even when NGOs are successful in project activities, these activities may not be multiplied.
4. NGOs themselves may have weak links with communities, tense relationships with community leaders and little capacity to organize and support the poorest citizens.[91]

Mitlin (2001) has listed the difficulties related to the relationship between NGOs and local organizations:

1. NGOs may impose their agendas on some of the local self-help organizations with which they are working.
2. NGOs may be insensitive to political power struggles within the community, failing to work effectively with existing organizations and/or failing to transform them into more representative organizations.
3. NGOs are overactive, undertaking most of the activities themselves, with the consequence that the abilities and skills of local organizations are not developed.

According to Mitlin, taken together, these concerns suggest that NGO staff may be reluctant to delegate power and responsibility to local residents. As a consequence, they may be failing to strengthen independent and capable agencies.[92]

In the World Bank report 'Can Anyone Hear Us', the poor

indicated that the NGOs have become important providers of basic services and charity in the absence of State services and where they are present they are often praised as the only groups concerned about poor people.[93] In many places NGOs are clearly more trusted by the poor than the government. Even so, researchers have found many examples of ineffectiveness, irrelevance, and favouritism amongst NGOs.

1.5 Matching Government Policies with Collective Action

The role of the government in developing countries from the 1950s until now has changed considerably. Initially the State was perceived as being the ruling actor and its role was to provide its citizens with all the basic needs, illustrated by the first paradigm in Table 1.1. But during the economic crisis of the 1980s, it

TABLE 1.1: EVOLUTION OF THE PLANNING PROCESS IN THE TWENTIETH CENTURY

	Nature of Planning	*Planning Techniques*	*Predominance in Planning*	*Division of Power*	*Assumed Nature of Relations*
First paradigm	Fixed version of future ('blueprint')	Master plans, zoning	State planners	Government	Common consensus exists
Second paradigm	Flexible vision and specific action	Structure plans, action plans, special development areas	Public-private partnerships	Government with private sector	Common consensus has to be created
Third paradigm	No fixed version	Above techniques with participatory planning	Negotiation forums	Government, private sector and civil society	Conflict needs negotiation

Source: Jenkins and Smith, 2001: 25.

became clear that the State failed to provide. In urban areas it had failed to provide adequate housing, basic physical and social urban services or employment opportunities. Gradually the perception of the role of the State shifted from 'provider' to 'enabler'[94]; i.e. the government should set the framework to enable others—the poor themselves, the private sector or others such as NGOs, or civil society organizations—to provide the services,[95] illustrated by the second paradigm in Table 1.1. Participation was welcomed as a new opportunity for cost-recovery.[96] Over the last two decades, the process of urban governance in the developing world has been shaped by three major trends: decentralization of responsibilities from the central to the local level, privatization of State assets and public utilities, and an attempt to increase participation by sharing the planning process.[97] Rather overshadowed by these economic factors was a continuing recognition of the need for greater participation of the poor themselves in development projects, in order to achieve greater local ownership.[98] The third paradigm in Table 1.1 is based on collaborative consensus building rather than on competitive interest bargaining, thus embedding planning practise in its social context. This planning paradigm is still in the development and planning stage in the US and Europe, and evidence of its practise is still thin on the ground.[99] The evolution of planning in the twentieth century is illustrated in Table 1.1.

In the process of urban governance there are different stakeholders.[100] According to Devas (1999), they can be subdivided into four groups, namely:

1. *Households and individuals.*
2. *NGOs, community-based organizations and civil society organizations:* Internationally connected NGOs, formal civil society organizations like trade unions, churches and other religious organizations, political parties, and local community-based organizations.
3. *The government:* Central government, municipal government, development corporations or authorities, locally based central government agencies (e.g. district commissioners, police), traditional authorities (e.g. chiefs) and State-owned public utilities.

4. *Businesses:* Local, national and international formal sector and informal sector.[101]

The assets and vulnerabilities of the urban poor have already been discussed in Section 1.1. In analysing the space for matching local initiatives with State policies, the assets of that State have also to be formulated. Gonzales et al. (2000) distinguish the following capital of the government sector:

1. *Physical capital:* Financial, technological and material resources which are expressed in budget allocation and infrastructure.
2. *Organizational capital:* Human resources, capacity to manage, management structure, leadership and training, which are expressed in formal linkaging and coordination both vertical and horizontal, the bureaucratic structure, creation of rules, procedures and directives.
3. *Political capital:* Power, authority, law making, influence and legitimacy (and the law itself, of course).
4. *Intellectual capital:* Knowledge or know-how; mastery of relevant laws, policies and institutional context; technical expertise on specific subjects.
5. *Socio-cultural capital:* Government ideals, values and ideology, civic mindedness.[102]

Dia (1996) in his analyses of the disconnect between what he calls 'informal indigenous institutions' and institutions rooted in the region's history and culture on the one hand, and formal institutions mostly transplanted from outside on the other hand, says that because these formal institutions are not rooted in local culture they 'fail to command society's loyalty or trigger local ownership'. According to him, both these phenomena are important catalysts for sustainability and enforcement.[103]

1.5.1 COMMUNITY PARTICIPATION IN DEVELOPMENT PROGRAMMES

The concept of participation of local target groups in urban governance can certainly not be claimed as new. Conventionally, however, this participation has meant direct participation by small groups in well-defined activities, generally confined to specific development projects and the delivery of urban services. These two areas encompass slum-improvement related projects, the provision of community-level infrastructure facilities as well as employment programmes, and social and environmental services. Organizations like the World Bank have often used the concept of community participation in urban projects. But attempts at capacity building, empowerment, and participation in the actual decision-making have been only modest.[104]

Dia (1996) pays attention to the cultural aspects of community participation: 'If there is considerable pressure within the community for strict adherence to traditional, socially acceptable behaviour, individuals may be reluctant to adopt innovations that tend to alienate them from the group. (. . .) In such a setting, it may be necessary to adopt 'extension methods' that make the group, rather than individuals, the focal contact point.'[105]

Indian experiences in participatory governance are at best weak and fragmented. According to Mehta (1999), community participation in development projects is the most widespread form of participation in urban governance to be found in India, and it relates mostly to the urban environment, encompassing water, sanitation and solid waste management, and several urban community development programmes and employment programmes. These programmes are meant to be participatory, at least on paper, but in reality many of them lack any form of participation.[106]

TABLE 1.2: LEVELS OF PARTICIPATION IN DEVELOPMENT PROGRAMMES

Level of Participation (in Descending Order)	*Participation in Practise*
Empowerment	This may take the form of community members having a majority of seats or genuine specified powers in formal decision-making bodies over a particular project or programme involving community participation, when municipal authorities are unable or unwilling to

contd.

TABLE 1.2 (contd.)

	undertake improvements themselves. Communities are expected to initiate their own improvements, possibly with the assistance of outside organizations such as NGOs. These possibilities of actually controlling the situation and making allies, with governmental support, constitute the main characteristics of empowerment.
Partnership	Members of the community and outside decision makers and planners agree to share planning and decision-making responsibilities about development projects involving community participation through such structures as joint policy boards, planning committees and eventually other informal mechanisms for resolving problems and conflicts.
Conciliation	Conciliation occurs when the government devises solutions that are ratified by the people.
Dissimulation	In order to achieve a semblance of participation, people are placed on rubber-stamp advisory committees or boards. The express purpose is educating them, or more frequently, engineering their support.
Diplomacy	The government, for lack of interest, lack of financial resources or for incompetence, is likely to expect the community itself to make the necessary improvements, usually with the assistance of an outside organization. When there is a possibility that the community by itself accomplishes real improvements or when NGOs are involved, the government may change its attitude, frequently for tactical reasons, providing limited amounts of aid.
Informing	This consists of a one-way flow of information from officials to the community, or their rights, responsibilities and options, without allowance for feedback or negotiation, in projects that have already been developed.

contd.

TABLE 1.2 (contd.)

Conspiracy	No participation in the formal decision-making process is allowed or even considered, as the government often rejects any idea of helping the poor.
Self-management	Self-management takes place when the government does nothing to solve local problems and the members of the community, by themselves, plan improvements to their neighbourhood and actually control the projects.

Source: Arnstein, 1969 and Choguill, 1996: 435-41.

As mentioned above, community participation has often meant direct participation by small groups in specific development programmes and in the delivery of urban services. It is seen as a means to enable people to get, through mutual-help initiatives and possibly with outside help, the basic necessities that otherwise would not be available to them. In a ladder developed by Arnstein (1969), community participation is seen as a means for the poor to influence decisions in the political arena about issues that affect them.

As can be seen in Figure 1.1 in the fortunate case of supportive governments, initiatives may lead to one of the three levels of

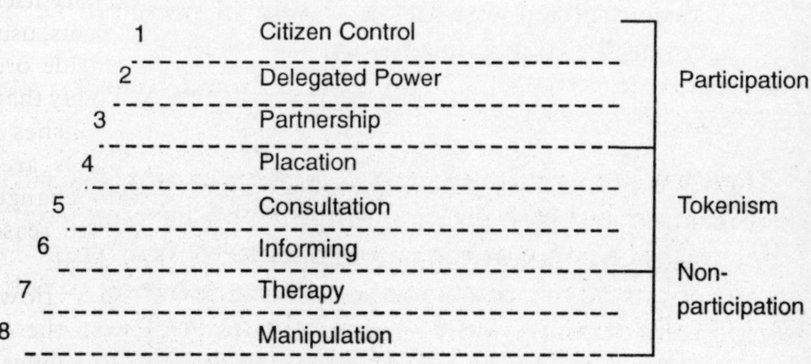

Source: Arnstein, 1969.

FIGURE 1.1: A LADDER OF COMMUNITY PARTICIPATION FOR UNDERDEVELOPED COUNTRIES

participation, depending on the degree of governmental willingness and/or confidence in the community's ability to contribute to its own improvements and of the residents' ability to initiate activities themselves or with the support of outside agencies. At the next four levels of participation, the government tries to control community participation. At the conspiracy level, the poor are seen as an inopportune and unwelcome group to be eradicated at any cost. This usually manifests as destructive governmental top-down projects. And in the last rung of the ladder, when rejection is manifested as governmental disregard or neglect, self-management emerges as a reaction of the poor to their situation.

1.5.2 PARTICIPATION THROUGH DECENTRALIZATION

As already explained, during the 1980s concern grew about the inability of many governments to deliver development programmes to their people at the local level. Decentralization was thought to be the alternative way to address poverty. The reasons why so many countries have adopted decentralization strategies are:

1. Decentralization can ensure an efficient response to the variation in demand.
2. Services that are locally financed and provided can be produced at lower costs.
3. A decentralized institution should in principle be more accountable to its constituents.
4. Many local services can be combined, which reduces costs.[107]

There has been a rising interest in decentralization also because liberalization and globalization in the 1990s have undercut the scope for governance at the national level.[108] As a result, many organizations advocate democracy, decentralization of administration and planning, more responsibility for local communities, and increased involvement of civil society, including non-governmental organizations and popular movements.[109] Decentralization has therefore become a standard approach to addressing urban service and urban development needs. The vast majority of developing countries at least claim to have a decentralization agenda, and donor agencies are funding many decentralization programmes.[110] There are four major variants of decentralization:

1. Deconcentration, or the transfer of functions, but not power, from a central unit to a local administrative office. This is one of the 'weakest' forms of decentralization and has become a common response by higher levels of government to deflect the blame for inadequate service provision from central to local authorities.
2. Delegation, which involves, in most cases, the transfer of certain powers to agencies closely related to the central state. While these agencies have certain autonomy in day-to-day management, ultimately, government controls them.
3. Devolution is considered by some as real decentralization, since power and functions are actually transferred to sub-national political entities, which, in turn, have real autonomy in many important respects.
4. Privatization, which involves the transfer of responsibility for certain state functions to private groups or companies.[111]

Decentralization is not a new idea in India. The ancient Indian village is described as an autonomous republic where the panchayat governed the affairs of the village. It was usually assumed to have once been a democratically constituted body, its members being chosen by the people. But these self-governing institutions appear to have disintegrated over time. In order to provide a more comprehensive decentralized and democratic administrative set-up for rural development, a three-tier Panchayati Raj system was introduced during the late 1950s in various States in India.[112] Recognizing the importance of community participation in urban governance and development, the Government of India in 1992 passed the 74th Constitutional Amendment, which relates to decentralizing urban governance to a newly created layer of urban local bodies. Similar to the 73rd Amendment relating to rural governance,[113] the Act declares that the state government should delegate more powers to the municipalities in the areas of urban planning, regulation of land use and construction of buildings, planning for social and economic development, water supply, and slum improvement and upgradation.[114] The 74th Amendment also provides for 'ward committees' at the local levels in municipal bodies with a population exceeding 300,000.[115] The members of these ward committees are directly elected from and by the ward population. One-third of the elected members are to be women, while a certain fixed number of membership is reserved for people belonging to the Scheduled Castes and Scheduled Tribes.[116] All the members of the ward committee are nominated. They comprise all the municipal councillors from within the territorial area of the committee and other prominent members of the society. They are nominated by the chairperson of the committee, the municipal council, the state government or a combination thereof. The functions of the ward committee include identification of problems and priorities of the ward, supervision of the municipal works, planning and undertaking development activities, convening annual general meetings, submission of administrative and financial reports and resolutions adopted by the municipality.[117] At the community level, participation is stimulated through the help of local NGOs.[118] Two other important aspects of the 74th- (as well as the 73rd) Amendment are the regular conduct of elections and limited period of supersession and the arrangements for adequacy of finance through fiscal review, assignment of revenue authorities and fiscal transfers.

The 74th Amendment specifies the categorization of urban areas to be limited to three: transitional urban areas will have town councils, or nagar panchayats; smaller urban areas would have municipal councils; and larger urban areas would be covered by municipal corporations. The state governments would decide the criteria for different types of municipal institutions.[119]

One of the weaknesses of the decentralization efforts is that many urban development authorities and other functional agencies continue to operate outside the framework of the local bodies and remain answerable only to the State, and not to the people.[120] Also, the Amendment Act provides for devolution of financial resources to ward committees, but there are understandable fears based on past experience about money transfers to the decentralized rural local bodies,[121] as well as the knowledge that municipal finance is very poor in almost all Indian municipalities.[122] Therefore, a further dependence on Central Government subsidies is expected, which raises doubts regarding the actual devolution of powers.[123] An even more critical question is whether ward committees can be expected to be effective in alleviating urban poverty, which is a complex, multi-faceted, deep-rooted problem with economic, social, gender, and cultural aspects.[124] Another point of criticism is that decentralization does not always lead to the desired participation of marginalized sections of society. Empirical research has shown that decentralization can reinforce vested interest in existing patterns of patronage if there is no synergy between local government, civil society, and an active Central Government that is committed to support the mass of the local people in the struggle against local power-holders.[125] At the end all decentralization programmes are top-down measures. The question is whether any of them create the conditions in which local initiatives may fruitfully develop.

An interesting case for this study is the comprehensive decentralization programme in the state of Kerala as described by Véron (2001). This programme, which is described below, encourages comprehensive citizen participation in decision-making and in project implementation. Even though here democratic decentralization has explicitly included environmental goals, the process of citizen participation in the planning, decision-making, and implementation can be of use for this study.

In August 1996 the newly constituted Kerala State Planning Board launched the 'people's planning campaign' for initiating decentralized planning, and it trained voluntary resource persons to assist the local bodies. This 'planning from below' started in September 1996 with 14,147 meetings at the ward level in Kerala's 991 village panchayats. In these meetings, more than two million people expressed their felt needs and discussed their local development problems. To complement these discussions, development volunteers carried out participatory rapid appraisals and organized village development seminars. On the basis of this information, selected voluntary experts and ward representatives identified the main problems and drafted panchayat development reports, which contained socio-economic and environmental assessment. Based on these general reports, project proposals were drafted by local officials, voluntary experts and resource persons. The elected representatives, often people with little education and heavy time constraints, were trained and assisted to prioritise the project proposals and draft the local plan document. Even then, most projects showed little qualitative difference to earlier projects, although there were some important exceptions. The lessons that can be learned from this model for community-based sustainable development are the following: 1. Community participation has received mixed results. Decentralization does not ensure empowerment and village development plans may not fairly reflect the concerns of marginalized voices. 2. Decentralized planning created a new space for committed government officials and social activists. The panchayat gives local government officers and development volunteers the institutional frame to mediate between different groups and propose innovative new institutions. 3. The priorities of scientists and activists are often not the same as those of the local people, and 4. Village development plans made by local bodies are likely to neglect spatial externalities as well as temporal externalities. Therefore, these plans require coordination at higher levels, and some sort of top-down planning.[126]

Although this is an interesting case study, the main question, which is also raised in the conclusion, is whether the voices of all groups in the village were heard and listened to. It is doubtful whether the poorest and marginalized people attended meetings and were selected as representatives. If we return to the ladder of community participation as formulated by Arnstein (1969), the New Kerala Model can be categorized as a 'partnership'.[127]

1.5.3 PARTNERSHIPS

It is becoming increasingly clear that governments acting alone cannot meet the continually growing demand for water, waste management, and energy demand. Governments are finding that their tax revenues are not providing sufficient resources to meet these needs, and official development assistance has not been able to fill the gap. Since the 1980s, the World Bank and the International Monetary Fund (IMF) have strongly promoted a neo-liberal paradigm. The new truth is that the private sector would implement urban development policies more efficiently and effectively than the public sector. Therefore, government should move away from direct provision of services and limit itself to setting the regulatory framework for private companies. This has been called the 'enabling approach'.[128] Public-private partnerships are one of the most promising forms of such collaboration in that through these partnerships the advantages of the private sector—innovation, access to finance, knowledge of technologies, managerial efficiency, and entrepreneurial spirit—are combined with the social responsibility, environmental awareness, and local knowledge of the public sector, in an effort to solve urban problems.[129]

The distinguishing features of a partnership are:

1. It involves two or more actors.
2. It refers to a more or less enduring relationship between the actors based on a written or verbal agreement.
3. The relationship is mutually beneficial, without assuming equality between actors.
4. It finds expression in concrete, physical activities.
5. It contributes either directly or indirectly to a public goal.[130]

Three common types of partnership are:

1. Those between government and the private sector companies.
2. Those between communities and the private sector.
3. Those between community-based organizations, NGOs and local government.[131]

Another type of partnership is:

4. Those between international donors and the government.

The five most common types of public-private partnerships for the provision of water and waste services are the following:

1. *Operation, maintenance and service contracts:* Under such contract the public sector essentially hires a private organization to carry out one or more specific tasks or services for a period of five to seven years. The public sector remains the primary provider of the infrastructure service and only contracts out portions of its operation to the private organization. The private sector must perform the service at the agreed upon cost and must typically meet performance standards set by the public sector. Examples are the provision of water distribution services and waste collection.

2. *Build-operate-transfer (BOT) contracts:* BOT contracts are designed to bring private investment into the construction of new infrastructure plants. Under a BOT, the private sector finances, builds, and operates a new infrastructure facility or system according to performance standards set by the government. The government retains ownership of the infrastructure facilities and becomes both the customer and the regulator of the service. Governments generally issue BOT contracts for the construction of specific infrastructure facilities such as drinking water or waste-water treatment plants, waste transfer stations and waste disposal stations
3. *Concessions:* Under a concession, the government awards the private contractor (concessionaire) full responsibility for the delivery of infrastructure services in a specified area, including all related operation, maintenance, collection and management activities. In essence, the public sector's role shifts from being the provider of the service to the regulator of its price and quantity. Contracts are usually awarded for time periods of over 25 years. In the waste sector the government might award a concession to build and run a recycling or waste-to-energy facility. In the water sector, a concession might entail the full provision of water services for a designated geographic area.
4. *Joint ventures:* Under a joint venture, the public and private sector partners can either form a new company or assume joint ownership of an existing company that provides urban infrastructure services. In either case, it is essential that the company be independent of the municipality. Under a joint venture, the government is the ultimate regulator, but it is also an active shareholder in the operating company.
5. *Community-based provision:* Community-based provision starts when financial limitations prevent the government from providing adequate water and waste services to sections of the population, forcing these residents to rely on their own means of serving their needs. Community-based providers might include individuals, families or local micro-enterprises. In many cities, however, where local governments, and/or NGOs have recognized, organized, and

assisted these informal groups, service has improved. Many poor residents make their living through community-based solid waste management as, for instance, door-to-door collectors, waste pickers, or traders and dealers in waste materials. In the water sector, community-based providers might buy water in bulk from the local utility and sell it in their community in buckets. They might also install 'group taps' to provide service to households. Other options include 'communal water point service' where households install metered taps off the main system and regulate their own water use, paying the bill collectively.[132]

There is another form of partnership which consists of an arrangement between households and the private sector, not involving the government at all, for instance in slum improvement, or water, sanitation and drainage provision.[133] Such 'unplanned privatization' occurs widely in cities, especially in those areas where local governments exclude unauthorized settlements from basic provision, which leaves local inhabitants to their own devices.[134]

Let us now return to Dia (1996). He talks about the 'disconnect' between formal and informal institutions. He states that 'formal institutions need to be adapted to the local context in order to build the legitimacy needed for enforceability; informal institutions, although rooted in local culture, also need to adapt to the changing outside world to maintain their relevance in a more challenging and competitive global arena'. In order to improve their 'matching', which he calls 'reconciliation', he has identified three major requirements for what he calls 'successful implementation of the reconciliation paradigm'. The first is the need for a new, genuinely participatory process that focuses on building convergence between formal and informal institutions and on empowering beneficiaries and local communities. The second requirement is a new communications system that ensures access and voice for a larger number of beneficiaries and stakeholders who are quasi-illiterate. The third requirement is a stable institutional and political environment.[135]

In India, partnerships for service delivery are established. In some cases, local governments are not able to provide many of the services for all of its citizens. In such situations, partnership arrangements with NGOs or the private sector may improve the coverage or effectiveness of services.[136] These partnerships involving two or more actors working together are increasingly seen as an effective way to manage urban development.[137] In Bangalore, for instance, the municipal corporation has privatized part of its solid waste collection, in an arrangement whereby the corporation provides financial support and the private contractor provides the labour, transport, and disposal services.[138] In Chennai, the Chennai City Municipal Corporation has hired a private company for waste collection in three of the ten zones, for a fixed period of seven years, which started in March 2000. Different types of public-NGO and community alliances are also found in the city. The corporation decided to introduce a new alliance between the public sector, the private sector, and the community under the Clean and Green Madras City project, whose main aim was to help rehabilitate street children by paying them through NGOs to take care of cleaning and maintenance of the streets. Another example is Exnora International, a community-based voluntary organization which has created a community-private alliance. When the corporation introduced neighbourhood waste containers, Exnora took the responsibility of making sure the system would work. It has incorporated local rag pickers for sweeping and collecting, and named them Street Beautifiers. It has obtained a bank loan, bought tricycle carts for the Beautifiers' activities, and provided them protective clothing and equipment. The collected garbage is segregated and all the materials are sold to dealers for recycling. The households pay the minimal amounts per month required for the street service, and a street unit collects funds for the Street Beautifiers' salaries, repayment of the bank loan, and to build-up a reserve fund against defaults.[139]

According to Lee (1998), reorienting the conventional method of State-delivered infrastructure and services to an alternative community-based approach in Asia however, requires the development of readily available funding as well as technical and legal assistance to individuals, households, and communities.[140] This implies the need for intermediary institutions which can provide funding and technical support to community-level initiatives on a continuing basis. Lee (1998) states that there is a limit to self-help or community-based schemes, and that external intermediary institutions are needed to provide support to communities in mobilizing internal resources and gaining access to outside inputs that enhance their capacities to improve their living conditions.[141]

An example of a partnership between an international donor and the government is the Sustainable Chennai Programme. Chennai was selected as one of the cities to join in the Sustainable Cities Programme, a worldwide initiative established in 1990 and focusing on the stimulation of local participation and decentralized sustainable development. The Sustainable Cities Programme is a joint initiative of UN–Habitat and UNEP. The worldwide programme works towards developing a sustainable urban environment, building capacities in urban environmental planning and management and promoting broad-based participation.[142] The Chennai Metropolitan Development Authority (CMDA) is the implementing agency for the project. The Sustainable Chennai Project started in 1994 and the three-year term ended in 1997, but was extended up to October 1998. UNDP provided Rs. 2 crore as grant funds, which were mainly used for technical consultancy.[143] The following issues were prioritized for Chennai better liquid waste management and improvement of waterways; reduction of traffic congestion and improving the air quality; improving solid waste management in the poor and suburban areas of the city.[144]

One of the ideas behind the Sustainable Cities Programme is that the community itself should play an active and constructive role in development planning and implementation. It was determined that any truly sustainable development for Chennai will necessarily involve a greater participation of its people in the planning and, especially, implementation of effective and environmentally sensible development programmes and projects.[145] This implies a top-down approach where the policy makers set priorities. The phrase 'greater participation' is also very vague because, as noted before, there are many different levels of participation and the programme is not very clear as to what approach it favours.[146]

There were problems in the cooperation between UNDP and the Indian authorities, and UNDP did not want to proceed with the funding of the third phase of the project after October 1998. According to the *Hindu*, a combination of factors have led to the stoppage of UNDP funding including bureaucratic delay in decision-making and the lack of top level political patronage in the state for the project.[147] After a six-month closure, the project was eventually revived following state government intervention in May 1999 and ended in October 1999.

1.6 Conclusion

The conventional method of measuring poverty through measuring income at the household level has been criticized. It has been replaced by a new approach which acknowledges that poverty is not only due to lack of income and employment but a combination of deprivations. In this new approach the poor are seen as active 'actors' who are engaged in many types and scales of association in order to build-up their assets and decrease their vulnerabilities. Even though they may be hindered by social inequalities (Mitlin, 2001; Eckstein, 1990; Devas et al., 2001; Schuurman and van Naerssen, 1989), many local organizations are active in poor urban areas. The discussion on local initiatives and collective action is somewhat confusing as different authors use the same expressions but, in practice, mean different things. Also, they do not provide clear definitions of the concepts they use. A distinction should be made between the different levels at which collective action occurs. There is collective action which takes place at the local level, for instance in poor urban neighbourhoods, and which is instigated by (amongst others) the need to secure land tenure (Mitlin, 2000). Also, there is collective action which takes place at higher levels, is more formal and organized, and tries to achieve 'higher' or more abstract targets like influencing policy (Della Porte and Diani, 1999; Ghosh, 1995; and partly Schuurman and van Naerssen, 1989). Given that my research deals with such informal forms of collective action at the local level, namely at a relocation site where poor urban households reside, the studies by Mitlin (2001), Eckstein (1990) and Desai (1999) are particularly useful. Authors use different terms when they speak of various local organizations. Moving from formal to less-formal organizations, the following terms are used; community-based organizations, community organizations, grassroots organizations, citizens' organizations, self-help groups or organizations, and residents associations. This study focuses on informal types of organization that are formed at the local level, and the term 'local organization' is preferred and defined as 'an informal group of persons that join to achieve a common goal at the local level'.

By now it is common knowledge that in order to reach the (urban) poor, local perceptions and priorities should be listened to and addressed. Participation by the beneficiaries is therefore needed at all levels. Nevertheless, not many studies have been undertaken regarding the urban poor's perception and expectation of government and NGO policy formulation and implementation. The 'Voices of the Poor' study makes it clear that the poor are very negative about the role of the government and the NGOs in general as they are not accountable to them and are characterized by widespread ineffectiveness and corruption. The poor state that for their survival, they depend on their own organizations. More studies are needed on perceptions and expectations of poor urban households concerning concrete policies of the government and NGOs, and local initiatives. This study aims at making a contribution to that discussion.

The attitude of the State towards housing and slums has changed drastically over the years. From slum clearance in the 1950s to self-help in sites-and-services-and slum upgrading schemes of the 1970s, it evolved to a more integrated approach in the mid-1980s and to an emphasis on enablement and provision by the market, NGOs and CBOs (Mengers, 1997; Choguill, 1995; Steinberg, 1996). Still, there is an enormous shortage of suitable housing, and many of the urban poor reside in slums or on the pavement. The reasons listed by Cernea (1993b) explain why the urban poor have been/are forcibly relocated from illegal slums and pavements in the cities. It is not clear whether alternative housing was offered in all these cases, but this study focuses on a relocation site to which the relocatees were forcibly shifted. The literature points out many impoverishment risks relating to displacement (Cernea, 1993a,

1997, 2000; Mertens, 1996; Mathur, 1998; UNCHS, 1991; Mahapatra and Mahapatra, 2000). However, these authors did not study whether the urban poor are also able to build-up assets after they are relocated. In order to achieve to a more balanced assessment on relocation, the present study will also focus on this issue.

As discussed above, the role of the State has gradually changed from being the 'provider' to being the 'enabler'. Over the last two decades, the process of urban governance has been shaped by decentralization, privatization, and participation. As is clear from the work of others, participation can assume many different meanings, and each time it is discussed, it should be made clear how the concept is being defined. In India, through the implementation of the 74th Amendment, participation is said to be stimulated by local NGOs at the community level. This research will explore what this means in practice and whether it is actually happening.

Devas et al. (2001) and Mitlin (2001) have listed the major problems of NGOs in working with the poor. These arguments are formulated on a rather theoretical level. In this study the main focus will be on the critique, negative as well as positive, of the role of NGOs in the relocation site, as formulated by the urban poor themselves.

In conclusion, there is the question of matching of government and NGO initiatives with local initiatives. As already stated, there is a discussion on the presence of a 'disconnect' between formal and informal institutions, due to many different reasons. Requirements to stimulate the matching between the formal (State and NGO) programmes and the informal initiatives are listed.

The conclusion of this chapter has led to the following academic problem, namely, can local initiatives and forms of collective organization of the urban poor be matched with the implementation of formal development programmes, and if so, how can this be done more effectively? This question will be dealt with and subdivided into more specific research questions in the next chapter, which also includes the methodology used in addressing these questions.

NOTES

1. Ravallion, 1992, as quoted in Moser, 1998: 2; see also Sen (1997).
2. Satterthwaite, 1997: 13-14.
3. Chambers, 1995a, as quoted by Satterthwaite, 1997: 13.
4. World Bank, 2000: 15.
5. Wratten, 1995: 16.
6. Chambers, 1992 and 1995b, as quoted by Moser, 1998: 2.
7. Moser, 1998: 2, 3.
8. Lipton and Maxwell, 1992: 10, as quoted by Moser, 1998: 3.
9. De Soto, 1992, as quoted by Wratten, 1995: 26.
10. Wratten, 1995: 23-28.
11. Moser, 1996: 24.
12. De Haan, 2000: 15.
13. Or, as McLeod calls it 'environmental capital' which also includes wildlife, bio-diversity, and environmental resources (McLeod, 2001: 2).
14. Morris (1998: 6) makes a distinction between formal and informal social capital. Formal social capital refers to formally defined patterns of behaviour, norms of exchange, networks and institutions. Informal social capital refers to those networks which operate outside this formal system; it refers to things such as kinships, informal networks between individuals, families and groups.
15. McLeod, 2001: 3-4.
16. In the early 1980s, the term 'survival strategy' was introduced to indicate that the poor do not only passively resist developments that threaten their situation, but actively and creatively try to manipulate the conditions of their existence. However, the connotation 'survival' is balancing on the edge of life and death, whereas most poor households do not find themselves in such a harsh situation. The term livelihood is more neutral and refers to the struggle of individuals, households and/or organized groups to achieve an acceptable existence regardless of their assets and capacities (*Livelihood and Environment*, 1990 as quoted by Post, 1996: 16).
17. Rakodi, 1999: 318.
18. Douglass and Zoghlin, 1994, as quoted by Hordijk, 2001: 111.
19. Douglass and Zoghlin, 1994: 177.
20. Douglass, 1998: 122, as quoted by Hordijk, 2000: 28.
21. Douglass and Zoghlin, 1994: 177.
22. Hordijk, 2000: 27-9.
23. Chambers, 1995b, as quoted by De Haan: 2000: 13. Tangible assets are, for instance, cattle, stock and equipment; intangible (or non-tangible) assets consist of claims and access (De Haan, 2000: 15).
24. Moser, 1998; De Haan, 2000, as quoted by Hordijk, 2001: 111.

25. As quoted by Hordijk, 2001: 111.
26. Douglass, 1992: 24.
27. Douglass and Zoghlin, 1994: 186.
28. Verhagen, 1987: 22.
29. Mitlin, 2001: 153-4.
30. Rakodi, 1993, as quoted by Baud, 2000: 10.
31. Eckstein, 1990, as quoted by Douglass, 1992: 25.
32. Desai, 1995: 56 ; Castells, 1997: 62-3.
33. Baud, 2000: 10.
34. Narayan, et al., 1999: 220.
35. Dia, 1996: 1.
36. Therefore each time collective action occurs, the question needs to be asked which community is referred to, who it includes and who it excludes (Baud, 2000: 10).
37. Baud, 2000; De Wit, 1993.
38. At that time still called Madras.
39. Clientelism is defined as 'the dispensing of public resources as favours (or the promise to do so) by political power holders/seekers and their respective parties, in exchange for votes or forms of popular political support, being a strategy of elite controlled political participation fostering the status quo' (Banck, 1986, as quoted by De Wit, 1989: 63).
40. Douglass, 1992: 24.
41. Narayan et al., 1999: 221.
42. Mitlin, 2001: 157.
43. Leach et al., 1997b: 91.
44. Devas et al., 2001: 30.
45. Dia, 1996: 1-2.
46. Della Porte and Diani, 1999: 3. Castells (1983: xviii) speaks of urban protest movements, which according to him are developed around three major themes: (1) Demands focused on collective consumption, that is goods and services directly or indirectly provided by the state, (2) Defense of cultural identity associated with and organized around a specific territory, and (3) Political mobilization in relationship to the State, particularly emphasizing the role of the local government.
47. Della Porte and Diani, 1999: 6-9.
48. Saschikonye, 1995, as quoted by Jenkins, 2001: 186.
49. Jenkins, 2001: 186.
50. Local initiatives are also sometimes referred to as 'grassroots initiatives'. The term 'grassroots' has been used to mean 'people' and 'people in a local setting'. But it has been equated with various marginalized groups like dalits, women and even children. It has also come to mean people subjected to dominance, injustice and exploitation; or people associated with heterogeneous social

movements—human rights, ecology, gender, health, literacy and so on (Ghosh, 1995: 9).

51. Ghosh, 1995: 2-3.
52. Schuurman and van Naerssen, 1989: 2-3.
53. Schuurman, 1989: 9.
54. Burgwal, 1995: 17-18.
55. As quoted by Hordijk, 2001: 111.
56. Chambers, 1998: 1.
57. Rakodi, 1999: 315-16.
58. Moore et al., 1998: 3.
59. <www.worldbank.org/poverty/voices/listen-findings.h> [accessed in December 2001].
60. Narayan et al., 2000: 281.
61. Narayan et al., 1999: 222.
62. Kumar et al., 1999: 38-9.
63. Moore et al., 1998: 3.
64. Moore et al. use deprivation and ill-being as concepts with a broader meaning than poverty (DFID, 1997; UNDP, 1996, as quoted in Moore et al., 1998: 10).
65. Moore et al., 1998: 10-13.
66. UNDP, 1998: Chapter 3.
67. Mengers, 1997: 12.
68. Aldrich and Sandhu, 1995: 27.
69. Choguill, 1995: 404-5.
70. Berner, 2001: 3-5.
71. Pugh, 1997: 91-100.
72. Steinberg, 1996: xxix.
73. For definitions on relocation see Chapter 2.
74. Cernea, 2000: 3659.
75. Cernea, 1993b: 13-14. By non-urban programmes Cernea means 'projects that infringe upon existing urban settlements, requiring their integral or partial relocation, e.g. new reservoirs that extend beyond the dams and submerge or threaten to submerge existing towns' (Cernea, 1993a: 16).
76. UNCHS, 1991, as quoted by Cernea, 1993a: 16-18.
77. As put together by the author from: Cernea, 1993a: 22-4; 1997: 1575; 2000: 3363-7; Mertens, 1996: 89; Mathur, 1999; UNCHS, 1991: 40; Mahapatra and Mahapatra, 2000: 437.
78. Kundu, 1993: 63.
79. Berner, 2001: 14.
80. UNCHS, 1991: 34-40 , 44; Bijl et al., 1992: 117-18.
81. Davidson et al., 1993: 2.
82. UNCHS, 1991: 34-40.
83. Hundsalz, 1993: 11.

84. Gorman, 1984; Korten, 1990; Clark, 1991, as quoted by Mitlin, 2001: 151–12.
85. Mitlin: 2001: 152.
86. Hyden, 1998, as quoted by Mitlin: 2001: 151-2.
87. Korten, 1991: 21.
88. Put, 1998: 39.
89. Turner, 1988 as quoted by UNCHS, 1996: 428.
90. UNCHS, 1996: 428-9.
91. Devas et al., 2001: 31.
92. Mitlin, 2001: 159-60.
93. From the 'Voices of the Poor' report: Narayan et al., 2000, 219-20.
94. The enabling approach for promoting urban development in general has come from a much earlier discussion on public sector housing provision, in which Turner (1976) strongly promoted the idea of urban residents being given more room by the government to organize housing provision for themselves. The later, more general concept of government enablement was brought forward by several international agencies like the World Bank, UNCHS and UNDP (Baud, 2000: 14). The concept of enablement is based on the understanding that most human investments, activities, and choices, all of which influence the achievement of development goals and the extent of environmental impacts, take place outside the 'government'. Most are beyond the control of governments, even when governments seek some regulation. In southern cities, the point is particularly valid since most homes are created outside the government and often in contravention of official rules and regulations. The emphasis on 'enabling policies' has received considerable support from the growing recognition that democratic and participatory government structures are not only important goals of development but also important means for achieving such development. Participation and enablement are inseparable since popular priorities and demands will be a major influence on the development of effective and flexible enabling policies (UNCHS, 1996: 424). Community enablement means external, especially government, support for community participation and community management (Wils and Helmsing, 2001: 8). Government enablement of community action may be defined as (local) government(s) creating appropriate legal, administrative (including financial) and planning frameworks to facilitate community organization, management, and action (Helmsing, 1999, as quoted by Wils and Helmsing, 2001: 8).
95. Hordijk, 2001: 3.
96. Mitlin, 2001: 152.
97. Devas, 1999; Baud and Hordijk, 2000, as quoted by Hordijk, 2000: 21.
98. Hyden, 1998, as quoted by Mitlin, 2001: 152.

99. Jenkins and Smith, 2001: 25.
100. Urban governance connotes the process of governing in urban areas. It includes the functioning of the urban government as well as the relation between it and the civil society (Mukhopadhyay, 1999: 109). Others emphasize that urban governance deals with the power relationship between the State and the different groups in society, particularly the poor (Porio, 1997, as quoted by Devas, 1999: 25). An urban governance process may or may not be participatory depending on the social actors involved, and how they are involved (Werna, 2001: 216).
101. Devas, 1999: 20.
102. Gonzales et al., 2000, as quoted by Hordijk, 2001: 112-13.
103. Dia, 1996: 1.
104. Mehta, 1999: 176. For more information on participation in development projects, see also Galjart and Buijs, 1982: 2-3.
105. Dia, 1996: 118-19.
106. Mehta, 1999: 186.
107. UNCHS, 1996: 162.
108. Evans, 2000, as quoted by Véron, 2001: 604.
109. Véron, 2001: 604.
110. Dillinger, 1994; Fox, 1994, and van der Hof and Steinberg, 1992, as quoted by Devas, 1999: 4.
111. UNCHS, 1996: 162-3.
112. Gnaneshwar, 1995: 295. According to Blair (2000: 22) the actual year of the introduction of the Panchayati Raj was 1959.
113. De Wit, 1997: 9.
114. Subramanian, 1998: 57-8.
115. Chennai has 155 wards and 10 ward committees (Singh, 2001: 41).
116. De Wit, 1997: 9.
117. Singh and Maitra, 2001: 90.
118. Gnaneshwar, 1995: 313.
119. Datta, 1999: 89; 90.
120. Subramanian, 1998: 57.
121. De Wit, 1997: 10.
122. De Wit, 1996 and NIUA, 1994, as quoted by De Wit, 1997: 10.
123. Steinberg, 1996: xxxviii.
124. De Wit, 1997: 10.
125. Tendler, 1997; Crook and Manor, 1998, as quoted by Véron, 2001: 604.
126. Véron, 2001.
127. Choguill, 1996: 435-41.
128. Baud, 2000: 14.
129. Bennett et al., 1999: 3-4.
130. Baud and Post, 2001: 132. Baud, in her inaugural address (2000: 4),

speaks of alliances instead of partnerships. She prefers alliances as 'the term alliance or coalition indicates that such relations inherently contain both elements of conflict and cooperation'.

131. Baud, 2000: 4-5.
132. Bennett et al., 1999: 6-14.
133. Batley, 1996, as quoted by Baud, 2000: 16, and Batley, 1996: 727.
134. Baud, 2000: 16.
135. Dia, 1996: 1, 241.
136. Mehta, 1999: 199-202.
137. Schübeler, 1996; Baud et al., 2001, as quoted by Baud, 2000: 4-5.
138. Huysman and Velu, 1994: 39.
139. Baud et al., 2001: 7.
140. Douglass and Zoghlin, 1994; Hardoy et al., 1992, as quoted by Lee, 1998: 993.
141. Lee, 1998: 993.
142. <www.unchs.org/scp/scphome.htm> [accessed in December 2001].
143. The *Hindu*, 2 May 1999.
144. Doss, 2001: 185.
145. Dattatri, 1991: 3.
146. See also Table 1.2 on the different levels of participation. This programme will be discussed in depth in Chapter 5 as one of the non-governmental organizations in Ambedkar Nagar was selected to implement a pilot project in the area under this scheme.
147. *The Hindu*, 12 November 1998.

2

Research Framework and Methodology

The academic problem, which has already been mentioned in Chapter 1, focuses on local initiatives and government and NGO programmes in order to investigate whether these can be matched. This chapter discusses the four specific research questions that were drawn from the academic problem. We will first formulate the research questions as well as their operationalization. The scheme of actors and agencies will then be presented, followed by a definition of the major concepts and figures of slums and inhabitants of Chennai. The different research methodologies that were used to collect the data will also be discussed.

2.1 Research Questions and their Operationalization

The overall academic problem bears repeating: can local initiatives and forms of collective organization of the urban poor be matched with the implementation of formal development programmes, and if so, how can this be done more effectively? This academic problem has led me to raise the following, more specific questions: What are the initiatives and forms of collective organization of the urban poor? How do poor urban households perceive policy and implementation with regard to their habitat and what are their expectations in this area? What policies have the government and NGOs developed and implemented with regard to relocated urban poor? Are current initiatives of collective action and government and NGO programmes accountable, effective, and appropriate?

2.1.1 LOCAL INITIATIVES AND COLLECTIVE ORGANIZATION

As is clear from the literature discussed in Chapter 1, poor households are combining different strategies in order to decrease their vulnerabilities and build-up their assets through 'livelihood strategies', which cover different domains and different themes. For instance, households are actively engaged in many types and scales of association, the so-called self-help organizations. As is described in Chapter 1, the extent to which the community can be considered an asset that reduces vulnerability or increases opportunities depends on its stock of social capital. It refers to the benefits of membership within a social network. Poor people invest heavily in social relations for their psychological, cultural, and economic well-being.[1]

Collective action or organization is any voluntary action undertaken by a group of persons, which aims at the satisfaction of collective needs or aspirations.[2] Eckstein (1990) states that there is a positive relation between the occurrence of collective action and the sense of shared destiny amongst people in a community, like for instance a sense of shared economic deprivation and a common sense of limited alternatives.[3] Collective action can occur at different levels within the community.

Communities are heterogeneous as there are social divisions and conflicting interests within any community—between men and women, between young and old, between leaders and inhabitants.[4] Furthermore, in India there are differences based on religion, caste and class, which hinder social cohesion.[5] 'Historically, socio-economic cleavages in India have created a segmentary society in which the various segments are "cellular", i.e. separate, each having a distinct life of its own.'[6] Therefore collective action mostly and most easily occurs at the level of primary social groups, which in this study are family networks based on caste. Another reason why social cohesion is difficult to achieve in India, according to De Wit (1993), is the 'vertical orientation (reliance on patrons/brokers) rather than horizontal orientation (class organization) of slum people and their social handicaps, including a low esteem of the efficacy of individual efforts which appears to apply even more to Harijans (Scheduled Castes) than to other, higher caste groups'.[7]

Whenever the sense of shared destiny is higher social cohesion will emerge. Or as Baud puts it: 'when partners identify strong common interests, collective action will emerge beyond local divisions'.[8] Verba et al. (1978) emphasize this point: 'groups with a consciousness of common purpose are likely to form organizations'.[9] This is also found in India, where according to the country study of the 'Voices of the Poor' (1999), homogeneity along class lines appears to be the rallying factor in community dynamics, and that instances of inter-class collusion are rare, but whenever transactions across class lines occur, they are mostly driven by the need for survival.[10] A study in the Indian Himalayas concluded that fewer levels of stratification and much less rigidity exist in inter-caste relationships in the villages studied there, possibly because of the enforced isolation of village communities, especially through the winter months.[11] Social cohesion is the connectedness among individuals and social groups that facilitates collaboration and equitable resource distribution at the household, community, and state level. It is essential for societal stability and for easing the material and psychological strains of poverty. It also affirms individual and group identities, and includes rather than excludes less powerful groups. Among poor households, social connections are used to build social solidarity, to receive and give emotional support, to obtain help in daily tasks, to access small loans and job leads, and to collaborate to accomplish otherwise impossible tasks such as house building. At the community level, cohesion is an asset that provides security, regulates behaviour and improves the standard of living of the community as a whole in matters that include but are not limited to material wealth.[12]

Since most societies are not homogeneous, groups differ in their access to resources and power. Members may be helped by high social capital, which Narayan (1999) calls 'bonding social capital' within a group, but they may be excluded from other groups; in other words, they 'lack bridging social capital'. Cross-cutting ties between groups open up economic opportunities to those belonging to less powerful or excluded groups. And they also build social cohesion, a critical element in social stability and economic welfare over any extended period. According to Narayan (1999), social cohesion requires not just high social capital, but also dense, though not necessarily strong cross-cutting ties among groups. Networks and associations consisting of primary social groups without cross-cutting ties lead to the betterment of only those groups, whereas voluntary cross-cutting networks, associations and related norms based on everyday social interactions lead to the collective good of citizens.[13]

It can be concluded that collective action occurs at different levels and that when people identify strong common interests within a community, collective action will emerge beyond local divisions like caste.

Collective action in a relocation site has been one of the central issues of this study. A precondition for selecting collective initiatives was that they had to be undertaken and developed by members of the local community and they had to be locally based. A distinction is made between collective action undertaken by primary social groups and action undertaken at the secondary level where more social groups join together. As mentioned earlier, caste is a major element leading to heterogeneity in Indian society. Primary groups are social groups that distinguish themselves from others based on their caste identity, and it is expected that caste is one of the elements on which the primary social groups are formed in the study area. Another distinctive element leading to heterogeneity is the location background of the different relocated groups. As a report of the UNCHS has already highlighted, 'involuntary relocation frequently leads to serious problems of adaptation and social integration and organization in the new site'.[14] As people in the relocation site under study came from many different (slum) areas in Chennai, it was assumed that the new community would also be differentiated according to the location they were relocated from, which is in the study also defined as a primary social group.

2.1.2 PERCEPTIONS AND EXPECTATIONS OF POLICY AND IMPLEMENTATION

In short, not much attention has been paid to poor people's own ideas and knowledge of development issues. Development policies were designed and implemented top-down, without consulting the target groups; 'their voices were not heard'. Many of those policies failed, or did not reach their target groups. And although people's participation appears to be a reoccurring theme echoed in successive plans in India, the programmes taken up to achieve these objectives were ill-conceived, ad hoc and obsolete.[15] The anti-poverty programmes ignored the beneficiaries: 'anti-poverty programmes are planned centrally at the national level and at the state level and even at the donor level, based on the perceptions of these agencies of the assumed felt needs of the poor. There was no opportunity given to the poor families or communities to identify their own needs and problems, to make their own plans and to manage and implement programmes and activities for their own betterment'.[16]

In this study, it is assumed that in order for policies to be successful, meaning that they benefit the target group, it is necessary for the beneficiaries to participate in the design and implementation of those policies. Therefore we need to know the perceptions and expectations of the poor with regard to development. Perceptions are defined as beliefs or opinions that people have as a result of realizing or noticing something, especially something that is not obvious to others. In this study, it refers to the opinions of the inhabitants of the relocation site on relocation itself and on their access to poverty alleviation schemes and the provision and maintenance of basic services in the area and the role of NGOs in the area. It focuses on three aspects:

1. Relocation and its effects on employment, education, market facilities, and social cohesion.
2. The provision and maintenance of basic services in the relocation site: water and sanitation, health care, drainage and waste disposal, transport, electricity, and employment programmes.
3. Social security programmes targeting the urban poor and therefore also the inhabitants of Ambedkar Nagar, such as vocational training facilities offered by the NGOs in the area, the Public Distribution System (PDS), loans and old age pensions, and the Noon Meal Scheme.

Expectations indicate what the members of the target group

expect from the government and the NGOs, or better said, what they are entitled to as a basic human right and what they expect the government and the NGOs to provide them with.

2.1.3 POLICIES OF THE GOVERNMENT OF TAMIL NADU, THE CHENNAI CITY MUNICIPAL CORPORATION, AND THE NGOS

The policies studied in this research question focus on three aspects already mentioned above. Over the last few years, housing has no longer been seen as an isolated matter. Instead, international development thinking stresses on an integrated approach in order to develop sustainable settlements with sufficient infrastructure and services. A problem with many of the anti-poverty programmes of the Indian Government is that they are highly compartmentalized, each identifying the poor in its own way and each addressing one or two issues related to poverty. The implementing agencies themselves work in a very compartmentalized manner with no coordination or interaction between them. Besides, these programmes do not focus on the multiple aspects of poverty conditions in a comprehensive and integrated fashion but usually address only employment or income generating issues.

India's development programmes have caused an aggregate forced displacement of more than 20 million people over roughly four decades, and 75 per cent of these people have not been rehabilitated. Their livelihoods have not been restored; in fact, the vast majority of the development resettlers in India have become impoverished.[17] In India, people have been affected by relocation and displacement in many different areas, as will be described in Chapter 3. This study focuses on relocation in the urban area of Chennai. The term 'relocation' means forced physical movement from the actual living place to another location. The Tamil Nadu Slum Clearance Board forcibly relocated slum dwellers to a place in the outskirts of the city, and the slums they were living in were to be destroyed and used for an urban development project, namely the construction of a railway. Pavement dwellers were also relocated to the site. The research question will focus on how the relocation plan was drafted, and by whom; how the area was developed and by whom; how the area has changed overtime; which facilities existed when the slum dwellers were relocated to the site, how they changed over time, and by whom they are provided; and which poverty alleviation schemes the inhabitants can apply for and by which agencies are they provided. The financial aspects of the plan will also be discussed.

2.1.4 Accountability, Effectiveness and Appropriateness

The initiatives of collective action, government and NGO programmes (selected on the basis of the criteria mentioned above) are analysed based on their accountability, effectiveness, and appropriateness. These concepts are defined as follows:

1. *Accountability:* In the context of governance, it refers to holding the bearers of public office responsible for their performance and the results of their decisions. The criterion for determining if an initiative of collective action or a government programme is accountable is whether the target groups are informed and consulted. For instance, were meetings organized, what was the level of inclusiveness (did it only include the leaders or the whole community), and was there actually a choice left to be made by the target group?
2. *Effectiveness of the activities:* The degree to which the activities produce a decided, decisive, or desired effect, from the perspective of the provider/initiator.
3. *Appropriateness:* This indicates the priorities given to the activity by the target group itself. When it excludes part of the community, the perspective of the excluded is also evaluated.

2.2 Actors and Agencies

Figure 2.1 illustrates the theoretically assumed relations between different actors and agencies (individuals/households, collective initiatives, government, NGOs, and partnerships).

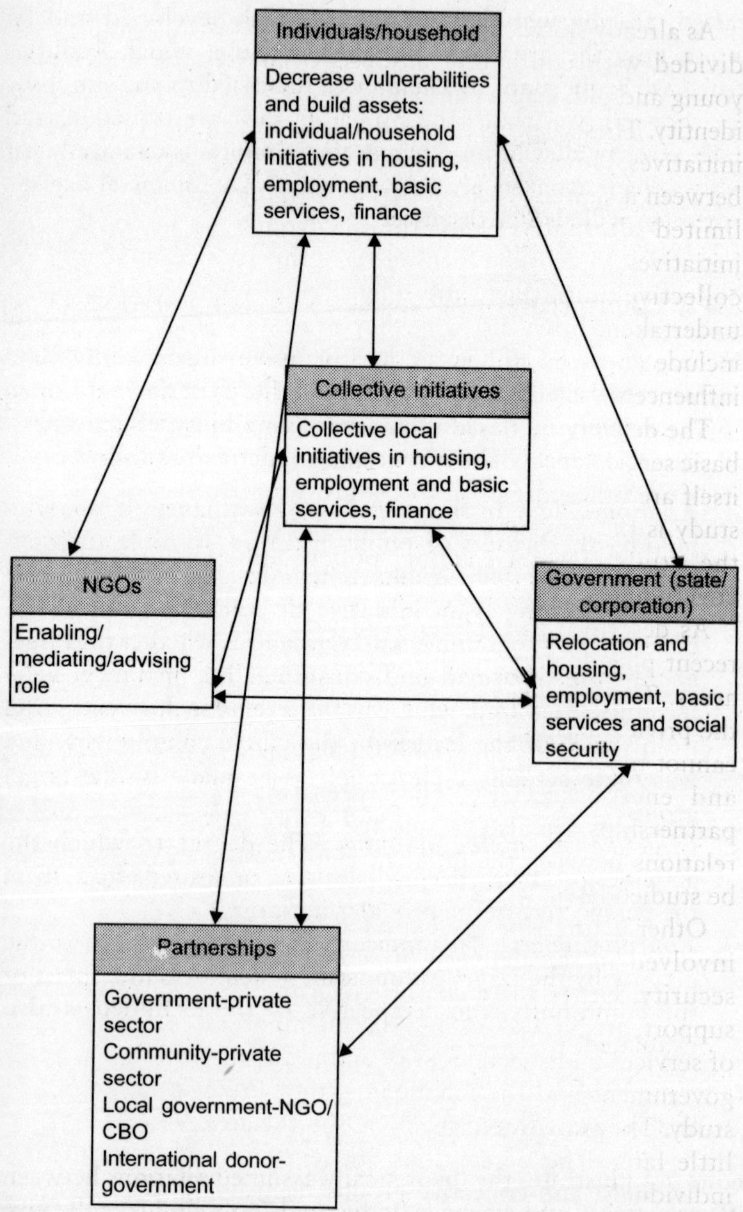

FIGURE 2.1: ACTORS, AGENCIES, AND RELATIONSHIPS

As already stated, communities are heterogeneous and socially divided with conflicting interests between men and women, young and old, leaders and inhabitants, rich and poor, and caste identity. These aspects hinder the development of collective local initiatives. However, it is assumed that there is a positive relation between a shared sense of identity, a common understanding of limited alternatives and the occurrence of collective local initiatives. One of the focus areas of this study is analysing local collective initiatives and identifying which initiatives are undertaken, how and why they are established, who do they include and who they exclude. It is assumed that these factors influence the delivery of services to the study area.

The delivery by the government of housing, employment and basic services, social security schemes, and the relocation process itself are other targets of this study. Another main aspect of the study is the perceptions and expectations of the inhabitants of the study area regarding policy implementation by the government.

As described in Chapter 1, private-public partnerships are a recent phenomenon in the delivery of services in India's urban areas. These partnerships are increasingly established between the private and the public sector,[18] as governments acting alone cannot meet the continually growing demand for water, waste, and energy services. Therefore it is expected that these partnerships are also established in the relocation areas.[19] The relations between the different actors in the partnership(s) will be studied later.

Other actors who are expected to be present in the area and involved in the delivery of services and provision of social security, either through the government or through outside support, are NGOs. As they play an important role in the delivery of services and social security and in the mediation between the government and the inhabitants, they are also included in the study. The activities of the NGOs in the area will be described a little later. The perceptions and expectations of households, individuals, and collective groups regarding NGOs, as well as the relationship between the NGOs and the government are also points of study.

2.3 Definitions and Figures

2.3.1 Collective action, community, and community-based organization (CBO)

Collective action is any voluntary action undertaken by a group of persons and which aims at the satisfaction of collective needs or aspirations.[20]

A community is defined as a group of people with face-to-face contact, a sense of belonging together, and having shared interests and similar values. In the context of urban low-income settlements, it refers to people who reside in a geographical area, identify with that area and share an interest in the betterment of that area.[21]

A CBO is 'any type of organization, formal or informal, which is based on a group of people living or working together who associate to pursue common interests. They are characterized by being local in focus and being directly accountable to their constituents'.[22] CBOs can also be defined as 'grassroots organizations managed by members on behalf of members'.[23]

2.3.2 Defining slums

The Tamil Nadu Slum Areas Improvement and Clearance Act of 1971 defines slum areas as:

1. Any area that is, or may be, a source of danger to the health, safety or convenience of the public of that area or of its neighbourhood, by reason of the area being low-lying, unsanitary, squalid, overcrowded or otherwise, or,
2. The building in any area used or intended to be used for human habitation is:
    a. In any respect, unfit for human habitation, or,
    b. By reason of dilapidation, overcrowding, faulty arrangement and design of such buildings, narrowness or faulty arrangements of streets, lack of ventilation, light or sanitation facilities, or any combination of these factors, detrimental to safety, health or morals.[24]

Wiebe (1981) correctly argues that this definition covers many of the regular residential areas in India.[25] A suitable definition of slums, which is also used in this study, is that slums are neighbourhoods in which the living conditions are so bad that they endanger the health of the dwellers.[26] The majority of these slums are squatter settlements, i.e. illegal occupations of public and to a lesser extent private land.

2.3.3 HOUSEHOLDS

It is impossible to provide a universal definition of households. A common definition, which is also used in this study, is 'a group of people who pool resources or eat from the same pot'.[27] The term households can also be applied simply to co-residence, a task-oriented unit or the site of shared activities. Households may involve close family, wider kin networks, and unrelated co-residents such as lodgers. It is important to note that the terms family and households are not coterminous, although they often have features in common.[28] Baud (1989) speaks of family-based households, which means 'the unit within which reproduction is organized and in which the relations between members are often thought of in terms of kin'.[29] Douglass and Zoghlin (1994) formulate it as follows: 'the household is the key unit of production, reproduction and consumption, and the unit where decisions on pooling and allocation of labour and resources, both financial and other resources, are made'.[30] Inevitably, groups of people who would consider themselves a household do not fall within the criteria set while others who do not consider themselves a household are characterized as such. Consequently, classifications of the household tend to be rather arbitrary and the more uncommon forms tend to disappear from accounts altogether. The definitional problem is highlighted by the tendency to gloss over the difference between the structure of the family or households and household compositions. The former simply models family/household morphology (nuclear/joint, etc.) while the latter describes who is in the household, how they are related and on what terms they are included. By itself, the household structure is not a reliable indicator of rights and relations within the household. For example, households with identical structures, one being based on a nuclear family, and including the husband's mother, and the other, also based on a nuclear family but including the wife's mother, have entirely different compositions. In the Tamil context, the husband's mother has an unquestionable right to incorporation within the household while the wife's mother has no right whatsoever unless she is the widowed or deserted sister of the daughter's husband [i.e. a women is married to her maternal uncle (mother's younger brother)]. Consequently, these mothers' access to household resources will be markedly different, as will their experience of and insertion to domestic power relations.[31]

The head of the household is the main breadwinner or key decision maker in the household, or the person defined as such by the household's members.[32] A nuclear household is a commensal unit consisting of a single married couple and their non-adult children, or of a married couple without children. A sub-nuclear household or single adult is a commensal unit consisting of a single parent and his or her non-adult children, or a single adult living alone. A special form is the female-headed household, which is a household where a male partner is absent.[33] The female head of the household is either widowed, divorced, or abandoned by her husband, never has lived together with her husband in the same house nor has a husband who lives in another place.[34] Moser (1993) makes a distinction between *de jure* households, which are households where the male husband is absent due to death or separation, and *de facto* female-headed households, where the male partner is temporarily absent.[35] A joint household is a commensal unit having as a core two or more married couples. A supplemented nuclear household is a commensal unit which has as a core a married couple and, in addition, at least one widowed parent, adult sibling, or adult child. It can also consist of one adult parent living with an adult child, and any other situation where a sub-nuclear household has been added to, or supplemented by, the presence of additional relatives.[36]

2.3.4 INDIGENOUS KNOWLEDGE OR LOCAL KNOWLEDGE

Local knowledge is the sum total of the knowledge and skills which people in a particular geographic area possess and acquire and which enable them to get the most out of their environment[37] and their community, for instance chit funds. Local knowledge is more often referred to as 'indigenous knowledge'. As the term 'indigenous' implies that it is knowledge passed down from one generation to the other without being crucially influenced by outside factors, and this of course is not the case in urban areas where people are influenced by many outside factors, I prefer to use the term 'local'. The initiatives studied in this research are locally based and initiated and developed by local people in the study area. Since they are not initiated or stimulated by NGOs, I specifically speak of 'local' knowledge.

2.3.5 POPULATION FIGURES FOR THE CHENNAI METROPOLITAN AREA AND THE CHENNAI CITY MUNICIPAL CORPORATION

The Chennai Metropolitan Area (CMA)[38] comprises the area under the jurisdiction of the Chennai City Municipal Corporation. It includes eight municipalities, one township, 27 town panchayats and 10 panchayat unions. In all, it comprises 304 revenue villages and extends to 1,177 square kilometres. The population was 7.5 million in 2001, and the Chennai City Municipal Corporation accounted for 4.9 million inhabitants. The Chennai Metropolitan Area is expected to grow to 9.5 million by 2011, of which 6 million are expected to be in the city of Chennai.[39]

2.3.6 RELOCATION DISPLACEMENT, RELOCATION PROJECTS, RESETTLEMENT REHABILITATION

The term relocation (or displacement) implies physical movement from the actual place of habitation to another location, where the evicted communities are not necessarily provided with housing and basic services. However, relocation projects are specific settlements for evicted slum and pavement dwellers where housing and basic services are provided. Resettlement or rehabilitation is defined as 'a process in which a community (or family) is resettled and establishes a new living situation in all its aspects. No matter if the new living place is located on the former living site (on-site resettlement) or at another location (off-site resettlement)'.[40]

2.3.7 SLUMS AND THEIR COMMUNITIES: SOME FIGURES

It is very difficult to give an accurate figure of the number of people living in slums because many slum dwellers live in illegal settlements and they are not registered. An estimate of the number of slum inhabitants based on surveys conducted by the National Sample Survey Organisation (NSSO) during 1988 and 1989, places the total slum population in India at 14.7 per cent of the total urban population.[41] This, according to Mathur (1994), is a gross underestimate given that in 1981, the slum population accounted for 17 per cent of the total urban population and that there has been no indication of any decline in the slum population since then. About 15 million urban households are homeless, and more than half of them occupy a single room with an average occupancy per room of 4.4 persons.[42] Table 2.1 provides an overview of the number of slum inhabitants in Chennai between 1991 and 2001.

A majority of 81 per cent of the migrants to the Chennai slums are from within Tamil Nadu. A minority of 13 per cent have migrated from other states, and 6 per cent from countries like Sri Lanka.[43] Apart from the households living in slums, approximately 20,000 households live on the pavements in Chennai.[44]

TABLE 2.1: NUMBER OF SLUM INHABITANTS IN CHENNAI 1991-2001

Year	*Total Population*	*Slum Population*	*Slum Population as Percentage of Total Population*
1991	5,420,000	1,530,000	28.2
2001	6,980,000	1,980,000	28.4

Source: Urban Statistics Handbook.[45]

The slums in Chennai are distributed throughout the entire area of Chennai city and the CMA. However, it may be seen that there are concentrations of slums in certain areas, especially along Buckingham Canal and in the northern industrial area. The size of the slums enumerated in a survey conducted in 1986 by the Chennai Metropolitan Development Authority (CMDA) ranges from 5 to 901 shelter units, with an average of 90 huts.[46]

2.3.8 SOCIAL CAPITAL

To possess social capital, a person must be related to others, and it is these others, not himself, who are the actual source of his or her advantage.[47] As an attribute of the social structure in which a person is embedded, social capital is not the private property of any of the persons who benefit from it.[48] It exists only when it is shared. A definition of social capital as given by Narayan is: 'the norms and social relations embedded in the social structures of society that enable people to co-ordinate and to achieve desired goals'.[49] Another useful definition used in this study and which comes from the World Bank is: 'social capital refers to the norms and networks that enable collective action'.[50]

2.4 RESEARCH METHODOLOGIES

Selection of the Research Location

As Chennai is the capital of Tamil Nadu, there would be numerous policies being implemented and therefore Chennai was selected as the city where the research would take place. One of the reasons for selecting the study area of Ambedkar Nagar (Velacheri) was that a relocation policy was being implemented there.

A relocation site was selected as it was clear that such policy affects everyone who is being relocated. Therefore, information was collected on relocation in Chennai. At the start of this study there were six relocation sites; two to which people were still being moved, the other four relocation schemes were being completed. Relocation to Velacheri had taken place between 1990 and 1993. This was a big advantage as the communities relocated to this site had had some time to get adjusted to their new environment and to develop collective action. Another reason to select this site was that a Dutch researcher De Wit, had undertaken a Ph.D. study in one of the slums in the city centre of Chennai, which was later relocated to Velacheri. Much information about the background of one of the groups that was relocated to Velacheri was already available from his dissertation (1993), as well as information on the preparations for the relocation. Moreover, I was very lucky that he had given me the

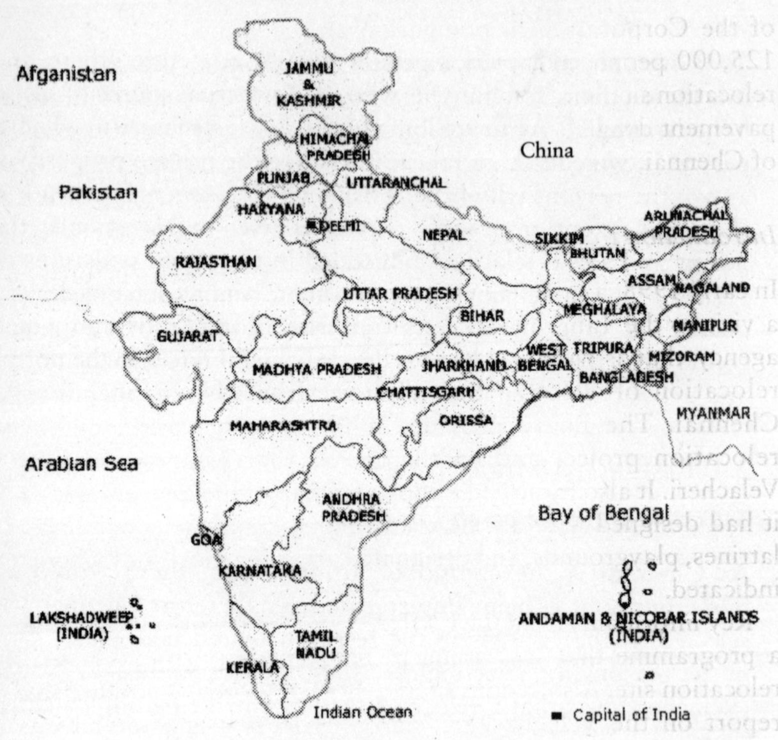

MAP 2.1: INDIA AND TAMIL NADU

opportunity to use some of his data, which allowed me to make comparisons between his and my findings on this particular group. Before selecting the area however, it had to be established that local initiatives had been undertaken on the site. The literature reviewed in Chapter 1 makes it clear that collective action by poor households is widespread in many settlements. Nonetheless, in order to be sure, Velacheri first needed to be visited. Pilot interviews revealed that many initiatives were being undertaken there (as explained later), and so it was chosen as the study area.

Velacheri is located in ward number 153 of the Corporation of Chennai, in the south-west part of the city. It is the biggest ward of the Corporation in population and size: it has more than 125,000 people and approximately 75 colonies. Velacheri is a relocation site bordered by a lake. In all, 2,640 families, slum and pavement dwellers who were previously living in the city centre of Chennai, were relocated to this site between 1990 and 1993.

Introduction to Chennai

In early 1998, a first field visit was paid to Chennai, starting with a visit to the Tamil Nadu Slum Clearance Board (TNSCB), the agency that is responsible for the clearing, improvement and relocation of slums in the whole of Tamil Nadu, including Chennai. The Board provided a lot of information on the relocation project and on the NGOs that were working in Velacheri. It also furnished a copy of a map of the relocation area it had designed with all the roads, plots, community buildings, latrines, playgrounds, and designated areas for shops and schools indicated.

Key informants from the CMDA[51] were interviewed regarding a programme that was going to be executed in the Velacheri relocation site. Also, a consultant who had written an evaluation report on the Velacheri relocation process was interviewed. Through these interviews, information was collected on the history of the relocation policy, on the way the relocation was executed and on the specific characteristics of the area, like the number of people that were relocated, where they were relocated from, when had this taken place, and their response to the plans and the actual relocation (from the perspective of the implementing agency).

Selection of Research Assistant

It was very important in this study to build a rapport of trust between the researcher and the assistant on the one hand and with the respondents on the other. Therefore one of the main requirements for the assistant was that he or she would have to be very enthusiastic about spending most of her or his time in the study area. As most of the respondents belonged to the Scheduled Castes, the assistant preferably would have to have a low-caste

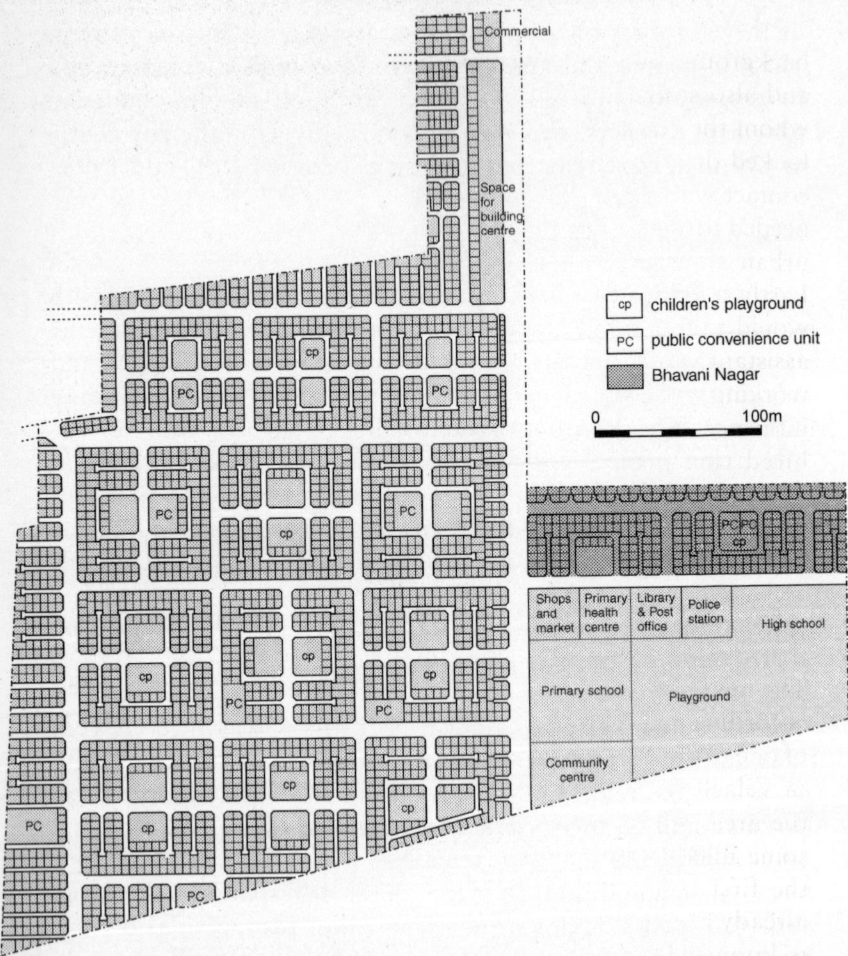

MAP 2.2: LAYOUT OF THE RELOCATION SCHEME

background and be familiar with low-caste culture and language, and also speak English. It was important to find a person with whom the respondents would be at ease and not feel judged or looked down upon, as this is what they normally experience in contact with other (higher caste, non-slum) people. The assistant needed to have at least some experience in executing fieldwork in urban slum areas, like carrying out questionnaire interviews. Lastly, a female assistant was preferred, as many of the interviews would take place in the households, an area to which a male assistant would not have access. Besides, being a woman myself, working with a male assistant could create problems, which could influence the research negatively. A female assistant was therefore hired through MIDS. She already had much experience in executing fieldwork in slum areas. She belonged to a Most Backward Caste group and was very enthusiastic about the study and working with me in the research site.[52]

Introduction to the Study Area

The next step was a visit to the head-offices of two NGOs that, according to TNSCB, were working in Velacheri. A staff member of one of the NGOs was willing to introduce me to the inhabitants of Velacheri. First a visit was paid to their community centre in the area, where we met the local staff. While talking to them, some inhabitants and one local slum leader dropped in and so the first contacts were made. Later a staff member who had already been working in the area for a few years and who seemed to know many people in these took us around and introduced us to the local slum leaders. My assistant and I were briefly introduced, after which we visited them a second time for a proper introduction.

After that second visit, we won the slum leaders' approval. Then I immediately decided to go my own way, not wanting to be identified with either the NGOs or the slum leaders. This was because my earlier work experience in India and slum literature had both made it clear that leaders and NGOs have a trivial role in slum areas. I think it was an advantage that my assistant and I were both women because after the introduction the slum leaders most did not interfere in our work and let us go our own way.

This was because they did not feel threatened by young women on the one hand, and on the other they also did not feel they could benefit from us. Although one of the leaders kept asking me for money and was rather rude whenever we passed his house, he did not create real trouble.

Rapid Urban Appraisal

In order to get an idea of the area, the facilities available, and the locations of different types of local initiatives (like the construction of local temples, etc.), I decided to execute a rapid appraisal using the map that I had received from the TNSCB. Apart from the houses which were already on it, I decided to mark all other facilities available in the area, from services provided by the corporation and TNSCB like wells, water taps, water tanks, public convenience units,[53] to shops, temples, mosques and churches, centres of the different NGOs, the police outpost, and the Sangam hall[54] of the local slum organization.

When the map was finished, with the help of a checklist, inhabitants were randomly interviewed throughout the area, especially along the main roads. The purpose was to get an idea of the issues that were relevant to ask in the questionnaire on relocation, development issues and local initiatives, and to get a general impression of the area and its inhabitants. Another reason was to build rapport with the inhabitants. Forty people were interviewed throughout Ambedkar Nagar, both men and women. In addition, information was collected, more systematically, about the temples, mosques and churches in the area, and from the staff of two major NGOs.

Household Survey

Information collected through the use of the checklist was used to design a questionnaire. I already knew that in total 2,640 families were relocated to Velacheri. From the primary interviews it was clear that not everyone relocated was still living in the area. In fact, some of them had never done so. They had rented out or sold off their plot. Thus, led me to safely presume that most of the plots on the map were inhabited. Therefore, I decided

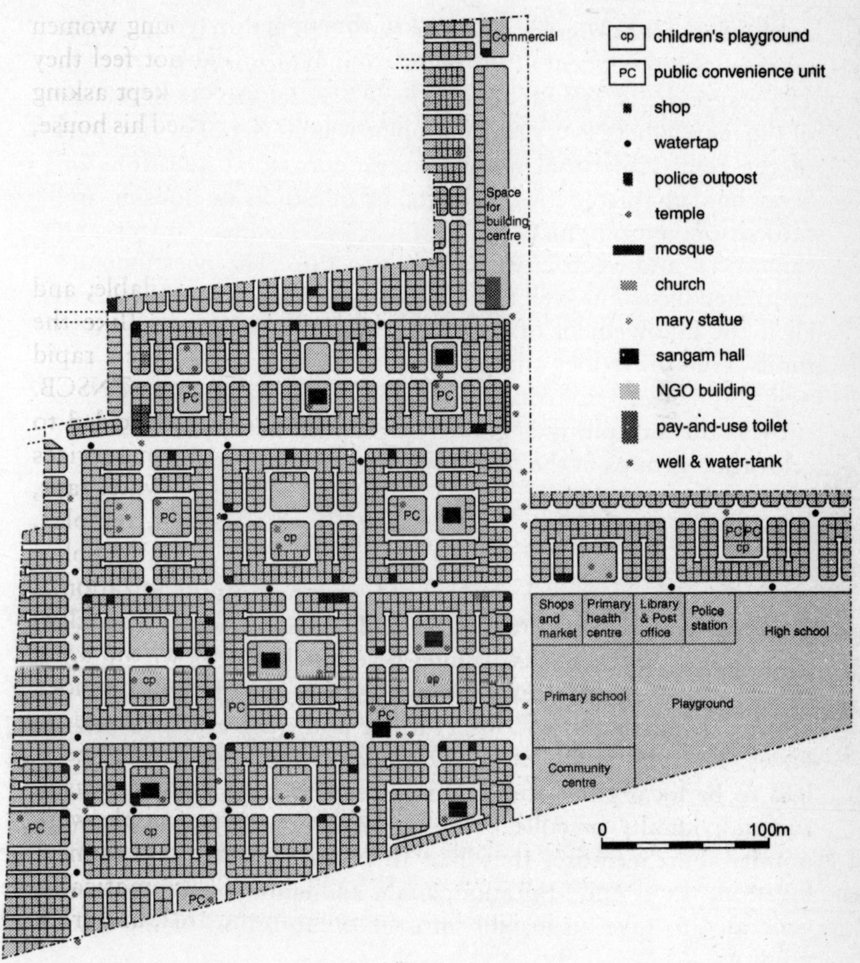

MAP 2.3: DESIGNED MAP OF THE RELOCATION SCHEME

used the map as provided to me by the TNSCB to select a sample representing 6 per cent of the population, which meant a total of 158 respondents. A systematic sample was selected with the use of the map, where every sixteenth plot was chosen. The first part of the semi-structured questionnaire contained questions on household characteristics, followed by questions on housing and relocation, employment and education, finance, water and sanitation, and electricity and infrastructure. The questionnaire contained closed as well as open questions and was designed to elicit the involvement of local organizations, slum parties, chit funds, NGO activities and people's own initiatives (for instance, neighbourhood environmental management). As Table 2.2 shows, the sample is a good representation of the different relocation groups in the relocation site.

Case Studies of Local (Collective) Initiatives

Case studies were selected based on the outcome of the questionnaire, observations in the field, and discussions with key informants. For these case studies several techniques were used: open interviews, interviews through the use of a checklist, rapid appraisal, participatory observation, and questionnaire interviews. The criteria for selecting these case studies were that they had to be locally initiated and undertaken, and developed and run individually or collectively by members of the local community. Furthermore, they had to relate to housing and relocation, water and sanitation, credit and employment, or more generally, to give an insight into the organization of the community.

In order to be present at strategic moments, we had to be in the area on an almost daily basis throughout the year. Key informants were visited on a regular basis, often for informal chats. They would inform us whenever something 'special' was going to happen, like the auctioning of a chit fund. As these appointments were always very informal and subject to change, double-checking was very important and flexibility on our side a must, because 'that is the way things go'. For other case studies like water distribution, it was more obvious whenever there was

TABLE 2.2: COMPARISON BETWEEN THE RELOCATION BACKGROUND OF THE TOTAL NUMBER OF RELOCATED HOUSEHOLDS AND THE SAMPLE SIZE[55]

Name of Previous Location	*Total Number of Relocated Households*	%	*Sample (Abs. Numbers)*	%
TBR	638	24	27	23
CN	520	20	32	27
KNW	42	2	–	–
GP	30	1	1	1
AK	107	4	4	3
SN	64	2	6	5
NBO	291	11	12	10
PN	163	6	8	7
KS	97	4	1	1
LT	192	7	8	7
SS	30	1	1	1
ASN	353	13	12	10
NK	64	2	3	3
Others	49	2	4	3
Missing	–	–	1	1
Total	2,640	100	120	100

something happening as we could see the water tankers enter the area. But as the area was very large we could not always be 'at the right place at the right time'. Sometimes we were just lucky to come across an event, such as the have we ran into a group of women going to demonstrate at the office of a private company in charge of the water supply in the area. Being there on a regular basis for an extended period of time was of prime importance when studying local initiatives and getting a grip on what was going on and what were the main issues in the area. This strategy also led to more reliable data, as people opened up more readily once we had become a familiar face in the area, and once they had spoken to us often enough. There were six case studies undertaken in this study, consisting of both individual and collective initiatives; two focused on relocation (the 'Chitra Nagar' group and plot transfers); the others on water, chit funds, shops, and temple festivals.

Data Collection on Government Intervention

Interviews were held with informants from the Chennai Corporation, the Zonal Office and the Division Office under which Velacheri falls, the Government of Tamil Nadu, and the autonomous boards that are active in slums, like the Chennai Metropolitan Water Supply and Sewerage Board (CMWSSB), the TNSCB, as well as with the Civil Supplies Office.

From the questionnaire, people eligible for government support were selected; these included people above the age of 65, or leprosy-affected people above the age of 60, widows of all ages who were not remarried, and deserted wives above 30 years of age. These people were interviewed to determine whether or not they received government assistance, and how they had applied (through the help of others or not) for the same. This information provided deeper insight into whether or not government schemes directed towards specific target groups were reaching them.

The six major local leaders in Ambedkar Nagar were interviewed on the history of the site, the role and background of the local slum organization, their own role in the community as mediators in applying for government programmes, and their contact with outside politicians.

Informal Conversations

Many informal conversations happened while we were in the area; they focused on a number of topics that were of interest to the inhabitants, such as family problems, problems of physical environment in the area, social problems, and the inhabitants' opinion of the activities of NGOs. When my assistant and I had become familiar faces in the area, people just came to chat with us and often invited us over to their house for an informal conversation. Also, group discussions with women were held to learn their perception of the availability of services in Ambedkar Nagar. These conversations provided valuable insights into the lives of the people in the area.

In addition to these conversations, in-depth interviews were held with religious leaders like the president and the imam of the local mosque and members of the local apostolic church.

Library Research

In Chennai, all the relevant libraries were visited (the library of the Madras University, Anna University, the library of the Madras School of Economics, the Swaminathan Foundation and the library of the Madras Institute of Development Studies), and many useful books and reports studied. Moreover, discussions were held with researchers from research institutes involved in development studies.

NOTES

1. Narayan et al., 1999: 39, 101.
2. Derived from a definition on self-help by Verhagen, 1987: 22.
3. As quoted by Douglass, 1992: 25.
4. Baud, 2000; De Wit, 1993.
5. See amongst others the studies by Fuller (1992), Béteille (1992), and Srinivas (1962).
6. Saberwal, 1995, as quoted by Pai, 2001: 649.
7. De Wit, 1993: 165.
8. Baud, 2000: 10.
9. Verba et al., 1978, as quoted by Desai, 1995: 56.
10. Praxis, 1999: 38.
11. Jayal, 2001: 656.
12. Narayan et al., 1999: 175.
13. Narayan, 1999: 1, 13.
14. UNCHS, 1991: 38.
15. Gnaneshwar, 1995: 313.
16. Srilatha and Gopinathan, 1996: 208. These anti-poverty programmes will be discussed in Chapter 3.
17. Fernandes, 1991; Fernandes et al., 1989; Mahapatra, 1999, as quoted by Cernea, 2000: 3659.
18. Examples are described in the solid waste sector in Chennai: Baud and Post, 2001: 143-4.
19. Baud, 2000: 14.
20. Derived from a definition on self-help by Verhagen, 1987: 22.
21. Yap in Lee, 1994, as quoted by Hordijk, 2000: 31.
22. Davidson et al., 1993: 13.
23. Edwards and Hulme, 1992, as quoted by Narayan et al., 1999: 111.
24. TNSCB, 1997b: 3-4.
25. Wiebe, 1981: 16.

26. Baken and Rao, 1995: xi.
27. Robertson, 1984, as quoted by Beall and Kanji, 1999: 1.
28. Beall and Kanji, 1999: 1-2.
29. Baud, 1989: 20.
30. Douglass and Zoghlin, 1994, as quoted by Hordijk, 2000, 27.
31. Vera-Sanso, 1997: 73.
32. Moser, 1996: 49.
33. The opposite of a female-headed household is a male-headed household: a household where the male and female are married and where the male partner is the main earner (Kromhout, 2000: 81).
34. Kromhout, 2000: 81.
35. Moser, 1993: 17.
36. Beck, 1972: 209.
37. Derived from Indigenous and Development Monitor, 1998: 1. For more on this topic see Chapter Six.
38. At the time of the publication Chennai was still called Madras.
39. <http://www.cmdachennai.org>[accessed in February 2007].
40. Bijl et al., 1992: v.
41. This figure depends upon the definition of what is urban, which is not elucidated; does it include the metropolitan area or only the city?
42. Gnaneshwar, 1995: 298.
43. TNSCB, 1997a: 11.
44. De Wit, 1993: 79.
45. Urban Statistics Handbook, 2000.
46. Bunch, 1994.
47. Portes, 1998, as quoted by Narayan, 1999: 6.
48. Coleman, 1990, as quoted by Narayan, 1999: 6.
49. Narayan, 1999: 6.
50. <www.worldbank.org/poverty/scapital/index.htm> [accessed in April 2001].
51. The CMDA was created in 1975 (at that time still called MMDA) as a planning authority, leaving the executive development work to the Tamil Nadu Housing Board (TNHB) and the Tamil Nadu Slum Clearance Board (TNSCB). But CMDA's role could be extended to formulating the shape of low-income housing programmes and to monitoring progress made by the executive boards TNHB and TNSCB (Pugh, 1990: 232). CMDA has the monopoly on physical planning inside the Chennai Metropolitan Area (CMA).
52. As she was a Human Geographer who had just finished her Ph.D. thesis on housing for low-income groups, she was very experienced in doing fieldwork in low-income settlements. Besides, she knew many people at the different government and corporation offices, which was another big advantage.

53. Latrines.
54. The local association hall.
55. Throughout all the tables in the report presenting the research data, the percentages are rounded off to whole figures.

3

Government Policies

The present chapter provides an overview of the selected policies focusing on the poor in the areas which are: relocation and housing, employment, basic services and social security. It describes the policies that are implemented at the Central, state and corporate levels, over the last 10 years in order to get an overview of policy implementation, changes in policies, existing gaps, and the urban poor's eligibility for programmes. The role of NGOs is also discussed.

3.1 Overview of National Housing and Urban Development Policies Since Independence

The movement for political independence in India has been strongly linked to ideas of social and economic development. The Constitution, drafted by a committee chaired by Dr Ambedkar shortly after Independence in 1947, contained many articles that aimed at the securing of fundamental human rights, equality and fraternity as well as 'the state's duty', within the limits of its capacity, to make effective provision for securing the right to work, education, and public assistance in cases of unemployment, old age, sickness and disablement, and in other cases of undeserved want.[1] The notion that the State should intervene on behalf of the underprivileged is also embedded in the Directive Principles of State Policy and in the mandatory provisions for positive discrimination in favour of Scheduled Castes and Scheduled Tribes in the Indian Constitution. While the former is no more than a declaration of intent, the concerns it embodies have been invoked in the formulation of state policy and are reflected in the five-year plans.[2]

In 1950, the National Planning Commission was established

and made responsible for the planning process in India.[3] The Constitution delineates the powers and the responsibilities between the Union (Central Government) and the states in the Seventh Schedule, referred to as the 'Union List', or List I, and the 'State List', or List II. There is also a 'Concurrent List', or List III, containing subjects over whom both Parliament and the state legislatures have the power to legislate, but the Centre has overriding powers in all matters relating to this List.[4] The ultimate instrument of the Centre to control state politics is the President's Rule, which can be imposed in a state for problems of law and order or political unrest.

Urban development policies are articulated in various policy papers, legislative acts, by-laws, government guidelines and orders, and are laid down in the annual and five-year plans. India has annual and five-year plans at both the national and the state levels. Such plans and policy documents constitute a public statement of government plans over a period of time, and include

TABLE 3.1: THE DIFFERENT LISTS AND THE SUBJECTS THEREUNDER

List	*Functions*
List I (Union List)	Defence, foreign affairs, and sectors and industries of strategic importance such as the railways, post and telecommunication, national highways, shipping and navigation in inland waterways, air transport, and detailed plans which are prepared for these sectors by the Central Government.
List II (State List)	Public order, police, administration of justice, agriculture, water supply and irrigation, education, public health, land rights, and industries other than those in the Union List. These areas are elaborated in state plans for which the Central Government prepares a global policy and programme outlines and provides general outlays in the five-year plans.
List III (Concurrent List)	Electricity, newspapers, criminal law, marriage and divorce, stamp duties, trade unions, price controls, etc.

Source: Mengers, 1997:8; 52; www.meadev.nic.in/govt/govt.htm#g7

general objectives, main activities and details of the proposed budgets. Secondly, they constitute political documents that express the outcome of political debate and compromises in the Cabinet between ministers, and are the result of intra- and inter-departmental discussions. Thirdly, they are administrative documents that will guide the departments in their activities over the coming years. The plans and policy statements are also monitoring instruments, i.e. to assess the performance of the government and form a reference for regular process reporting.[5]

In the early years of planning, stimulating economic growth was considered to be the appropriate method to alleviate poverty,[6] and to redistribute resources for social development. It was soon realized that the benefits of economic growth did not 'trickle down' to the poor and that additional policies would be required to better their lot. During the 1950s the 'minimum needs' of people were identified.[7] From the Fifth Plan in 1974,[8] 'the target group approach' was adopted whereby poverty was to be tackled by specific programmes. These programmes were grouped into those that provided income yielding assets and skills, those that ensured wage employment opportunities and those that improved the quality of life.[9]

In addition to the shift of emphasis from economic growth to the target group approach and to endeavours to increase employment, opportunities were sought to raise the poor above the poverty line. There was a new emphasis on the provision for needs that improve the quality of life, such as health, education, nutrition, and housing. Moreover, as against the 1970s, the initial strategy of slum removal shifted towards an approach based on sites and services projects and slum upgrading.[10]

The National Housing Policy (NHP) of 1992[11] recognized that despite considerable public investment and efforts, the housing problem had remained unsolved by the Government of India: 'the resource requirement for meeting the goal "shelter for all" by the year 2000, as envisaged in the Global Shelter Strategy of the United Nations, is beyond the means of the public sector'. The policy suggested that 'the crucial role of the government at different levels is not to seek to build houses itself, but to make appropriate investment and create conditions where all women and men, especially the poor, may gain and secure adequate housing, and to remove impediments to housing activity'. The thrust of NHP is consistent with the macro-economic policy of advocating a supportive and facilitative role of government in housing, 'creating an enabling environment for housing activity of various sections of the society by eliminating constraints and by developing an efficient and equitable system of delivery of housing inputs'. But the market sector did not provide housing for the poor due to the latter's inability to pay, and the fact that the existing building regulations did not encourage the use of low-cost building materials. The impact of macro-economic policies of industrial and trade liberalization is likely to be an accelerated pace of urbanization. Larger cities with better infrastructure will attract more investment, and the surpluses in the economy will get invested in real estate, which will lead to rapid increase in land and property prices. Thus the poor, who will not benefit from the market-led growth, will be hard hit by rising real estate prices as well.[12] The state governments' budgetary support to Public Housing Agencies (PHAs) to meet operational expenses and debt obligations, decreased significantly during the 1980s and the early 1990s. As a result, the PHAs have come to depend increasingly on their internal resources. This has forced many of them to take up housing schemes largely on a self-financing basis, resulting in the construction of more upper- and middle-income housing. The impact of specific housing schemes targeting the poor, like the Scheme of employment through Housing And Shelter Upgradation (SHASU), which comes under the Nehru Rozgar Yojana (NRY) (see Section 3.3) have been extremely limited.[13] Another theme shaping housing policies in the 1980s and 1990s was the almost worldwide effort to engage civil society and its institutions, such as community groups and NGOs, in the housing delivery process.[14]

Until the 1990s, most programmes pertaining to basic services were financed primarily through the Central Government. Thereafter there has been a shift of responsibility from the Central to the state governments and local bodies. Kundu (1996b) has shown that these changes have had an adverse effect on the availability of basic services to the urban population and especially to the poor, because many state governments have suspended the programmes due to the discontinuation of Central assistance.[15]

The responsibility for the provision of basic services in the post-Independence period was placed on the states. Furthermore, a few specialized agencies like slum clearance boards were created for the purpose of providing basic services to the poor and slum dwellers. In some of the metropolitan cities, slum and squatter wings came up within the administrative structure of development authorities or municipal bodies. The total fund made available to these specialized agencies was however meagre. Other state government departments, not specifically targeting the poor, have therefore taken up most of the projects for the provision of basic services. As the role of vested interests and local elites is important in the general administration of civic bodies this influences the selection of infrastructural projects and their maintenance. According to Kundu, it is therefore not at all surprising that the civic bodies' very design discriminates against the low-income population, particularly those residing in low-income slum colonies.[16]

Anti-poverty programmes have received a great deal of attention. The plans have generally been well accepted, but their implementation has received much criticism for having failed to reach intended goals.[17] Amongst other conclusions, Kundu (1993) finds that 'the reach of the programmes was limited, even the main targets were missed, and there was a high degree of inflexibility in the programmes and schemes'.[18] The main points of critique on poverty alleviation schemes, according to Vaidyanathan (1995) are that the benefits of the programmes are not reaching the intended beneficiaries because it is easy for the better off, by virtue of their superior connections with the local bureaucracy, to appropriate a sizeable part of the benefits. Even when the beneficiaries are part of the target group, their selection is often biased, and intermediaries tend to siphon off a substantial part of the resources: The intended beneficiaries lack knowledge and information about the programmes under which they could seek assistance. They are not organized to press their claims, to correct biased selection and other defects, and many anti-poverty programmes lack integration and are fragmented.[19] Most importantly, many development programmes are not designed to fulfil the needs and priorities of the target group. Mengers (1997), in his Ph.D. thesis on housing and urban development policies in the state of Karnataka, concludes that the outcome of housing policies has not been very successful due to uneven financial assistance in the state. The production of houses remains a fraction of the estimated demand and there is no coordination between the agencies responsible for slum upgrading. In general, the main causes for the current problem of urban development are, according to Mengers, the deterioration of the political system and increasing corruption.[20] Put (1998), in his doctoral thesis on rural development in India concludes that the intervention strategies of the Indian state have not been successful as they are very bureaucratic, top-down oriented, and often technocratic.[21]

3.2 Relocation in India and Tamil Nadu

After gaining Independence in 1947, the official Indian policy with respect to slums was mainly clearance and resettlement. This policy was embodied in the Slum Clearance and Improvement Scheme (1956) and legally backed by the state Slum Improvements Act. It was financed by the Central Government, and state governments and local bodies implemented it on a limited scale. Baken (2000) mentions that the Fourth Plan (1969-74) proposed a change in policy from 'clearance and resettlement' to on-site improvements.[22] This stand was repeated in all official government documents published since then. However, over the years, deterioration in structural quality and services affected many inner city residential areas. The number of squatter settlements and slum dwellers was increasing, as was the number of pavement dwellers. It was in this context that the NHS (1992) was developed.[23] The policy recognizes the obligation of a democratic state to ensure conditions under which men and women can secure access to shelter and services, and to remove constraints to housing activity, especially by the poor and disadvantaged sections.

With respect to slums and squatter settlements it is mentioned that 'the approach will be to avoid forcible relocation, to confer occupancy rights wherever possible, to extend basic services, finance and shelter inputs, but to arrange for relocation, where unavoidable, with the involvement of the community and of voluntary agencies'.[24] What is meant by full involvement is not elaborated and is open to many different interpretations.

In India, people have been affected by relocation and displacement in many different areas. People were forced to move as a consequence of large development projects. Mines, for instance, have displaced over 2,100,000 persons over the last 40 years.[25] People are also affected by changes in land use and loss of livelihood caused by environmental pollution.[26] In urban areas, the major causes of displacement are economic growth, environmental improvements, slum upgrading and non-urban programme, or a combination of causes. In some cases people are affected by multiple displacement, like for instance in Orissa, where residents of a village were displaced three times from the early 1980s onwards.[27] India's development programmes have caused an aggregate displacement of more than 20 million people during roughly four decades, and 75 per cent of these people have not been rehabilitated.[28] In fact, according to Cernea (2000), the vast majority of development resettlers in India have become impoverished.[29] Apart from impoverishment, a study on rural resettlement in Orissa has highlighted latent conflicts in the resettlers' patterns of marriage alliance. This along with estrangement in the family, weakening of kinship ties, and mounting inter-caste tensions has become a characteristic of the resettled villages.[30]

Before turning to relocation in Tamil Nadu, we will study relocation projects in other places in India. Two major relocation schemes were initiated in Bombay (now called Mumbai) and in Delhi as long-term strategies to improve the living conditions of slum dwellers. In Bombay, the Bombay Municipal Corporation established 15 resettlement colonies during the 1970s and 1980s to rehouse about 20,000 families. The scheme aimed at providing alternative developed plots and creating as least the minimum civic amenities in new colonies established in city suburbs. Under the scheme, all slum dwellers residing on plots needed for urgent civic amenities were relocated.[31] Patel et al. (2002) describe resettlement programmes in Mumbai that took place from 1989 onwards, where relocatees were resettled from their dwellings along the railway tracks in the city.[32] In Delhi, like in many other cities in the 1950s and 1960s, the resettlement of squatters was the dominant policy.[33] In 1960, resettlement programmes in Delhi were initiated under the Jhuggi-Jhompri Removal Scheme (JJRS) to remove 50,000 families squatting on public land and to provide alternative accommodation. During 1975-6, 14 resettlement colonies were developed, covering an area of 900 ha., and 139,520 plots. The number of people settled in these colonies in 1981 was approximately 597,000. In the decade between 1980 and 1990, the population in the 14 resettlement colonies had risen to 944,000, which was mainly due to encroachments on the vacant spaces in the colonies.[34] Both schemes in Bombay and Delhi were initiated in order to relocate squatters and make available the vacated plots for development of civic amenities in the city. People were shifted to far-off places, which had the effect of depriving them of previously established mutual-help networks and employment opportunities. There was no advance planning or consultation with the affected population in the selection of sites or design of basic amenities.[35] The impact study carried out in Delhi brought out the comparative living standards in the new colonies versus the previous location and found out that the overall living conditions deteriorated in the new colonies.[36] I found studies of relocation projects in four other cities in India. In his Ph.D. thesis on Vijayawada, a city with 845,305 inhabitants (1991), and Visakhapatnam, a city with 1,057,118 inhabitants (1991), both located in the southern state Andhra Pradesh, Baken concludes that from the start of the Fourth Plan in 1969 slum and pavement dwellers in both cities were relocated to approximately 27,091 plots in 31 relocation settlements.[37] He mentions that compared to the pre-1980 era, the period between 1980-94 witnessed more frequent and larger squatting-related relocation drives involving shifts to more distant areas in both cities. In Hyderabad, forced relocation took place under the Hyderabad Water Supply and Sanitation Project, which was financed by the World Bank and relocated 50,000 people in 1990.[38] Mertens

(1996) described a relocation project in Bangalore, where from 1987 onwards inner city slum dwellers were forcibly shifted to a project on the outskirts of the city.

According to Reddy (2000), there are currently new approaches to involuntary resettlement in urban infrastructure projects, namely that 'resettlement and rehabilitation are increasingly treated as inseparable components of the earliest stages of project design and they are being given priority in terms of advance planning, institutional support, and adequate budgetary resources'.[39] Fernandes and Chatterji (1995) mention that the Government of India has finally realized the need for a rehabilitation policy for displaced persons 'because they pay the price for development', but that in practice only one corporation has actually developed such a policy, namely the National Thermal Power Corporation. Three other rehabilitation policies are under preparation: by the Department of Water Resources Development, the biggest displacing agency; Coal India; and the Ministry of Rural Development.[40] These bodies all undertake large development projects in the rural areas. And although Tamil Nadu has experience in implementing rehabilitation programmes in World Bank assisted projects, there is no state-level policy for resettlement and rehabilitation.[41] This study will be restricted to relocation in the urban context.

In 1970, as a consequence of the fast growing slums in Chennai, the Tamil Nadu Slum Clearance Board (TNSCB) was formed.[42] It was given a statutory footing through the Tamil Nadu Slum Areas (Improvement and Clearance) Act of 1971.[43] Initially, the main responsibility of the TNSCB was 'slum clearance'. By 1976 though, the Government of Tamil Nadu realized that if the slum families continued to grow as fast as they were growing, and if the TNSCB continued to lay emphasis on their costly programme of slum clearance and rehabilitation, the problem of shelter for households could not be solved. Accordingly, the Board shifted its emphasis from slum clearance to slum improvement.[44] The objectives of the Board are:

1. To clear the slums in flood-prone and other vulnerable areas within the city of Chennai and to provide self-contained hygienic tenements or serviced plots in safe places.

2. To prevent the growth of new slums and encroachments.
3. To prevent private landowners from evicting slum dwellers from their huts and to provide tenants with security of tenure.
4. To provide basic amenities like drinking water, street lights, storm water drains, sewer lines, etc. to all slums.[45]
5. To improve the standards of slums and to ensure a better quality of life to all slum dwellers.[46]

Since the 74th Amendment, the state government may endow powers to municipalities for performance of functions and implementation of schemes including urban planning and slum improvement and upgradation. Since then, the Tamil Nadu Housing Board (TNHB) and the TNSCB have been under the jurisdiction of the Chennai City Municipal Corporation.[47]

In terms of ownership, the location of slums in Chennai can be broadly classified into those on land owned by the state (36 per cent); land owned by the corporation (8 per cent); land owned by the TNHB and the TNSCB (13 per cent); land owned by religious institutions (9 per cent) and; private land (32 per cent). In addition, 2 per cent of the slums are located on objectionable land like water margins, road margins, and railway margins. Different authorities own this land.[48]

In 1986 there were 1,417 slums in the inner city, with a population of 765,000. In the periphery there were 430 slums with a population of 253,000. The Chennai Metropolitan Area had a total of 1,847 slums with a population of 1,018,000.[49] While most of the slums on public lands have been taken up under the clearance programme or under improvement schemes, the slums on private lands have hardly been touched. A survey conducted by the TNSCB in 1986 revealed that there were 46,550 families living on private land. Due to paucity of other lands for putting up huts, slums have also emerged on the banks of waterways as well as along road margins. It was found that there were 22,700 families living in 142 locations along the four waterways running through Chennai city. Similarly, 24,117 families were identified as living along road margins, railway margins and the like.[50]

TNSCB's policy is that slums along road margins, water

margins, railway tracks and low lying areas have to be relocated. Also, as a Mass Rapid Transport System (MRTS) is being constructed in Chennai, all the slums located on the track are being relocated. Pavement dwellers are also being relocated to 'relocation areas'. About 17,582 families were and are being resettled to various locations, as is illustrated in Table 3.2.

TABLE 3.2: RELOCATION SCHEMES IN CHENNAI

Name of Scheme	*Number of Families*	*Completed or Ongoing*
Velacheri	2,640	Completed
Kodungaiyur	1,046	Completed
Korrukkupet phase I	1,010	Completed
Korrukkupet phase II	434	Completed
Tamilar Nagar	132	Completed
Pallikkanarai	2,520	Ongoing
Okkiam Thoraipakkam	9,800	Ongoing
Total	17,582	

Source: TNSCB, date not given. Information on the last scheme was given in July 2001 by Mr Zafrullah, Community Development Officer, TNSCB.

The Chennai Urban Water Supply and Sanitation projects cause forced relocation of many persons, especially in rural areas. The first two projects have affected 3,528 persons in rural areas. The Government of Tamil Nadu formulated the third project in 1998, with the assistance of the World Bank; the Government of Tamil Nadu and the Chennai Metropolitan Water Supply and Sewerage Board are the implementing agencies. The project aims at improving and expanding the water supply, sanitation and solid waste systems of Chennai city, and will cause relocation. A rehabilitation action plan has been designed. In the rural areas, 1,023 families have been declared to be eligible for rehabilitation assistance under this programme. As the proposed sites where water and sewerage works are to be undertaken in Chennai, are not, according to the report, occupied by slum dwellers, resettlement and rehabilitation would not be needed in

Chennai.[51] A look at the proposed locations casts doubts on this conclusion.

3.3 Central and State Government Housing, Employment and Basic Services Programmes for the Urban Poor

The Central Government institution that plays an important role in housing and urban development policies is the Ministry of Urban Development (MOUD). It was created in 1985 and has a number of important agencies under its control: the Central Public Works Organisation, the Town and Country Planning Organisation and the Housing and Urban Development Corporation Ltd. Though housing and urban development are a state subjects, the union ministry is responsible for the formulation of policies for programmes and implementation strategies of housing and urban development schemes.[52] Besides framing policies and guidelines for the Union Territories and states, MOUD formulates and implements a number of schemes through state governments, of which the most important are the Integrated Development of Small and Medium Towns (IDSMT), Nehru Rozgar Yojana (NRY), Swarna Jayanti Shahari Rozgar Yojana (SJSRY), Urban Basic Services for the Poor (UBSP), the Environmental Improvement of Urban Slums (EIUS),[53] and Self-Employment Programme for the Urban Poor (SEPUP), as well as the major state government schemes.

In Tamil Nadu, housing and urban development come under the responsibility of the Housing and Urban Development Department. Since the introduction of the 74th Constitutional Amendment Act in 1992, the CMDA, the TNSCB, and the CMWSSB, which provides water to the whole of Chennai including the study area, fall under the responsibility of the Chennai City Municipal Corporation.[54] The Public Distribution System (PDS) comes under the Food, Civil Supplies and Consumer Protection Department, education under the Education Department, and social security under the Social Welfare Department.[55] Employment programmes fall under the responsibility of the Housing and Urban Development Depart-

TABLE 3.3: JURISDICTION AND OWNERSHIP OF SPECIAL AUTHORITIES WITHIN THE METROPOLITAN AREA OF CHENNAI

Function	*Jurisdiction*	*Ownership*
Water and sewerage	Metropolitan	State
Bus transport	Metropolitan	State
Suburban railways	Metropolitan	National
Electricity	State	State
Town planning	Metropolitan	State
Area development	Metropolitan	State
Housing	Metropolitan	State
Slum improvement	Metropolitan	State
Telecommunications	Metropolitan	National
Industries	State	State
Employment	State	State

Source: Derived and adjusted from Datta and Chakravarty, 1981, as quoted by Datta, 1999: 92.[56]

ment. Table 3.3 shows the jurisdiction and ownership of special authorities in Chennai.

Environmental Improvement of Slums (EIS), Accelerated Slum Improvement Scheme (ASIS) and Environmental Improvement of Urban Slums (EIUS)

The EIS was launched in 1972.[57] It was a major programme financed by the Central Government, designed solely for the physical improvement of existing and legalized slums through the provision of basic facilities like tap water, drains, toilets, and streetlights.[58] Although generally the schemes were restricted to slums located on government lands, in a few cities even slums on private lands were brought under the scheme. The programme was initiated in 11 major cities with populations above 3 lakh.[59] Eventually though, during the Sixth Five Year Plan (1980-5) it was scaled up to be implemented in all urban areas, irrespective of their size.[60] The per capita sum sanctioned was only Rs 120 in the initial years, but was raised in 1985 to Rs 300.[61] In 1990-1 the scheme for the Environmental Improvement of Slums (EIS) was renamed the Environmental Improvement of Urban Slums (EIUS). The modalities remained, however, more or less the same.[62] In Tamil Nadu however, as can be read below, EIUS was financed completely by the state and the local governments.

In 1972, the TNSCB started to implement the EIS in Tamil Nadu, a programme financed by the Central Government.[63] In Chennai, the programme provided for a limited number of slum improvements and ensured water supply, community baths and streetlights.[64] The scheme was concluded in 1977 and the TNSCB stated that a total of 54,654 families had benefited at a cost of Rs 40 million.

A new scheme, which can be considered a continuation of EIS, was started in 1977 in Tamil Nadu, and was called the Accelerated Slum Improvement Scheme (ASIS).[65] It provided for public convenience units, water taps, and street lights. According to the TNSCB, a total of 99,558 families benefited from the scheme, at a cost of Rs 87 million (up to March 1990).[66] In Chennai the programme ended in 1991.[67]

Another scheme started in Tamil Nadu in the 1990s. Called the EIUS, it was financed completely by the state and local governments. It provided for baths, toilets, public fountains, streetlights and roads. The scheme was meant for cities where the Tamil Nadu Urban Development Project (TNUDP) was not implemented.[68] The exception was Chennai, where both programmes were implemented.[69] A policy note of the Government of Tamil Nadu in 1999-2000 mentions that the TNSCB planned to implement slum improvement works within the EIUS, and that its objectives were that these works benefit 30,000 families living in slums in Chennai and other cities at a total cost of Rs 6 crore (Rs 60,000,000).[70] According to an official of the TNSCB, this programme ended in 2000 as the money had been spent.[71]

Sites and Services Scheme and Slum Upgradation-cum-Improvement Schemes

In the Sites and Services Scheme (S&S) launched by the Central Government during the Fifth Five Year Plan (1974-9), the poor themselves attempted to build their dwellings.[72] The programme envisaged the provision of small plots with certain minimum facilities to the urban poor on a hire-purchase basis. The sites and services schemes are generally implemented by the state housing agencies, whereas the slum improvement schemes are implemented through slum clearance boards or slum wings of development authorities or local bodies.[73] Mengers (1997) mentions that although several successes are known of sites and services projects, the general outcome has not been very satisfactory. Failures are due to poor administration, low commitment of executing agencies to non-conventional and less 'profitable' approaches, non-conducive building and settlement-planning by-laws, problems of acquiring land, and poor response from urban dwellers to settle in often distant, under-serviced and more expensive settlements.[74]

In the Fifth Five Year Plan (1974-9) the following slum development programmes were launched by the Central Government:

a. The Slum Improvement Programme (SIP) involves merely physical improvement of the slum by the provision of a standard package of basic facilities.
b. The Slum Upgradation Programme (SUP) provides shelter and basic services.
c. The Slum Reconstruction Programme (SRP) is designed to re-house the slum population after reconstruction of houses with a proper layout plan on the same site.[75] It has only been adopted in a few cities.

In 1977, a World Bank supported scheme started in Chennai: the Madras Urban Development Programme (MUDP I and MUDP II). This programme signified an important policy change. The emphasis in low income housing policy shifted from the provision of readymade tenement units to relying on the self-help of slum dwellers in the field of shelter provision through the SIP and S&S schemes.[76] Under MUDP I and II the slum improvement projects undertaken by the Madras Metropolitan Development Authority had covered 322 slum areas, benefiting about 75,000 families.[77]

In 1985-6, when MUDP II came to a close, the World Bank co-financed a programme that covered Chennai and nine other major cities of Tamil Nadu under the Tamil Nadu Urban

Development Project (TNUDP).[78] Like MUDP I and II, two of the components are S&S schemes and SIP.[79] This programme envisages the improvement of existing slums through, amongst others, the provision of basic services like roads, water supply, drains, sanitation, street lights, and community facilities,[80] the improvement of the transport system in Chennai and the provision of financial assistance to municipalities so that they may improve their administrative functioning. The programme was due to finish in September 1995.[81] However, the S&S component was still proceeding in 2001.[82] Under this scheme, land acquired by the TNSCB is plotted and provided with infrastructure and services. These plots are allotted to slum families living in objectionable areas on a hire-purchase basis, the cost being recovered over 20 years.[83]

Integrated Development of Small and Medium Towns

The Central Government's Integrated Development of Small and Medium Towns (IDSMT) programme, established at the start of the Sixth Five Year Plan (1980-5), focuses on the development of small and medium towns and aims to reduce migration to the major cities. It encompasses slum improvement and low-cost sanitation. Initially, its scope was restricted to towns with a population of less then 1 lakh, as per the 1971 Census. At present, however, a few towns with a population more than 1 lakh, but less than 3 lakh have been brought under the programme. Fast growing centres that are also district or sub-divisional head-quarters have generally been selected under the programme. The local bodies implement the programme, although state government departments such as the Public Works Department (PWD), the town and country planning department, the housing board and the slum clearance boards share this responsibility.[84]

By 1999, 53 housing schemes had been implemented in small and medium towns of Tamil Nadu, generating 10,550 houses and 7,040 developed plots. Schemes for the construction of 492 houses and 6,882 plots were underway in 1999 and during the year 1999-2000, another 328 houses and 1,572 developed plots were slated to be constructed in 42 towns.[85]

Urban Basic Services and Urban Basic Services for the Poor[86]

The Urban Basic Services (UBS) scheme was launched by the Central Government in 1986, and it involved the provision of basic services to poor urban households with community participation. It originated in the conventional urban community development programmes, and its central idea was that participation and leadership were crucial elements in the effective use and management of services such as primary health, primary education, basic sanitation, water supply, and income generating activities for poor women.[87] The programme involved the financial participation of the Central Government, state government, the municipality and the UNICEF. In 1990-1, the UBS scheme was modified and renamed Urban Basic Services for the Poor (UBSP).[88] Since 1992, the programme funds have been provided fully by the state governments and municipalities. UNICEF has retained a role in the field of training. By 1997 the programme had been implemented in about 280 towns.[89]

Whilst the UBSP delivered material benefits to many slum communities and helped women realize that they could overcome some of the problems affecting them, effective implementation was undermined by poor efforts to integrate it with the services of different development departments, and to involve NGOs in certain areas. Another problem was the severe financial constraints imposed on the programme when state governments failed to release funds in time and municipalities could not contribute their share. The programme was discontinued in 1997 and replaced by a new scheme: Swarna Jayanti Shahari Rozgar Yojana.[90]

Self-Employment Programme for Urban Poor (SEPUP), Nehru Rozgar Yojana (NRY), and Swarna Jayanti Shahari Rozgar Yojana (SJSRY)

The SEPUP was launched by the Central Government in 1986 as the urban counterpart of the IRDP.[91] Under this programme, the urban poor living below the poverty line get financial assistance up to Rs 5,000. The objective of the scheme is to encourage the urban poor to undertake self-employment ventures in small business, artisan crafts and service-oriented activities through the provision of subsidized loans.[92] Between 1987 and 1992, the programme is said to have assisted a large number of beneficiaries in urban areas and to have helped some of them to cross the poverty line.[93] According to Reddy, however, due to the failure of SEPUP, the government in 1992 decided to merge this scheme with the Nehru Rozgar Yojana.[94] Weaknesses of the scheme included inadequate assistance and misuse by the beneficiaries.[95]

The Nehru Rozgar Yojana, which started in 1989 and ended in 1997, was an urban counterpart of the Jawahar Rozgar Yojana that started in 1986.[96] It was the responsibility of the Union Ministry of Urban Affairs and Employment, Department of Urban Employment and Poverty Alleviation.[97] The financing of the scheme was shared by the Central Government, the state government, and the local authorities;[98] central, state and local bodies were all involved in implementing the scheme.[99] The programme sought to provide wage employment, self-employment, and skills for the urban poor. The target group was persons living below the poverty line in urban areas. The poverty line was based on an income of Rs 8,400 per annum in 1989-90, which was adjusted to Rs 11,850 per annum in 1991-2.[100] The scheme consisted of:

a. The Scheme of Urban Wage Employment (SUWE), which provided for employment for urban poor living in settlements having a population up to 1 lakh.[101]
b. The Scheme of Employment through Housing and Shelter Upgradation (SHASU), which was meant to assist economically weaker sections of the society in the construction or upgradation of their dwelling units, which was applicable to urban settlements with a population below 20 lakh. It consisted of a loan and subsidy component and provided for training and infrastructure support.[102]
c. Under the Scheme for Urban Micro Enterprises (SUME), the urban poor were encouraged to start micro-enterprises

in the informal sector with the help of subsidized bank loans and training. This plan intended to have a multiplier effect of generating wage employment and to reduce the dependency on the informal moneylender.[103] The scheme consisted of a loan and subsidy component and provided for training and infrastructure support. It was applicable to all urban settlements.[104]

The impact of SHASU has been limited. This is because of the requirement of a land *patta* (title), demanded by the funding agencies, and the lack of urban land available for this purpose. Getting a clear land title or the state government's guarantee that the people residing in the slums taken up for upgradation would not be relocated for the next 15 years were the other major bottlenecks.[105] Also, the funds provided under SHASU were extremely limited.[106]

Six years after the introduction of NRY, 742,541 beneficiaries had received bank loans, whereas the number of people who had completed training courses was much lower: 188,235. According to official figures, by the end of 1995, a total subsidy amount of Rs 133.30 crore was sanctioned under SUME, calculated on the basis of reported performance by the states and Union Territories.[107] The Government of India then stated that NRY had not taken off as was expected and planned,[108] and towards the end of 1997 launches a unified poverty alleviation programme was called the SJSRY. This scheme replaced, amongst others, the NRY and the UBSP.[109] The SJSRY is funded on a 75:25 basis by the Central Government and the state governments. It consists of two major schemes:

a. The Urban Self Employment Programme (USEP) encourages urban poor, defined as those living below the poverty line, especially women, to set-up small service enterprises, petty businesses and manufacturing operations. It also provides training.
b. The Urban Wage Employment Programme (UWEP) seeks to provide wage employment to beneficiaries living below the poverty line. The programme applies to urban local

bodies with a population of less than 500,000, as per the 1991 Census. So it does not apply to Chennai.[110]

Under the NRY programme in Tamil Nadu, a loan of Rs 4,510 was issued to each family living below the poverty line by the TNSCB, which included a grant of Rs 800 from the Government of India and Rs 200 from the Government of Tamil Nadu and a loan of Rs 3,150 from HUDCO.[111] From the end of 1997, SJSRY replaced the NRY. This programme however was not implemented in Tamil Nadu in the period 1998-2000.

Pavement Dweller Housing Scheme and Resettlement and Rehabilitation Scheme

In pursuance of the National Housing Policy, the Union Planning Commission allocated Rs. 3 crore for the rehabilitation of pavement dwellers. The plan was first implemented in Bombay, Calcutta, Madras and Hyderabad, where shelter problems of the pavement dwellers were severe and called for immediate action. The Pavement Dweller Housing Scheme envisaged the provision of serviced plots to the displaced households in an organized layout with basic services and the construction of community shelters.[112]

In Tamil Nadu, the Pavement Dwellers Housing Scheme was intended to shift the pavement dwellers in Chennai city to different places in the Chennai Metropolitan Area and to provide for serviced plots with core houses to each family.[113] This programme continued into 2001 but under a different name: Resettlement and Rehabilitation Scheme, better known as the R and R scheme.[114]

Education

Primary education comes under the responsibility of the municipal authorities.[115] In India, elementary education is a shared responsibility of the Central and state governments. It appears on the Concurrent List, but in practice state governments are the main actors.[116] In 1989-90 the total spending on education by the central and state departments on education was

3.8 per cent, and in 1993-4 it came down to 3.5 per cent of the GDP. As a share of the GDP, spending on primary education was 1.6 per cent in 1993-4. There are now 67 million children between the ages of six and ten who are attending primary schools, but 28 to 32 million primary school-age children who are not.[117] Others mention that as many as one-third of all the children between the ages of six and fourteen, 23 million boys and 36 million girls, are out of school. In 1999, half of the population of India, 61 per cent of the women and 36 per cent of the men, was unable to read and write and less than 30 per cent of all adults had completed eight years of schooling.[118] There is a great diversity in performance between states and even within states, with some districts faring poorly even in states that are otherwise doing well, and vice versa. There also are gaps between groups of children, with education outcomes differing between boys and girls, between the poor and the better off, and between tribal or Scheduled Caste children and others.

There are private and public schools in India. The structure of public schooling varies across the states, although for the most part, it follows a similar pattern. Public elementary education covers grades one to eight, with upper primary school beginning at grade five in some states and grade six in others. Lower secondary covers grades nine and ten, and upper secondary covers grades eleven and twelve. All elementary subjects are compulsory, while some secondary subjects are optional in grades eleven and twelve. Schooling is nominally compulsory in 14 states and 4 union territories.[119] Public elementary schools are free, as directed in the Constitution in the sense that admission fees in government schools are negligible. This does not mean that education is free in the more relevant sense that it involves no expenditure for the parents. North Indian parents spend about Rs 318 per year, which is well below real costs, on items including fees, books, slates and clothes. This is a major financial burden, especially for poor families with several children of school-going age.[120]

Health Care

According to the Constitution, health care is the responsibility of the state governments, although in certain limited areas, the

Central Government exercises direct control. The Central Government as well as the states and corporations/municipalities run hospitals. There are also private clinics, run by, amongst others, companies and voluntary organizations. There are a number of health care facilities available for middle and higher income groups and special health care institutions for employees of public and private companies. In addition, there are public sector facilities free of cost for the poor, where the non-poor are required to make payments, but in practice free medical services are provided to everyone in these hospitals. Pricing of services then, has not been used to restrict use by the non-poor, which limits the availability to the poor.[121] The only facilities used by the urban poor are the dispensaries and hospitals at the local level run by the state or local governments. In the provision of basic medical facilities to the poor, a major problem is that of physical access. In some cities this problem has been met by the extension of the facilities to slum colonies through mobile vans. In other slums, medical facilities are provided through NGOs, but these are not free of cost.

Water Provision, Sanitation, Sewerage and Waste Disposal

As a large segment of the population in urban India remained without access to safe drinking water and sanitation facilities, many programmes from the 1980s focused on these areas.[122] However, even today many people remain without access to clean drinking water and sanitation. The 1991 Census showed that the percentage of households having access to safe drinking water had increased from 38 per cent in 1981 to 63 per cent in 1991, leaving 37 per cent without access.[123] The World Bank mentions that in 1995, 70 per cent of the urban population had access to sanitation, leaving 30 per cent without access.[124] According to Gnaneshwar (1995), cities like Chennai (still called Madras at that time) face acute water supply problems as its system is able to supply a mere 70-80 litres per capita per day, as compared to the norm of 125-200 litres. Moreover, he argues that the real problem appears to be the unequal distribution in different areas of the same metro cities.[125] According to Mathur (1994) in the lower income groups, the proportion of the population that is dependent on rivers, canals and water tankers for water supply is high. More than 60 per cent of those who use rivers, canals and water tankers for water belong to groups whose income is less than Rs 40 a day.[126] A study conducted in 1995 by Swaminathan in Mumbai (still called Bombay at that time) concluded that pavement dwellers consumed, on an average, about 15 litres of water per person per day. Moreover, slum and pavement dwellers pay more than other city residents for water.[127] In some cities part of the water supply is privatized, like for instance in some towns of Uttar Pradesh where the operation and maintenance of tubewells for water is contracted out to the private sector.[128]

After the 74th Amendment, water supply and sewerage came under the responsibility of the local government so that (from then onwards) the Chennai Metropolitan Water Supply and Sewerage Board (amongst others) came under the Chennai City Municipal Corporation. The Municipal Corporation is responsible for the maintenance of the drains in the city, which at times leads to one body accusing the other of not maintaining the system, especially during the monsoon, when in many areas of the city there is stagnation of either rain or sewage.[129]

Regarding sanitation facilities, the 1991 Census also showed that while 64 per cent of the urban population in all of India had access to a toilet, only 38 per cent of the Scheduled Caste households had such a facility.[130] Even if they have access, this may mean that many people may have to share one latrine and they are often not well maintained, without access to running water.[131] In Chennai, the sewerage system serves only 31 per cent of the metropolitan population.[132]

Waste collection, which is one of the tasks of the local authorities, is inadequate in most cities in India. Slum areas have little or no garbage collection at all. So often the only alternative for slum dwellers besides selling the valuable materials to the recycling sector, is to burn the waste, or throw it in storm water drains and open spots. As mentioned before, in some cities in India, part of the waste collection and transportation is privatized. NGOs and community-based organizations are also active in the field of waste collection, composting and recycling activities, though only in a few cities. The informal sector likewise plays a major role in waste collection and recycling.[133]

The management of urban infrastructure is the responsibility of the Chennai Metropolitan Development Authority (CMDA), which is nominated by the state government, and is, according to Mukhopadhyay (1999), bureaucratic, unaccountable to the local people, and heavily influenced by state politics.[134]

Specific State Government Schemes for the Urban Poor in Tamil Nadu

a. Shelter for Shelterless. Shelter for Shelterless was a programme under which houses were constructed with loans from HUDCO on serviced plots for families living in slum areas. The houses were given on a hire-purchase basis.[135] This programme is no longer operational.[136]

b. Fire-Proof Shelters. During 1999-2000, the resettlement of families living in objectionable areas in Chennai city was planned by the TNSCB, as was the upgradation of the sewage system in four slum areas. A new programme of the TNSCB was the provision of asbestos roofs to slums to prevent the fast spreading of fire.[137] In early 1999, the Board converted 4,432 huts into fire-proof shelters.[138] The fact that asbestos poses a grave health concern, especially in cases of fire, is not an issue, and many people are not aware of the dangers.[139]

3.4 Central and State Government Social Security Programmes for the Urban Poor

Public Distribution System (PDS)

One very large programme is the PDS, a joint responsibility of the central, state, union territory, and district administrations. It involves the procurement of food grains and a few other items by the central or state government department/agencies at certain predetermined prices, storage and transportation to different parts of the country, and distribution among consumers through a system of ration shops.[140] Cards are issued so that holders can obtain food and kerosene from the ration shops. The cardholders are dependent upon the supply of 'their ration shop', i.e. they are attached to one particular shop.[141] Kundu (1993) pointed out that the procedure of issuing ration cards involves an implicit bias against the poor, illiterate, houseless, slum dwellers and temporary migrants as:

1. Most of these people do not satisfy the requirement of having legal ownership or tenancy over the place of their residence. Many do not even have a permanent address.
2. Their capability to cope with the administrative requirements of the system is extremely limited due to their socio-economic background.
3. Many of the poor are being pushed out of the more expensive localities in most cities, a large number of them live in colonies at great distances from the offices issuing ration cards. Also, most of these colonies do not have a fair price shop in the neighbourhood.
4. Engaged in a struggle for survival, they do not have the time to complete the bureaucratic requirements of obtaining a ration card.[142]

Another aspect of the PDS believed to be going against the poor is the periodicity of sale. A study by Kabra and Ittyerah (1986) shows that the system of issuing rations on a monthly basis is founded on the assumptions that the target populations under the PDS have regular incomes and can buy their provisions on a monthly basis.[143] A large majority of urban workers are employed in informal activities associated with construction and trade and commerce, and have an irregular and uncertain flow of income. Many of them get their salaries on a weekly basis.[144] They also find it difficult to purchase their monthly requirements in one instalment. Kundu (1993) mentions that a weekly or fortnightly system is therefore better suited to the urban poor.

Other points of criticism are related to the lack of targeting of the PDS: 'While large numbers of the poor do not have access to it, there is, on the other hand, little or no attempt to deny access to the affluent.'[145] Parikh (1997) mentions that the poor are not benefiting much from the PDS; they depend to a substantial extent on the open market for their consumption requirements.[146] The PDS is not effective in reaching the poorest 20 per cent of households. For every rupee spent, less than twenty *paisa* reach the poor in all states excepting Goa, Daman and Diu.[147] One of the other problems in the PDS is the amount of leakages of food grains and other commodities in the form of losses in the transport, storage, and diversion of food grains to the free market.[148] Baken (2000) mentions that the card system is 'one of the many welfare measures of the Indian Government that has fallen victim to the uneasy co-operation of public servants, politicians, dealers, and citizens, aimed at grabbing from society, inevitably leading to a fair degree of instrumental chaos'. This chaos is illustrated by the fact that in some areas in Andhra Pradesh for instance, there are many more card holders than households, while in others there are very few households holding cards.[149]

There is some confusion as to which colour of ration cards there are in Tamil Nadu, as can be seen in Chapter 5. The colours also change regularly, which may be the reason for the confusion. According to the Government of Tamil Nadu, in 2002 there were two cards, pink and yellow. In the urban areas, the criteria for obtaining a pink card are a family income under Rs 15,000 per year, applicable to people living generally in slums and daily wage earners like rickshaw pullers, porters, food and flower sellers on the pavement, domestic servants, construction workers, and others similarly placed.[150] All others obtain a yellow card.[151]

Old Age Pension Scheme

The National Old Age Pension Scheme (NOAPS) comes under the National Social Assistance Scheme, which was introduced by the Central Government in 1995. The NOAPS is meant for the poor elderly and is a Centrally sponsored programme with 100 per cent Union assistance to the states and Union Territories in accordance with the norms, guidelines, and conditions laid down by the Central Government. The Central Ministry of rural development manages the scheme.[152] The following criteria apply in the implementation of the scheme:

1. The age of the male or female applicant should be 65 years or more.
2. The applicant must be destitute in the sense of having little or no regular means of subsistence from his or her own sources of income or through financial support from family members or other sources.[153]

The amount of the old age pension will be Rs 75 per month for purposes of claiming central assistance. It was assumed that 50 per cent of the population below the poverty line in the above 65 years age group would qualify for the old age pension.[154]

On 19 March 1999, the Government of India announced another social assistance scheme called 'Annapurna' for the elderly destitutes who have no one to take care of them. Under this scheme, an elderly destitute was to be provided with 10 kilograms of rice or wheat per month free of cost through the PDS. The scheme aimed at covering those destitutes who were otherwise eligible for old age pensions under the national old age pension scheme.[155] The Ministry of Rural Development again implemented this scheme with the assistance of the Ministry of Food and Civil Supplies. However, in 2001 the amount of money allocated was released only to 15 states and 12 Union Territories, and half of them have not yet released it.[156]

The old age pension scheme in Tamil Nadu is subdivided into different schemes, which cover different groups of people. These are:[157]

1. *General old age pension scheme:* It covers old age persons who are destitute and do not have livelihood assistance. The minimum age to receive it is 60 years in the case of persons who are not getting earnings due to leprosy, insanity, paralysis or loss of limb. For others, the minimum age is 65 years.
2. *Old age pension scheme for destitute physically handicapped:* It covers physically handicapped persons whose disability is 50 per cent and above, and who are above the age of 45 years.

3. *Old age pension scheme for destitute widows:* For this group there is no age limit, the only criterion is that these widows should not have remarried, though they may have a legal heir of 18 years of age.
4. *Old age pension scheme for destitute deserted wives:* It covers women above the age of 30, but only those who do not have any link with their husband for over five years and who had obtained a legal separation certificate from the Court of Law. The deserted destitute wives who have legal heirs of 18 years of age are also eligible to get assistance under the scheme.

Old age pensioners are also eligible for a free *dhoti* or *sari* on Deepavali and Pongal, and, as will be discussed below, they are supplied daily with the Noon Meal Scheme in the Noon Meal Centres, and half a kilogram of rice a week. Those who do not take the Noon Meal are supplied with one kilogram of free rice a week.[158]

Although Prasad (1995) writes that the different schemes in Tamil Nadu have a considerable number of beneficiaries, she has noticed that in the district she studied there is a large unevenness in the coverage between the district headquarters and the more backward regions, located far from the district headquarters. She has also described the difficulties for widows to apply for a

TABLE 3.4: NUMBER OF RECIPIENTS OF OLD AGE PENSION IN 1997-8 AND 1998-9 IN TAMIL NADU

Scheme	*Number of Recipients*	
	1997-8	*1998-9*
General old age pension scheme	336,207	349,796
Old age pension scheme for destitute physically handicapped	34,554	39,015
Old age pension scheme for destitute widows	281,073	329,247
Old age pension scheme for destitute deserted wives	50,896	51,291
Total	702,730	769,349

Source: Government of Tamil Nadu, 1999b: 89.

pension; even obtaining an application form to seek state assistance in itself appeared to be a major problem.[159]

Specific State Government Programmes for the Urban Poor in Tamil Nadu

To attack malnutrition amongst children, nutrition programmes were introduced in Tamil Nadu way back in 1956. So far, the state has experimented with as many as 25 nutrition programmes. At present there are three main programmes in operation:

1. The Integrated Child Development Scheme (ICDS) provides supplementary food, non-formal pre-school education, health check-ups, immunization, nutrition and health education for children after birth until the age of six.[160]
2. The Tamil Nadu Integrated Nutrition Project (TINP) is implemented in many districts of Tamil Nadu but not in Chennai and the main components of the project are nutrition and health services.[161]
3. The Chief Minister's Nutritious Noon Meal Scheme (CMNNS).

The state government of Tamil Nadu finances the CMNNS. It started in 1982[162] as a personal initiative of the then chief minister M.G. Ramachandran (MGR), the leader of the All India Anna Dravida Munnetra Kazhagam (AIADMK).[163] The scheme was introduced in child welfare centres in rural areas for pre-school going children between the ages of three and five and for children between the ages of five and nine attending primary schools. In September 1982, it was extended to the nutritious meal centres in urban areas. In September 1984, it was further extended to the students between the ages of ten and fifteen. Old age pensioners and pregnant women are also included as beneficiaries under this scheme.[164] It is still operating and is the most ambitious of all feeding programmes and therefore selected to be evaluated in this study. It envisages providing midday meals to 8.5 million pre-school and school-going children. An extensive network of child welfare centres throughout the state has been established:

23,483 centres in rural areas and 4,840 centres in urban areas.[165] In Chennai, there are 697 such centres.[166] This is in addition to 35,510 school feeding centres that cater to almost 6.4 million pupils in classes one to ten. Besides the primary objective of direct nutrition intervention, the scheme also aims at improving school enrolment and attendance, as the free meal is perceived as a strong incentive to attend school.[167] According to the *Hindu* (2002), nearly 6,500,000 children are fed in 41,057 school noon meal centres daily, for which the government spends at least Rs 225 to 250 crore a year.[168]

The problem with the scheme is that two-thirds of the recipients do not really need the programme whereas the most vulnerable children are not reached because they do not go to school.[169]

3.5 The Role of NGOs in Poor Urban Areas

India, where tax incentives and a long history of donations to religious groups have supported the growth of independent organizations, has thousands of local NGOs, including an estimated 12,000 that focus on development.[170] In order to get an idea of the number of NGOs working in poor urban areas in India, data from a cross-section of 67 NGOs working in poor settlements in Mumbai was used to describe, amongst other elements their activities. It was found that the prime importance of the services delivered by these agencies to the poor are welfare activities, providing services, and creating access. All the sample NGOs work in ways intended to benefit the urban poor but concentrate on activities targeted at more specific groups of beneficiaries. The urban poor may be differentiated into women, street children, youths, and so on, and some NGOs aim to work with specific groups, whilst others do not have any particular targeting strategy. Most of the NGOs focusing on women are involved in the provision of services rather than with a wider emphasis on gender relations.

Most NGOs reported multiple external funding sources, and the median number of sources per NGO is two. Both the number of activities and, especially, total staff, seem to correlate with the number of funding sources. Some NGOs enjoy a high level of international funding whilst others are much more dependent upon domestic resources. Another source of funding is the user charges, which NGOs apply to their beneficiaries to sustain their activities.

The criticism levelled by many NGOs against government and donors is that they are unwilling to support long-term objectives, slow careful work, and gradual results which characterize successful local institutional development.

While most NGOs have linkages with municipal departments, interaction with state and Central Government departments seems less prevalent. NGOs tend to initiate links with government agencies when they come up against particular problems or when they identify a gap in government services either in terms of inefficient provision of services or the exclusion of particular sections of the population. Most interaction is initiated by NGOs, which seek to draw government resources into their programmes in order to influence government projects, strategy or policy to relieve constraints faced by the urban poor. The number of initiatives of this nature undertaken by government is much smaller.[171]

3.6 Programmes to be Covered in this Study

Table 3.5 presents an overview of the programmes selected to be studied in this research, the level of the administration responsible for them, the departments and boards these programmes fall under, and the target groups.

These programmes were chosen because they were still in operation at the time of the fieldwork and they targeted the inhabitants of the relocation area in the field of housing, employment, basic services, and social security.

3.7 Conclusion

Table 3.6 brings together the programmes implemented by the state and local government over the last 10 years in Chennai (as

TABLE 3.5: DEPARTMENTS AND BOARDS INVOLVED IN THE PROVISION OF HOUSING, BASIC SERVICES, AND SOCIAL SECURITY SCHEMES FOR THE POOR IN TAMIL NADU STUDIED IN THIS RESEARCH, AND THEIR TARGET GROUP

Provided	*Administrative Level*	*Department or Board*	*Functions Studied*	*Target Group*
Housing	Tamil Nadu State	TNSCB	Relocation, provision of basic services in the relocation site	Slum and pavement dwellers
Employment and basic services	All urban towns in Tamil Nadu	Housing and Urban Development Department	Swarna Jayanti Shahari Rozgar Yojana	Urban poor who live below the poverty line, especially women.
	Chennai Metropolitan Area (CMA)	CMWSSB	Water provision, sewerage	All inhabitants of CMA
	Tamil Nadu State	Education Department	Education	All inhabitants of Tamil Nadu
	Chennai City	Chennai City Municipal Corporation	Waste collection, maintenance of basic services in relocation site	All inhabitants of Chennai city
	Tamil Nadu State	Health Department	Health care	All inhabitants of Tamil Nadu

contd.

TABLE 3.5 (contd.)

Provided	*Administrative Level*	*Department or Board*	*Functions Studied*	*Target Group*
Social security	Tamil Nadu State	Social Welfare and Nutritious Meal Programme Department	Old age pension schemes	1. Old age destitute persons without livelihood assistance, minimum age of 60 years in the case leprosy, insanity, paralysis or loss of limb, for others, 65 years. 2. Old age destitute and physically handicapped, for physically handicapped with 50 per cent disability and more, and older than 45 years of age. 3. Old age destitute widows of all ages but not remarried, though they have legal heirs of 18 years of age. 4. Old age destitute deserted and legally seperated women of above 30 years of age.
			Noon Meal Scheme	1. Pre-school going children between 3-5 years 2. School-going children between 5-15 years 3. Old age pensioners 4. Pregnant women
Social security	Tamil Nadu State	Cooperation, Food, Civil Supplies and Consumer Protection Department	Public Distribution System	All inhabitants of Tamil Nadu

discussed in Chapters 1 and 3), the different types of partnerships that have developed, and the initiatives the poor themselves have taken up in the field of housing and urban development (as discussed in this chapter).

TABLE 3.6: MAJOR PROGRAMMES/INITIATIVES UNDERTAKEN BY THE GOVERNMENT, THROUGH PARTNERSHIPS OR BY THE POOR IN CHENNAI IN HOUSING AND URBAN DEVELOPMENT BETWEEN 1990 AND 2000

Initiator	*Programmes/ Initiatives*	*Short Description*
Government: (Central/ state/local/TNSCB)	Environmental Improvement of Urban Slums (EIUS)	Provision of baths, toilets, public fountains, street lights, and roads in slums
	Tamil Nadu Urban Development Project (TNUDP)	Provision of water supply, roads, drains, sanitation, street lights, community lights, community facilities in slums
	Shelter for Shelterless	Construction of houses for slum families
	Pavement Dweller Housing Scheme (renamed Rehabilitation and Resettlement Scheme)	Slum families and pavement dwellers shifted to relocation sites
	Provision of services, infrastructure, education	Water supply, sewerage, sanitation, solid waste disposal, health care, education
	Public Distribution System	Supply of food grains and other items at predetermined prices to the public

contd.

TABLE 3.6 (contd.)

Initiator	*Programmes/ Initiatives*	*Short Description*
	Old age pension schemes	Provision of pensions to the elderly, destitute women and handicapped persons
	Noon Meal Scheme	Providing midday meals to pre-school and school-going children
Partnerships	Sustainable Chennai Programme	Attacking surface water pollution, groundwater contamination, scarcity of potable water, solid waste management, air and noise pollution
	Green and Clean Madras City	Cleaning and maintenance of the streets by an NGO
	Privatization of parts of solid waste collection	Waste collection is handled by a private company
Collective action by poor alone	Squatting	Occupation of public and private land and objectionable areas by poor families
	Improving physical environment	Maintenance of roads, drainage systems, disposal of garbage, etc.
	Chit funds	Local savings system
	Water distribution	Organization of water provision and distribution

These three groups (government/partnership/collective action by poor alone) and their initiatives in the area of housing and urban development are the topics of this study and discussed in the following chapters.

3.7.1 HOUSING

In India, from the 1990s onwards, the importance of the market in providing housing gained more support, which led to a decrease in the specific housing schemes targeting the poor. The market sector did not provide for housing for this strata due to its inability to pay and the fact that existing building regulations did not encourage the use of low-cost building materials.

Also, due to economic liberalization, land prices in the urban areas increased enormously, which further lessened the possibilities for the urban poor to be provided with adequate housing.

In Tamil Nadu not many housing programmes have been implemented by the state and local agencies since the 1990s. In 2001, the TNUDP was still operational, as well as the Sites and Services Scheme, the Resettlement and Rehabilitation scheme and the scheme for the provision of fire proof shelters, but all on a very limited scale.

3.7.2 FORCED URBAN RELOCATION

With respect to slums and squatter settlements, the National Housing Policy (1992) mentions that forced relocation should be avoided, but whenever unavoidable, it should be arranged with the involvement of the community and voluntary agencies. However, what is meant by that is not elaborated upon. Even then, forced resettlement still occurs in India. In Chennai, slums located on sites needed for urban development projects and pavement dwellers are relocated. The relocatees are informed beforehand, but involvement of the community and voluntary agencies are not reported as being part of the relocation procedure.

3.7.3 EMPLOYMENT, BASIC SERVICES AND SOCIAL SECURITY

The main points of criticism of the government programmes and schemes for employment and basic services are: they do not reach the target groups due to ineffective targeting are inflexibility.[172] The target groups are not informed about the existence of schemes; and there is no coordination between the different agencies focusing on the same target groups. Starting in the 1990s, there was a shift of financial responsibility for providing basic services from the Central to state government and local bodies.[173] This has had an adverse effect on the availability of basic services as the total funds made available to these agencies was meager.[174]

Special programmes for the provision of employment and basic services for the urban poor were not implemented in Chennai in 1999-2000, due to spent budgets, and a programme that was set to take off has not started yet. Social security programmes that focus particularly on the poor like the PDS, the Noon Meal Scheme, and the old age pension schemes exist. From the literature it seems that some are efficient, although better targeting could improve their impact. Except for the Noon Meal Scheme, the bureaucratic procedures the target group needs to undertake to apply or to change conditions are elaborate, complex, and expensive. Whether this is also applicable to the research area will be one of the points under the study.

NOTES

1. Indian Constitution, Article 39, as quoted by Mengers, 1997: 49.
2. Vaidyanathan, 1995: 329.
3. Mengers, 1997: 52.
4. Mathur, 1999: 46.
5. Mengers, 1997: 82, 8.
6. Aziz, 1994: 4-5.
7. Van Kampen, 2000: 8.
8. According to Auclair (1998: 52), the Fifth Five-Year Plan started in 1975.
9. Aziz, 1994: 4-5.

10. Mengers, 1997: 124; Mehta, 1996: 43.
11. In 1992, the National Housing Policy (NHP) was formulated: it advocated a supportive and facilitative role of government in housing, by creating an enabling environment for housing activity of various sections of the society, by eliminating constraints, and by developing an efficient and equitable system of delivery of housing inputs (Mehta, 1996: 41). The policy will be discussed later in this chapter.
12. Mehta, 1996: 41, 46, 44.
13. Kundu, 1996a: 195, 199.
14. Mukhija, 2001: 2043.
15. Kundu, 1996b: 220.
16. Kundu, 1996a: 199.
17. Van Kampen, 2000: 8-9.
18. Kundu, 1993: 163.
19. Vaidyanathan, 1995: 339.
20. Mengers, 1997: 492-3.
21. Put, 1998: 372.
22. Baken, 2000: 439. Therefore from the 1970s onwards they had developed policies in order to improve slum areas like the Environmental Improvement of Slums (EIS) and the Urban Basic Services (UBS) (Baken, 2000: 86). For more information on these schemes see below.
23. As is also referred to in paragraph 3.1.
24. Sundaram, 1993: 52.
25. Asif, 2000: 2005.
26. Kothari, 1995a: 1.
27. Behura, 1996: 156.
28. Fernandes, 1991; Fernandes et al., 1989; Mahapatra, 1999, as quoted by Cernea, 2000: 3659. Rehabilitation, according to Asif (2000: 2005) is 'a total re-establishment of lost livelihood, i.e. recreation of physical, social and cultural environment required for a new life with dignity'.
29. However, Patel et al. (2002: 159) have described the resettlement of 60,000 low-income people in Mumbai who have, in contrast to most other projects, not become impoverished. This project was exceptional in two other aspects as well: the actual move was voluntary and the resettled people were involved in designing, planning and implementing the resettlement programme and managing the settlements to which they moved.
30. Behura and Nayak, 1993: 284.
31. Reddy, 2000: 169.
32. Patel et al., 2002.
33. Sundaram, 1993: 53-6.
34. Reddy, 2000: 169, Khan, 1995: 60-1, 64; Ali, 1990.

35. Reddy, 2000: 169.
36. Mishra and Gupota, 1981, as quoted by Reddy, 2000: 169.
37. Baken, 2000: 444-7.
38. Cernea and Guggenheim, 1993: 25.
39. Reddy, 2000: 172. Examples of this 'new approach' are given in Reddy, 2000: 174-82.
40. Fernandes and Chatterji, 1995: 29-40.
41. CMWSSB, 1998: 13.
42. According to Schenk (1986, as quoted in Baken, 2000: 86), 'even before the creation of the TNSCB, Madras had witnessed several slum clearance and resettlement schemes. With the creation of this agency however, ambitious plans were launched to eradicate all slums in the city within seven years and to construct multi-storey tenements containing some 164,000 heavily subsidised dwelling units to re-house the slum dwellers affected. The limits to this approach soon became visible. Instead of the planned average yearly construction of 23,500 tenement units, only 3,000 units were built. By 1980 the estimated number of slum households in Madras was 221,000'.
43. TNSCB, 1997a: 1.
44. Ramani, 1985: 133.
45. TNSCB, 1997a: 1.
46. Government of Tamil Nadu, 1999c: 48.
47. Subramanian, 1998: 57-58, 61.
48. TNSCB, 1997a: 9.
49. TNSCB, 1997b: 4-5.
50. TNSCB, 1997a: 2.
51. CMWSSB, 1998: 1-4. The solid waste management component will be implemented independently by the Chennai City Municipal Corporation (CMWSSB, 1998: 3).
52. According to Mengers (1997: 478) state governments are rather slow in recognizing emerging problems and even slower in conceiving solutions. Consequently, the Central Government has the urge to intervene, but because it is not able to do so, it gets around the problem by sponsoring schemes.
53. Mengers, 1997: 106.
54. As well as the Tamil Nadu Housing Board, the Tamil Nadu Pollution Control Board and the Transport Corporations (Subramanian, 1998: 61).
55. This was during the AIADMK rule, which was elected in 2001: <www.tn.gov.in/tnassemby/ministers.ht> [accessed in February 2002].
56. According to Datta (1999: 92), water and sewerage and slum improvement come under the responsibility of the state, but according to Subramanian (1998), after the introduction of the 74th Amendment Act, the CMWSSB and the TNSCB were placed under the responsibility

of the Chennai City Municipal Corporation. Table 3.3 was therefore changed by the author.

57. Kundu, 1993: 139; Aziz, 1994: 16; TNSCB, 1997a: 3.
58. Mengers, 1997: 124.
59. Kundu, 1993: 140.
60. Mengers, 1997: 127.
61. Kundu, 1993: 140.
62. Mengers, 1997: 135.
63. Kundu, 1993: 139, 140; Aziz, 1994: 16; TNSCB, 1997a: 3.
64. TNSCB, 1997a: 3.
65. De Wit, 1993: 86.
66. TNSCB, 1990, as quoted by De Wit, 1993: 86.
67. TNSCB, 1997a: 3.
68. TNSCB, 1997b: 10.
69. Dhanalakshmi and Iyer, 1999: 11.
70. Government of Tamil Nadu, 1999c: 62-3.
71. According to Mr Zafrullah, CDO of the TNSCB, in a conversation in July 2001.
72. Kundu (1993: 150), but according to Mengers (1997: 124), the programme was launched during the Fourth Five Year Plan (1969-74).
73. Kundu, 1993: 150, 156.
74. Mengers, 1997: 13.
75. Kundu, 1993: 162.
76. De Wit, 1993: 86-7.
77. Rao and Nelson, 1994: 167.
78. Kundu, 1993: 156, according to J. de Wit the programme started in 1988 (1993: 88).
79. Government of Tamil Nadu, 1995: 72.
80. TNSCB, 1997a: 4.
81. Dhanalakshmi and Iyer, 1999: 11.
82. According to Mr Zafrullah, CDO of the TNSCB, in a conversation in July 2001.
83. TNSCB, 1997a: 4.
84. Kundu, 1993: 146-8.
85. Government of Tamil Nadu, 1999c: 22-3.
86. It is not clear to me whether these programmes have actually been implemented in Tamil Nadu.
87. Mathur, 1994: 62-3.
88. Aziz, 1994; Mengers, 1997: 385, 135.
89. De Wit, 1997: 11.
90. Chaplin, 1999: 153.
91. Aziz, 1994: 17.
92. Reddy, 1994: 13.
93. Aziz, 1994.

94. Reddy, 1994: 52.
95. Aziz, 1994: 17.
96. Van Kampen, 2000: 279.
97. Of the Central Government (Government of India, a).
98. Mengers, 1997: 350.
99. Kumar, 1997: 17.
100. Mengers, 1997: 349.
101. In the first phase, but it is not mentioned how long this phase lasts and what happens afterwards, Government of India, a: 17.
102. Government of India, a: 17.
103. Kruse, 1997: 87-8.
104. Government of India, a: 17.
105. Planning Commission, 1992, as quoted by Kundu, 1996a: 198.
106. Kundu, 1996a: 198.
107. Kruse, 1997: 88.
108. Due to, amongst others, very low numbers of people completing the training courses. Government of India, 1994, as quoted by Kruse, 1997: 88.
109. Chaplin, 1999: 153.
110. Government of India, b: 1-6.
111. TNSCB, 1997a: 5. No information was found on whether SUWE and SUME were also implemented in Tamil Nadu.
112. Dattatri, s.a.: 4.
113. TNSCB, 1997a: 5.
114. According to Mr Zafrullah, CDO of the TNSCB, in a conversation in 2001. Under the scheme not only pavement dwellers were relocated, but also slum dwellers living in illegal slums.
115. Datta, 1999: 96.
116. Anuradha De et al., 1999: 12.
117. World Bank, 1997: 7, 2, 1.
118. Anuradha De et al., 1999: 9.
119. World Bank, 1997: 2, 17.
120. Anuradha De et al., 1999: 16.
121. Due to their limited capacity.
122. Kundu, 1993: 80-95, 135.
123. The figures are rounded off by the author.
124. World Bank, 1998/9: 192.
125. Gnaneshwar, 1995: 298.
126. Mathur, 1994: 49.
127. Swaminathan, 1995: 137.
128. Mehta and Mehta, 1992, as quoted in Lee, 1997: 144.
129. Subramanian, 1998: 61.
130. The author has rounded off the figures.

131. Chaplin, 1999: 152.
132. Gnaneshwar, 1995: 298.
133. There is much information on informal sector involvement in waste collection and recycling, see amongst others: Dhanalakshmi and Iyer, 1999; Baud and Schenk, 1994; Huysman, 1994; Van Eerd, 1995.
134. Mukhopadhyay, 1999: 122.
135. TNSCB, 1997a: 4.
136. According to Mr Zafrullah, CDO of the TNSCB, in a conversation in July 2001. He could not say when it started and stopped; no information could be found on this matter.
137. Government of Tamil Nadu, 1999c: 62, 62-6.
138. The *Hindu*, 18 January 1999.
139. Not all types of asbestos are equally dangerous. Blue and brown asbestos are the most dangerous types, but white asbestos (chrysotiel) can cause asbestosis and cancer. <www.geocities.com/RainForest/vines/5740/14asbest.html> [accessed in March 2002].
140. Kundu, 1993: 99, 95.
141. Baken, 2000: 144.
142. Kundu, 1993: 177-8.
143. Kabra and Ittyerah, 1986, as quoted by Kundu, 1993: 178-9.
144. Or, even more likely, on a daily basis.
145. Dutta and Ramaswamy, 2001: 1524.
146. Parikh, 1997: 67.
147. Parikh, 1994, as quoted by Parikh, 1997: 67.
148. Parikh, 1997: 67.
149. Baken, 2000: 145.
150. <www.tn.gov.in> [accessed in February 2002].
151. With a pink card you are entitled to more subsidized items than with a yellow card.
152. Rajan, 2001: 613.
153. Prasad mentions that a widow is considered destitute 'if she is without any regular income and if she has no relations of twenty years of age particularly a son, or grandson, or spouse. Widows without any relative and who do not own land or a house worth Rs 1000, who do not wear jewels worth Rs 500, who do not have any form of regular employment or who do not have helpful relations are also treated as destitutes' (1995: 794).
154. Rajan, 2001: 613.
155. It is not clear whether this scheme covers persons who are eligible to receive a pension under the NOAPS but in practise do not receive it, or whether it is over and above NOAPS.
156. Rajan, 2001: 614.

157. The old age pension does include one more scheme: the scheme for destitute agricultural labourers, but as it is not applicable to urban areas, it is not described here.
158. Government of Tamil Nadu, 1999b: 84-9.
159. Prasad, 1995: 794-5.
160. Government of Tamil Nadu, 1999b: 32-3.
161. Government of Tamil Nadu, 1999a: 30-5.
162. Government of Tamil Nadu, 1999b: 28. The scheme was also called Puratchi Thalaivar MGR Nutritious Meal Programme.
163. Harriss, 1991: 9.
164. Government of Tamil Nadu, 1999b: 28-30.
165. Samuel and Rayappa, 1994: 64.
166. <www.tn.gov.in> [accessed in February 2001].
167. Samuel and Rayappa, 1994: 64.
168. The *Hindu*, 24 May 2002.
169. Samuel and Rayappa, 1994: 63-5; Harriss, 1991: 84-5.
170. Lee, 1994: 160.
171. Desai, 1999: 248-57.
172. Kundu, 1993: 163.
173. Kundu, 1996b: 220.
174. Kundu, 1996a: 199.

4

The Relocation Project: Housing, the Government and the Households

In this chapter we will turn to the study area: a relocation site in south-west Chennai. The chapter will focus on the relocation project and its inhabitants. We will first draw a project outline and then turn to the inhabitants. Their household characteristics will be described with a focus on religion, caste, and the composition of the families living in the area. A discussion on how the inhabitants of the area obtained land and shelter and other issues related to housing in the relocation site will follow.

4.1 The Relocation Project

This section describes the location and layout of the project as well as the evolution of the site prior to this research. The relocatees' involvement in the relocation process will also be discussed.

4.1.1 Project Organization

The relocation site at Velacheri is located 15 km from the Chennai city centre. It used to be part of a tank with a total area of 106 ha. The lake would flood after heavy rains, then dry out during the dry season. In 1989 the TNHB started a Sites and Services scheme to benefit their target groups: the lower, middle and higher income groups of Chennai city. The scheme was developed on the highest and driest part of the Velacheri site. The lowest and most flood-prone part of the land, 13.7 ha., was handed over to the TNSCB, and it is here that they planned the relocation scheme.[1] As the project was designed to house the poor, the Tamil Nadu State Government allocated the land to the TNHB and the TNSCB and relaxed the ban on transfer of lands classified as watercourse (*poramboku*). The government, however, stipulated that the remaining areas of the Velacheri tank (30.3 ha.) should be deepened and preserved for flood moderation and for groundwater preservation.[2] As the area flooded during the monsoon, the Slum Board raised the land by three metres, but the area is still very low-lying. Also, a retaining wall was constructed as a barrier between the lake and land as well as a safeguard against flooding from other sides.[3]

The layout for the site was prepared and approved by the Madras Metropolitan Development Authority (MMDA) in close consultation with the TNSCB.[4] Designed as to what they called 'promote community interaction', 12 sub-neighbourhoods were created, each with a nursery school and a playground. It provided for 2,640 house sites measuring 4.5 m by 5.5 m each. The majority of the houses would have tiled roofs and brick walls. Plans were established for piped water and underground sanitation either from the start itself or at a later stage. Ten sites for the construction of public convenience units were planned throughout the area. Sites for all major community buildings were concentrated in one location, which provided for the construction of a primary school, a high school, a community centre, and public utilities. Sites for a market complex were also provided.

TABLE 4.1: LAND USE PATTERN OF THE VELACHERI RELOCATION SITE

Land use	*Area (ha.)*	%
Roads and access ways	3.2	23
Parks and open spaces	1.4	10
House sites	6.8	49
Public utilities	2.3	17
Commercial uses	0.1	1
Total	13.8	100

Source: Dattatri, s.a.: 11.

The Velacheri relocation project comes under the Pavement Dweller Housing Scheme, a scheme of the central government and the Tamil Nadu State Government, and was the first of its kind to be implemented under this programme throughout the whole country. The TNSCB was the implementing agency and the coordinator between all the different government departments, local bodies, and NGOs.

The costs of the project, apart from the construction of houses and land costs, were projected at Rs 5,000 per household, or Rs 132 lakh in total. Of this amount Rs 4,000 per household was financed by the central government and Rs 1,000 from the Tamil Nadu State Government. This amount was used for site preparation and the development of infrastructure. The state government was also asked to provide the land for the project free of cost.[5] Table 4.2 lists the estimate of costs for the different components of the project.

The development of the site and the construction of shelter units were carried out in phases over a period of four years between 1989 and 1993, which means that the area was still

TABLE 4.2: PROJECT ESTIMATE

Item		*Costs (Rs 100,000)*
Land Development works		220.32
	Filling low lying areas	54.82
	Storm water drains	12.23
	Building of roads	7.62
	Building of gravel pathway and sand gravel mix road	9.85
	Low lying tanks, open wells, and hand pumps	3.88
	Street lights	12
	Construction of public convenience units	13.05
	Culverts	6.71
	Construction of retaining wall	6.94
	Boundary, garbage bins, flood lights, tree planting, etc.	4.90
Total land and development works		352.32
Total project costs (excl. land and housing costs)		132

Source: Dattatri, s.a.: 14.

under construction when the relocatees were relocated to the area. In his study on an inner city slum that was going to be relocated to Velacheri, stories of the experiences of slum dwellers that were already relocated to the relocation site in Velacheri circulated in the area, making many of the inhabitants even less eager to move to the relocation site:

> Soon after arrival, the first Velacheri slum settlers faced heavy rains, which flooded a major part of the former lake, leading to abject misery. There were no facilities; even water was not brought regularly. People erected makeshift huts on demarcated plots allotted to them, many huts collapsing during rains. Moreover there were clashes between various groups of settlers, people of various castes, occupational groups and religions. For example one group tried to stop another group from slaughtering pigs. *Arrack* was freely available.[6]

4.1.2 PROVISION OF HOUSING IN THE RELOCATION SITE

The first settlers in the Velacheri relocation site erected huts on plots allotted to them against the cash payment of Rs 500 per household, given to them by the state government. Later people obtained cash loans of Rs 8,000 through HUDCO to construct their own dwellings.[7] Sixteen units were built with cash loan assistance. Sixty-four units were built with the additional help of an NGO, which supplemented the cash loan of Rs 8,000 with Rs 2,500 per household.[8] The NGOs consulted the target groups on which type of house was to be to built before starting construction.[9]

Some loans given to the relocatees were not used for the purpose they were meant for. The Slum Board, therefore, decided to build 1,656 independent core houses, the cost of which was met through the loan assistance provided to the beneficiaries. In addition, the Board also built other types of shelters on an experimental basis. The agreement was that the beneficiaries had to repay Rs 66 per month as land cost and Rs 10 per month for maintenance to the Slum Board for 21 years. After 21 years, when the full amount had been paid, the beneficiary would receive a sale deed, and the plot and dwelling become privately owned. Beneficiaries also had the flexibility of repaying the amount due before 21 years were over. In that case, they would receive a temporary sale deed for five years. In some individual cases the Slum Board would allow the allottees to leave the area after those five years. The Slum Board would then buy the plot and allocate it to another family.[10]

The resettlement of the 2,640 households in Velacheri, who came from different areas in Chennai city, started in 1990 and was completed in four phases, over a period of four years. Table 4.3 shows the number of households from the different areas in Chennai that were relocated to Velacheri.

Map 4.1 indicates the localities from where the relocatees were relocated. Also, all the other localities in Chennai that are mentioned in the dissertation are marked on the map.

An evaluation report undertaken by Dattatri for the Slum Board mentions that the relocation project was a success as, amongst reasons cited:

TABLE 4.3: CATEGORIES AND NUMBER OF HOUSEHOLDS RELOCATED TO THE VELACHERI RELOCATION SITE[11]

Category	*Number of Households*	*Distance from Velacheri Site (km)*
1. Pavement dwellers[12]	638	10
	520	14
	42	7
Sub-total	1,200	
2. Mass Rapid Transport System (MRTS)	30	13
	107	12
	64	12
	291	12
	163	11
	97	11
	192	10
	30	12
Sub-total	974	
3. River margins	353	8
4. Affected by calamities	64	–
Miscellaneous	49	–
Sub-total	113	
Total	2,640	

Source: Dattatri, s.a.: 13.

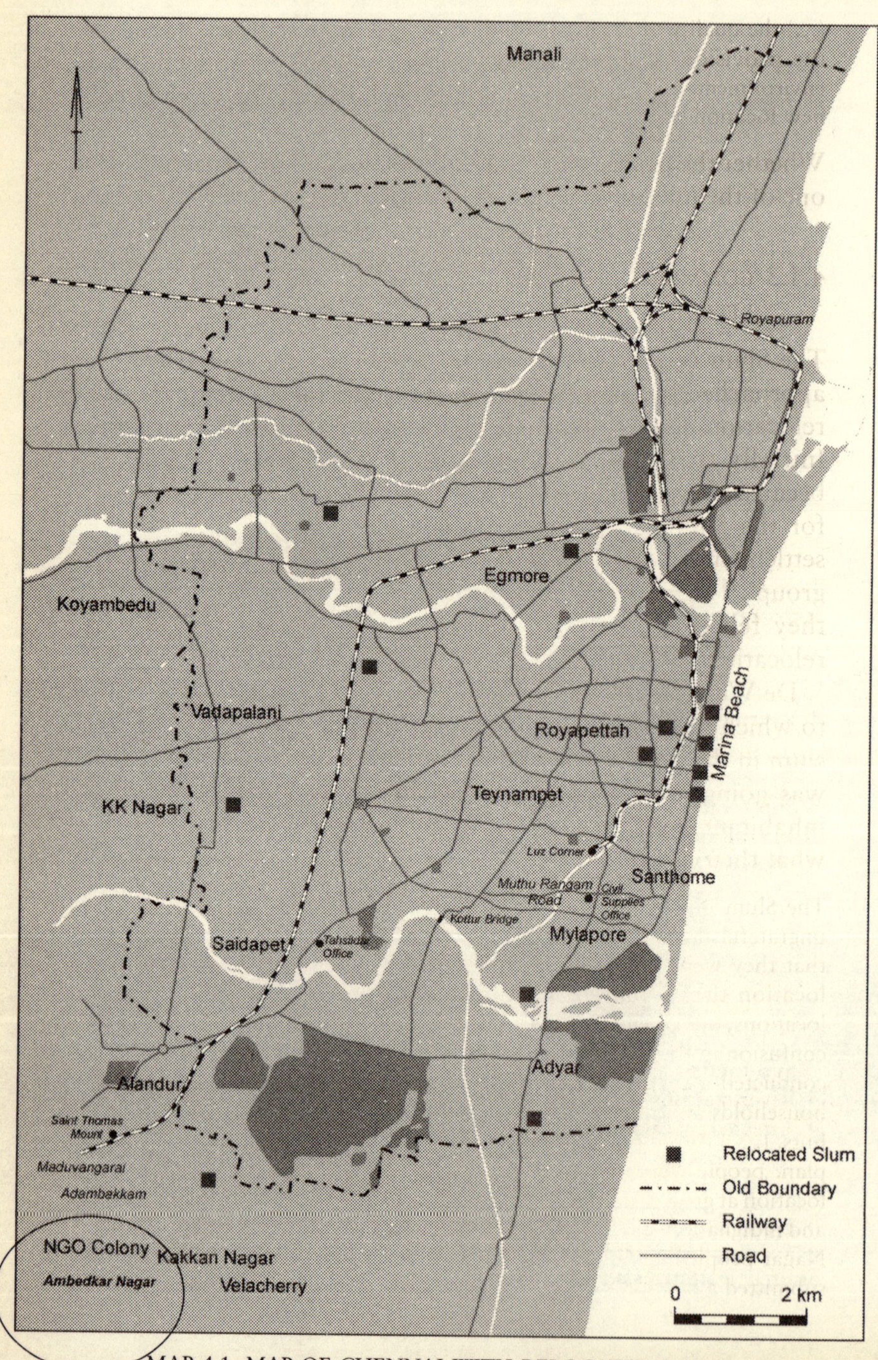

MAP 4.1: MAP OF CHENNAI WITH RELOCATED SLUMS

(...) the quality of the living conditions of the settlers is improved through the provision of durable shelters with basic amenities and a healthy environment, and because of the employment opportunities offered at the new location which is proximate to the industrial belt of the city.[13]

Whether the people relocated to Velacheri share this view will be one of the major topics of this research.

4.1.3 COMMUNITY PARTICIPATION IN THE RELOCATION PROCESS

The Slum Board carried out the actual resettlement. First, they approached the slum leaders to inform them of the necessity of relocation and subsequently the communities were informed.[14] Initially the different communities were hesitant to resettle because they feared loss of jobs. Dattatri, however, in the report for the Slum Board, states that eventually the process of resettlement was carried out with 'full cooperation of the target group'.[15] Whether this means that people were willing or whether they felt that there was no other option than to accept the relocation is described below.

De Wit (1993) undertook part of his Ph.D. research in a slum to which he gave the pseudonym Chitra Nagar. It was an illegal slum in the city centre on the banks of a small canal. This slum was going to be relocated to Velacheri. He describes how the inhabitants of that slum were informed about the relocation and what their response was.

The Slum Board first sent a CDW official to Chitra Nagar. She had the ungrateful task of informing the Chitra Nagar people in February 1988 that they were to be relocated. She was unable to say exactly to which location they would be sent, and could only indicate three possible locations, one of which was Koyambedu. (. . .) She managed only to create confusion in the slum and people were quite angry with her. (. . .) A team conducted a survey in Chitra Nagar in July/August 1988, registering all households and taking photos of all household members in front of their huts. (. . .) About one month later the Slum Board announced a change of plan: people were not to be relocated to Koyambedu, but to Manali, a location at great distance from the city centre. The news created much anger and indignation, and led to a small procession of approximately 125 Chitra Nagar people marching to the office of the Housing Secretary, where they submitted a petition.

Then the state elections came in January 1989 and policy planning and implementation were halted. In June 1989 a new meeting was held in Chitra Nagar, where the Community Development Officer of the Slum Board informed the people about the relocation plans. There he mentioned the new relocation site, Velacheri.

> He explained the details of the relocation plan and area. Velachery was a good place, easy to reach by bus. Employment would be no problem. Women could find work as domestic servants nearby; for men there were employment chances in nearby factories. The government would provide all the facilities needed: street lights, drainage, roads and if necessary additional transport. Hospitals and schools would also be built, depending on the existing facilities nearby. (. . .) Initially it appeared as if the meeting organized by the CDW official had raised more questions. (. . .) Only a few people understood all the details of the plans, and there were many misunderstandings.

De Wit mentions that eventually the majority of people in Chitra Nagar were willing to move to Velacheri, not so much because they were attracted to it, but more because they were unhappy with Chitra Nagar. Besides, many people felt they had no alternative.[16]

Besselink, an M.A. student, undertook her fieldwork in Velacheri in 1994-5 and she stated that many people were opposed to the relocation, and that in many cases they were threatened that their homes would be destroyed if they didn't cooperate. In some areas fights broke out between the police and the slum dwellers when they were relocated. One group even filed a court case against the Slum Board and obtained a stay order, but the court cancelled this one week later and people were ordered to move within 24 hours. When eventually the Slum Board and the police started to destroy their houses, the people decided to give in and were transported to the relocation site by lorries brought in by the Slum Board. One slum dweller in Besselink's thesis described the way they were informed by the Slum Board:

> One day people from the TNSCB came to our settlement and told us to shift. It was not a public meeting or that they came to each house. They just came and people gathered around these officials. They told us to move

because they (TNSCB) wanted to take mud from our place. For three months nothing happened. Suddenly one day they came and started removing the houses and putting them on lorries. They brought us to this area, where we got an allotment paper and a house number.[17]

Tokens were distributed: each household on the Slum Board's list was entitled to a plot in Velacheri but many irregularities occurred. It appeared that the most influential people managed to obtain more than one token, and that a small majority of households (the poor, the illiterate) obtained only one plot. Some people did not even know what the token was for but accepted it. An unknown number of households, mostly tenants and female heads of households who were not at home when the tokens were distributed, did not get a token.[18]

4.2 Household Heterogeneity

The relocation site has been given two different names by its inhabitants. The larger part of the area is called Ambedkar Nagar, while a smaller part is named Bhavani Nagar.[19] According to the inhabitants of Bhavani Nagar, this was done in order to keep them apart from the people in Ambedkar Nagar, who they said had a different (meaning lower) caste background. As these two areas are part of the same relocation site, and the name Ambedkar Nagar is more commonly used, in this dissertation Ambedkar Nagar includes Bhavani Nagar. In the first paragraph a general picture of the inhabitants of the research location will be drawn, focussing on religion, caste and family composition. A description of how the relocatees have dealt with the new situation will follow, after which the infrastructure of Ambedkar Nagar and the responses of its inhabitants and other important issues in the lives of the inhabitants will be analysed.

4.2.1 Religion and Caste

Of the 158 respondents, 87 per cent are Hindus,[20] 4 per cent Muslims, 7 per cent Christians,[21] and 2 per cent did not give an answer. Within Ambedkar Nagar there are 16 temples. Some of these are very small private shrines; others are bigger and have been built by a group of people. In addition, a big mosque has recently been constructed and there are two apostolic prayer halls. There is a statue of Mary too.[22]

Hindu society is, according to the Brahmin theory, divided on the basis of *varna*, which is the Sanskrit word for colour. The fourfold hierarchy has on its apex the Brahmins, who were traditionally ritual specialists, next come the Kshatriyas, who were the rulers and soldiers; then the Vaishyas, traditionally the merchants; and then the Shudras, who were the peasants and servants.[23] The outcastes, untouchables or Harijans (as Mahatma Gandhi renamed them and who are now commonly called Dalits) are outside the *varna* system.[24] Within and outside this largely theoretical system, there are thousands of endogamous groups or castes (*jati*). The Scheduled Castes, Scheduled Tribes and Other Backward Classes are grouped together as the Backward Classes, which are a large and mixed category of persons with boundaries that are both unclear and elastic. Together they comprise roughly one-third of the total population of the country. The Scheduled Tribes and Scheduled Castes are well-defined categories, comprising respectively around 7 and 15 per cent of the population. The Other Backward Classes (OBCs) are a residual category, their position is highly ambiguous and it is impossible to give an exact indication of their number.[25] In Tamil Nadu, the OBCs are subdivided into more categories: Scheduled Tribes and Scheduled Castes, Most Backward Classes and Backward Classes. A Census undertaken by the Second Backward Classes Commission in Tamil Nadu in 1984 concluded that in the whole of Tamil Nadu 19 per cent belong to Scheduled Castes and Scheduled Tribes, 24 per cent to the Most Backward Classes, 43 per cent to the Backward Classes and 12 per cent to the Forward Classes.[26]

As is shown in Table 4.4, 59 per cent of the respondents in Ambedkar Nagar are Scheduled Castes, or Adi Dravida.[27] Another relatively big group of 27 per cent belongs to the Most Backward Classes, 6 per cent to the Backward Classes, 6 per cent to the Forward Classes, and 2 per cent did not give an answer.

TABLE 4.4: CLASSES AND CASTES IN AMBEDKAR NAGAR

Classes	*Castes*	*Abs. Numbers*	*%*
ScheduledCastes/ Scheduled Tribes	Adi Dravida	88	56
	Arunthatiyar	1	1
	Love marriage (Scheduled Caste/other caste)	5	3
	Sub-total	94	59
Most Backward Classes	Vanniar	36	23
	Veera Kudi Vellalar	1	1
	Udayar	1	1
	Devar	3	2
	No name	1	1
	Sub-total	42	27
Backward Classes	Achari	3	2
	Gramani	1	1
	Labbai	1	1
	Syed	1	1
	Yadava	3	2
	Sub-total	9	6
Forward Classes	Chettiar	2	1
	Mudaliar	1	1
	Naidu	7	4
	Sub-total	10	6
No answer		3	2
Total		158	100

4.2.2 FAMILY COMPOSITION[28]

There is an average of 4.4 persons per household. Most of the households (120) are nuclear. Of those six are female-headed nuclear households, the women being widowed with young children. These are all, as Moser calls them, '*de jure* female-headed households'; households where the male partner is permanently absent due to death or separation. Female-headed households where the male partner is temporarily absent, Moser

TABLE 4.5: HOUSEHOLD SIZE, ABSOLUTE NUMBERS, AND PERCENTAGES

No. of Household Members	*Abs. Numbers*	%
1 member	1	1
2 members	7	4
3 members	26	16
4 members	53	34
5 members	44	28
6 members	18	11
7 members	8	5
8 members	1	1
Total	158	100

calls '*de facto* female-headed households'.[29] For more of the households in the survey the husband may have left permanently or temporarily but it is difficult to find out the real numbers, as some women do not like to reveal it. In families where widows have married sons or sons that have reached the age of 18, the mantle of household head passes to them.

Thirty-five households are extended families. In some of these extended households the children, especially sons, do not leave the house when they get married. Sometimes the children of a couple will first live apart after marriage, but the parent(s) will move into the son's house when they get old. In some cases, pregnant women returned to their mother's house for the delivery, especially for the birth of the first child. They stay there for a couple of months. For three households, it is unclear whether they are nuclear or extended households.

In a number of cases families had more children than those actually living with them. In some cases children lived with the family in the home village, others stayed with relatives in other parts of Chennai. One family mentioned that the children lived with relatives in Santhome[30] because the environment in and around Ambedkar Nagar was not good for children to grow up in, and in Santhome they were able to go to a good Christian school. As mentioned, these children are not incorporated into the household survey.

In some cases, when a woman could not conceive or when she did not bear a son, the husband found himself another wife. One respondent mentioned that her husband was also married to her sister, as she herself was not able to conceive. Her sister was living along with her and her husband, and had given birth to two children. The woman said that she agreed to this marriage under the condition that she would be allowed to live with her husband and his new bride. The two sisters take care of the children together. In another case, which is described below, a man had another wife, and he lived apart from his first wife. He only visited her occasionally, to give some money and to drink.

I met Shanti when we were interviewing people about chit funds and I was told that she was also organizing a chit fund. Initially we talked about the chit fund, but as she was in a lot of trouble, the conversation evolved into her life story:

Shanti was approximately 38 years old. She was married to Ravi, an *auto-rickshaw* driver, and they had two small daughters. From her first marriage she had two children: one son of sixteen years who was living with them, and one married daughter who was also living in Ambedkar Nagar with her husband and two children. Shanti's problems started when she first got married, about 20 years ago in a village near Tanjore, where she and her family were living. As they were very poor, her parents married her off to an old man, to become his second wife. They got two children together, a daughter and a son. When her daughter got married Shanti came to Madras to look for a job, as she said there was 'a problem' between her and her husband. She found a job as a construction labourer near Kottur Bridge. There she met her second husband. He was running a teashop near the construction site. They got married and she moved in with him in a slum near Adyar River. After a while they were relocated to Ambedkar Nagar. Initially they were happy, and reasonably well off, as her husband also owned a plot in another relocation site. He bought her nice jewellery and they got two daughters.

After a few years her husband wanted to buy an *auto-rickshaw* so she mortgaged some of her jewellery and the allotment order of the house. Her husband started drinking, and after a while she found out that he was having an affair. She was told so by one of the neighbours who had seen her husband with another woman in his *auto-rickshaw*. At the time we spoke to Shanti she was in a very bad shape; her husband only came home once in a while, in the middle of the night, drunk. Then he used to beat her up and throw her and her children out on the street. Other nights he came home with a few friends to drink. Then, as we discovered later, Shanti had also taken to drinking so that there was no money left to feed her children.

Shanti had no one to turn to because of her husband being a Nadar and she was a Vanniar, and her whole family was opposed to the marriage. Her brothers did not want to see her anymore; they said that she was responsible for her problems. Another related problem was that Shanti was at that time conducting a chit fund, but as everyone knew her problems, members were not paying their monthly deposit regularly. This meant that she, being the conductor, had to pay instead. In order to get the money back she had to persuade the defaulting members but this was getting more and more difficult as they had lost trust in her. So her debts were growing steadily.

When I returned to Ambedkar Nagar in 2001 and went to visit Shanti I found out that she had committed suicide. One night she poured kerosene over her body and set herself on fire. According to a neighbour her debts had increased over the years due to heavy drinking, and the fights with her husband had worsened. She saw no way out other than to end her life.

TABLE 4.6: NUMBER OF HOUSEHOLDS RESETTLED AND PREVIOUS LOCATIONS

Phase	*Year*	*Names of Previous Locations*	*Number of Households*
I	1990	SS	30
		AK	107
		NK	64
		NBD	291
		PN	163
		Sub-total	655
II	1991	KS	97
		GP	30
		SN	64
		Sub-total	191
III	1992	TBR	638
		CN	520
		ASN	353
		Sub-total	1,511
IV	1993	KNW	42
		LT	192
		Miscellaneous	49
		Sub-total	283
Total			2,640

Source: Dattatri, s.a.: 22.

4.3 Relocation from a Local Perspective: Obtaining Land and Shelter

As mentioned in Chapter 3, the policy of the Slum Board is that slums along road and water margins, railway tracks, slums in low lying areas, slums located on the tracks of the MRTS, as well as pavement dwellers have to be relocated. In 1990, the resettlement to Ambedkar Nagar of 2,640 households was taken up in four phases over a period of four years. The number of households resettled under each phase and their previous location are given below.

As mentioned before, the target group was first informed of the relocation through its leaders, after which public meetings were organized in the different slums.[31] Dattatri reports that initially the target groups were hesitant about the plans for relocation because of the fear of the loss of jobs, but eventually everyone agreed.[32] De Wit found that the majority of the slum dwellers he had studied were willing to go, not so much because they liked to be relocated, but because they did not like the area they were living in.[33] Dattatri states that the relocation process was a success.[34] The following paragraphs will examine from the responses and initiatives of the local communities, whether they regarded the process indeed to be a success.

4.3.1 Allottees, Tenants, and Buyers[35]

Table 4.7 shows how many of the respondents in 1998-9 were relocated to Ambedkar Nagar, and how many of them were tenants and buyers.

In the following table, we have only investigated how the respondents entered Ambedkar Nagar, as relocatees, tenants, or

TABLE 4.7: RESPONDENTS: NUMBER OF RELOCATEES, TENANTS, AND BUYERS

	Abs. Numbers	%
Relocated	120	76
Non-relocated tenants	8	5
Non-relocated buyers	30	19
Total	158	100

TABLE 4.8: RESPONDENTS: SUBDIVIDED NUMBER OF RELOCATEES, TENANTS, AND BUYERS

	Abs. Numbers	%
Relocatee living in allotted plot	106	67
Relocated but hiring a house	13	8
Relocated but bought a house/plot	1	1
Non-relocated tenant	8	5
Non-relocated buyer	30	19
Total	158	100

buyers. What became clear is that some of the relocatees did not actually live in an allocated plot but had either hired or bought a place. As can be seen in Table 4.8, thirteen of the relocated persons lived in Ambedkar Nagar as tenants and one relocatee had bought a place in the area.

Allottees

As is shown in Tables 4.7 and 4.8, of the 120 respondents relocated, 106 persons live on their own plot. The 14 respondents that were relocated but who live in Ambedkar Nagar as tenants and buyers are included in Table 4.8, but for the remaining part of this section they are included in the category of tenants and buyers and discussed in those respective sub-sections. As already mentioned, people were relocated from different parts of Chennai, as can be seen in Table 4.9.

When asked about the reasons for their relocation in 1998-9, many of the respondents knew the answers. It may be that at the time of relocation people were well informed, but it may also be that many people found out only afterwards the exact reasons for their relocation. As mentioned before, there was much confusion amongst the slum dwellers in one particular area about the reasons for the relocation and the choice of the site.

The majority of the relocatees moved into a house when they were relocated to Ambedkar Nagar, which means that they moved into a core house built by the Slum Board or got a loan from the Slum Board to construct their own house.[36] Some people never constructed anything, which is the reason that they had to rent a house in Ambedkar Nagar.

TABLE 4.9: LOCATIONS FROM WHERE RESPONDENTS WERE RELOCATED[37]

Name of the Previous Location	*Abs. Numbers*	%
TBR	27	23
CN	32	27
GP	1	1
AK	4	3
SN	6	5
NBO	12	10
PN	8	7
KS	1	1
LT	8	7
SS	1	1
ASN	12	10
NK	3	3
Others	4	3
Missing	1	1
Total	120	100

Of the total number of relocatees, 21 per cent did not invest in their house, and 79 per cent of the relocatees invested in the upgrading of their house. They had either built a compound wall, extended the front portion which was either constructed of thatches, walls of bricks with a thatched roof or walls of bricks with an asbestos roof. Some had also plastered their house. The minimum amount that was invested was Rs 500, the maximum

TABLE 4.10: AMOUNT OF INVESTMENT[38]

Rs	*Abs. Numbers*	%
0	22	21
500-5,000	39	37
5,000-10,000	17	16
10,000-15,000	4	4
15,000-20,000	6	6
20,000-40,000	5	5
40,000-60,000	5	5
60,000-80,000	3	3
80,000-100,000	4	4
200,000	1	1
Total	106	100

TABLE 4.11: SOURCE OF INVESTMENT

Source of Investment	*Abs. Numbers*	%
Loan from employers, relatives and friends	30	36
Personal savings, chit funds, loans and mortgaging	32	38
Loan from NGO, Slum Board, or sale of property	10	12
No answer	12	14
Total	84	100

Rs 200,000, with 58 per cent investing between Rs 0-5,000. The average investment by the total number of relocatees was Rs 20,295.

Personal belongings like jewellery and bronze vessels are amongst the objects that are given to a broker for mortgaging.

As mentioned before, the beneficiaries had to repay Rs 76 a month to the Slum Board. Many respondents never paid anything, others only paid once in a while. A reason commonly used to explain non-payment was the 'government forced us to live here so we should get it for free'. Those who had electricity or a No Objection Certificate (NOC) had paid the full amount to get it, but later stopped paying to the Slum Board. Some people said that it was a problem to go up and down to the office of the Slum Board in K.K. Nagar in order to pay the monthly instalment and would prefer the officers come to Ambedkar Nagar to collect it. According to an officer of the Slum Board ten bill collectors initially went to Ambedkar Nagar, but they stopped this as people refused to pay. However, once a year the bill collectors came to

TABLE 4.12: PAYMENT TO THE SLUM BOARD

Payment to Slum Board	*Abs. Numbers*	%
Nothing	43	27
Once a year (when they come)	3	2
Monthly	40	25
A small amount	21	13
To get NOC	2	1
Once	2	1
No answer	47	30
Total	158	100

Ambedkar Nagar for a 'drive collection' during which they tried to persuade the people to pay the accumulated amount due. Some respondents expected that following the elections they would get their plot for free, i.e. be declared owners.

Almost all respondents were neither happy nor unhappy about coming to Ambedkar Nagar. The relocatees explained that they did not have a choice but to be moved to the area and that is why 'they have to adjust to it'. When the three categories of relocatees, tenants and buyers are split up and compared, the following picture emerges (see Table 4.13).

As can be seen in Table 4.13, the number of non-relocated buyers that are relatively happy about coming to Ambedkar Nagar is 8 per cent higher than non-relocated tenants and 10 per cent higher than relocatees. As these buyers have almost all come to Ambedkar Nagar of their own free will, this was to be expected.

A comparison between Ambedkar Nagar and the area the respondents were relocated from was drawn regarding conveniences like medical facilities, the availability of water, public convenience units, employment opportunities, educational facilities, garbage disposal, electricity, the quality of roads, availability of transport, and market facilities. The overall majority replied that the facilities were poorer in Ambedkar Nagar in comparison with their former neighbourhood. Though it is likely that many people romanticize their former place of

TABLE 4.13: RELOCATEES, NON-RELOCATED TENANTS AND BUYERS: HAPPINESS OR UNHAPPINESS ABOUT SHIFTING TO AMBEDKAR NAGAR (IN PERCENTAGES)

Category	*Relatively happy Abs.*		*Relatively unhappy Abs.*		*Neither happy nor happy Abs.*		*Total Abs.*	
	Number	*%*	*Number*	*%*	*Number*	*%*	*Number*	*%*
Relocatees	4	3	6	5	110	92	120	100
Non-relocated tenants	1	5	1	5	6	90	8	100
Non-relocated buyers	4	13	–	–	26	87	30	100

living, this can also be interpreted as overall discontent with life in Ambedkar Nagar. While many people did not like to live here, they appreciated the ownership of a house. They also said that in the early days, life in Ambedkar Nagar was very bad, due to the reasons explained before, but it had gradually become better. When asked about the future of Ambedkar Nagar, many said that it was very difficult for them to think about the future as every day they had to struggle to survive. Others said it would only make them feel bad and worried to think about the future. Nonetheless, many hoped that in the near future all the facilities would be installed and 'Ambedkar Nagar would look like a small town'.

Sixty per cent of the respondents mentioned that their housing status had improved and the main reason for this improvement was the ownership of a plot, as now they no longer feared eviction. Furthermore, as almost all the respondents had brick walls instead of thatched ones, and appreciated the privacy they had obtained in Ambedkar Nagar. Forty per cent said their housing status had not improved and held that as the major reason for their economic status not improving. A reaction often encountered was: 'what is the use of a tiled roof when all our other problems are not solved?'. Some still feared eviction, as there was a persistent rumour in December 1998 that this was going to happen again. This rumour spread fast and caused much stress. A CDO of the Slum Board strongly denied this going to happen.

Ninety-five per cent of the allottees said they would not sell their place against the current land value, as they would not know where else to go.

Tenants

A small group of 21 respondents lived in Ambedkar Nagar as tenants, 13 of whom were relocated and 8 of whom came to Ambedkar Nagar without being relocated. This group was extra vulnerable, as their status was not legal. They were also the worst-off. They had no allotment order and would never become owners of the plots they lived on. In many cases, they also did not have a ration card because they could not get the necessary proof of tenancy, given that renting was illegal in Ambedkar Nagar.[39]

Some of the 13 respondents who were evicted were already renting in their previous location. As they were not able to get an allotment for a plot in Ambedkar Nagar and did not have the financial capacity to buy a plot or a house, they had no other option than to rent a house. Also, in some cases, a family got one plot, but after shifting to Ambedkar Nagar, the children got married, so they had to rent another plot. Some allottees who had their own plots had to sell it because of financial problems and became tenants. Others still had an allocated plot, but as they were not able to construct, they were forced to become tenants.

Five respondents came voluntarily to Ambedkar Nagar. Some of them lived very close to the slums that were relocated, and after the eviction they were told there were places for rent in Ambedkar Nagar. As rents were low, they moved to the relocation site. Other reasons to come to Ambedkar Nagar included the fact that friends or family lived there, or that rent was low. The tenants, like the allottees, came to Ambedkar Nagar from 1990 onwards. The average monthly rent was Rs 150.

Buyers

Thirty respondents were buyers. Also, one respondent who was relocated had bought a plot. Twenty-two of these buyers came from Chennai and six from outside the city. It is not clear where the other three buyers came from.

Even though the status of buyers is not legalized, they are, in general, economically better off than the others.[40] The major reason for buying a plot or a house in Ambedkar Nagar was the low price. Nowhere else in the city could they buy a place for the same price as in Ambedkar Nagar. Many thought that though the area then was underdeveloped, it would improve eventually and the land price would increase. Consequently, they expected the buying of a house to be a profitable investment. Sixteen respondents bought a plot with a complete house; one respondent bought a plot with a partially constructed house; eleven respondents bought a plot on which they themselves constructed a house; no information is available for two respondents; and for one respondent, it is not known whether he bought only a plot or a plot and a house.

Buyers also moved to Ambedkar Nagar from 1990 onwards. The price paid for a plot or a house depended on the location; near the main roads the price was often higher than in the alleys at the far end of the area. When a complete house was sold, the price also depended on its condition.[41] The price sometimes was lower than average when the plot or house was bought from relatives or friends. Due to many problems like illegal trade in drugs and liquor, and social problems between the different groups, in the early years of 1990-1, many allottees sold off, as they did not feel safe in Ambedkar Nagar.

Table 4.14 shows how much buyers paid for their plots/houses. The average amount paid for a plot was less than for a house, namely Rs 3,556 less. All the buyers invested in the construction of their house after they bought it, but the amount varied considerably. Of the 25 buyers who knew or wanted to reveal the amount invested in their house or plot, 12 invested up to Rs 10,000, five invested up to 20,000, two invested up to 30,000 and six more than Rs 30,000. The average amount invested in a plot was considerably more than in a house; namely Rs 18,948 more. Most of the buyers of both plots and houses had saved money for the investment; others had joined chit funds, borrowed money, mortgaged personal belongings or sold off other property.

Twenty-nine buyers said would not like to sell their place at

TABLE 4.14: YEAR OF PURCHASE, PRICES PAID FOR PLOTS AND HOUSES, AND INVESTMENTS MADE BY BUYERS

Year	*Number of Plot Buyer*	*Price Paid per Plot (Rs)*	*Investment in Plot (Rs) (Excl. Plot Price)*	*Number of House Buyers*	*Price Paid Per House (Rs)*	*Investment in House (Rs) (Excl. House Price)*
1990–1	2	5,000	15,000	2	20,000	Not given
		3,000	15,000		3,000	2,000
1992–3	1	11,000	7,500	4	Not given	75,000
					13,000	5,000

contd.

TABLE 4.14 (contd.)

					22,000	5,000
					20,000	15,000
1994-5	3	1,250	50,000	1	20,000	15,000
		10,000	50,000			
		11,500	6,000			
1996-7	5	11,500	42,500	5	8,000	5,000
		10,000	165,000		16,000	10,000
		25,000	5,000		17,500	25,000
		25,000	5,000		15,000	30,000
		35,000	35,000		22,000	1,000
1998-9	1	20,000	16,000	2	17,000	2,000
					35,000	10,000
Total	12			14		
No answer	5					
Average		14,021	34,333		17,577	15,385
N = 31						

the current land value, as such an inexpensive place was difficult to find in Chennai. However two buyers said they would consider selling it.

Safety

Of the 158 households, 72 faced a fire in their former area, whereas 8 households had a similar experience in Ambedkar Nagar. In June 1999, another fire broke out in Ambedkar Nagar:

On the 10th of June 1999 Vijayalakshmi and I were on our way to the area, when suddenly many women came running down the road, screaming and crying. 'There was a fire in Ambedkar Nagar and one child had burned to death,' they said. A thick cloud of smoke was hanging in the air. We went down the road where we saw a Metro water lorry filling up pots with water and throwing it on the burning huts. Many people had gathered around the fire and there was a lot of panic. As in this part of Ambedkar Nagar almost all the huts were made of thatches, and as it had not rained for a long period and there was some wind, the fire spread rapidly, and many huts had already burnt to the ground. Many men helped to throw water on the neighbouring huts to prevent the area from burning down completely. Later we were told that a baby that had died, the mother had gone to the ration shop to do her shopping when the fire started. The cause of the fire was short-circuiting and a total of 100 huts had burned to the ground.

Even so, many people felt safer in Ambedkar Nagar than in their former area, due to the fact that they would not be relocated again and to the improved construction of their house. Compared to the neighbouring areas however, they felt that Ambedkar Nagar was less safe. Women especially said they did not like to move around in the streets after dark, as by then many men were drunk and streets had no proper street lights.

Almost all respondents felt that they were part of the group they were originally relocated with and referred to themselves and each other as 'the Fishermen, the Egmore people, Vasantha College'. Even the majority of buyers and tenants felt themselves part of the group they were living amongst. Although when asked specifically many respondents did not admit that there was tension between the different groups, it seems that people in general were well aware of each other's backgrounds and normally 'stuck to their own group'. They normally did not like to mingle with other groups and felt that their own street was safer than other parts of Ambedkar Nagar.

4.3.2 PLOT TRANSFERS IN AMBEDKAR NAGAR

This case study investigates one randomly selected block in Ambedkar Nagar in order to find out whether the relocatees were still living in their allocated houses, as was the intention of the relocation project, or whether they had illegally sold them or rented them out.[42] This case study was selected because it was expected to provide more in-depth information, as the number of respondents was lower than the total sample of Ambedkar Nagar. Besides, as this case study covered a much smaller area, it would be easier to build rapport with the inhabitants.

The block contained 86 plots. The number of allottees, tenants, and buyers in this block are listed in Table 4.15 and compared with those in the whole of Ambedkar Nagar.

As can be seen in the table the number of allottees in the block is much lower than the number of allottees in the sample of Ambedkar Nagar, namely 40 per cent. The number of tenants is higher, namely 22 per cent, and the number of buyers is also higher at 17 per cent. It is not clear where these differences come from in the block but what is striking is the active involvement in

TABLE 4.15: NUMBER OF ALLOTTEES, TENANTS, AND BUYERS IN THE TOTAL SAMPLE OF AMBEDKAR NAGAR, IN THE BLOCK AND NUMBERS INTERVIEWED IN THE BLOCK

	Ambedkar Nagar Sample Abs. Numbers	%	*Abs. Numbers in Block*	%	*Abs. Numbers Interviewed in Block*	%
Allottees	120	76	31	36	17	31
Tenants	8	5	23	27	16	29
Buyers	30	19	31	36	21	38
No answer			1	1	1	2
Total	158	100	86	100	55	100

the 'plot business' of the local leaders of this particular area, which might explain part of the difference.

What is very remarkable in the block of 86 plots is that even though it is illegal, many people have sold off: 36 per cent of the households in the block are buyers. Also, 27 per cent are tenants, which means that allottees have rented out their plot; some of them had obtained two plots and rented out one. Others have never lived in Ambedkar Nagar or left after living there for a while, giving their plot on rent. Another 36 per cent are allottees. Five per cent of the houses, although it was traceable whether the owners were allottees, tenants or buyers and therefore included, were unoccupied.

Now we will turn to the sample study in this block. As a number of households were never at home during the day, including Sundays, 55 of the households of the block were interviewed, as can be seen in Table 4.15.

Allottees in the Block

The allottees could, before they were relocated, indicate to the Slum Board which neighbours they would like to have in Ambedkar Nagar. Therefore many people lived amongst the group of people they used to live with before the relocation. They came from different locations in Chennai: five allottees were relocated from Malleswaram, one from the pavement near Luz

Corner in Mylapore, one from the pavement of Muthu Rangam Road in Mylapore, one from Durga Nagar, seven from Indira Slum in Adyar and two from unknown locations.[43] Many people said they were not very happy to live in Ambedkar Nagar but a reply often heard was 'there was no other way, we just have to adjust to the situation'. Some recalled that during the early years after the relocation it was much worse as there were frequent fights between the different groups and between the leaders over the illegal trade of *arrack* and brown sugar.[44] Also, the facilities were not operational.

No one seemed to pay the monthly instalment to the Slum Board. Many had never paid anything, with the exception of three respondents who had an individual electricity connection. As discussed before, to apply for electricity connection, one needed to obtain a NOC from the Slum Board, which is only given when all bills are cleared.

Tenants in the Block

As renting out a house is illegal, the allottee is still responsible for paying the monthly amount due to the Slum Board and the Corporation. The allotment order is still owned by the allottee.

As already mentioned, there are a number of reasons why people came to Ambedkar Nagar as tenants. Some people lived in the neighbourhood of the evicted area and were told that the rent, as well as the advance to be paid, were low there. Others lived in slums that were going to be relocated, but were unable to get an allotment. Some people came to Ambedkar Nagar with their family but got married in the meantime and wanted to live on their own. Others came to the area as tenants because friends or relatives were living there and they were told the rents were low in Ambedkar Nagar. There is one person in this block who had his own allotment but debts forced him to move out of his house and become a tenant.

Some women did not know how much rent was paid as their husbands managed the money, but the average amount paid was approximately Rs 140 per month.[45] In some cases, before tenants could enter a house they had to pay an advance, which was normally returned when the tenant vacated. Eight respondents gave information on the amount of advance they had to pay before they could rent the house; the average was Rs 775.[46] One respondent mentioned that he was in the process of buying the house he was renting from the allottee and that a local leader was mediating for him. He said that the leader did not ask for mediation money or other favours, and although difficult to prove, it was most probable that one way or the other this leader would benefit from the mediation. Whether local leaders were involved in the mediation between the other tenants and allottees is not clear as some of them did not want to speak about it. Some respondents rented from a buyer, which means the plot was sold at least once. These buyers, as they had never lived in Ambedkar Nagar, just bought the plot as an investment. Some of them bought when prices were still low and they would come to live there when the area improved. Until then, they would rent out their house. Others are allottees that never lived in Ambedkar Nagar. Tenants came to Ambedkar Nagar from 1990 onwards. Many of the tenants were not very happy as they thought the environment was bad, although they appreciated the fact that at least the rent was low.

Devi works as a housemaid, and her husband Nataraj is an auto-driver. They have three children, the eldest is a son who is 18 years old and is working, another son is 10 years old and is physically not well and does not attend school. The youngest, a daughter, goes to the *balwadi.*[47]

Before they shifted to Ambedkar Nagar, Devi used to work as a housemaid but she had to leave her job when they were shifted to Ambedkar Nagar and It took her more then a year to find a new job in the neighbourhood of Ambedkar Nagar; only after she mingled with other people in the new area did she manage to find employment. It was even more difficult for her husband to earn money as he was now driving around Ambedkar Nagar and earned less than before. So both were not earning enough money.

They came to Ambedkar Nagar in 1997, moving from Teynampet[48] where they were paying a rent of Rs 750 a month. In Ambedkar Nagar they were paying Rs 150 a month. They have rented their house from a buyer and the house has already been sold three times. The owner of the house lives in Mylapore and Devi does not know whether he has more plots in Ambedkar Nagar. He only comes there to collect the rent.

Devi and her husband decided to shift to Ambedkar Nagar after Devi's brother bought a house in the area. She and her husband looked around the area when they visited her brother and found that this place was for rent.

She thinks the move was not such a good decision as besides the decrease in income, there were many problems in Ambedkar Nagar, like water provision, schools that are not as good as in Teynampet, and government hospitals that are too far. There are private clinics in the neighbourhood but are too expensive and since they don't want to help her son, she has to go either to Saidapet or Royapettah.[49]

Buyers in the Block

Houses in this block in Ambedkar Nagar were bought from 1990 onwards, though they were not meant to be houses be sold.[50]

TABLE 4.16: YEAR OF PURCHASE AND PRICE PAID FOR HOUSE OR PLOT

Year	*Number of Plot Buyer*	*Price Paid Per Plot (Rs)*	*Investment in Plot (Rs) (Excl. Plot Price)*	*Number of House Buyers*	*Price Paid Per House (Rs)*	*Investment in House (Rs) (Excl. House Price)*
1990-1	1	3,000	No answer	3	22,000	0
					20,500	Missing
					Missing	5,000
1992-3				3	8,000	35,000
					8,500	500
					10,000	Missing
1994-5				4	15,000	Missing
					20,000	Missing
					25,000	Missing
					40,000	85,000
1996-7				8	9,000	1,500
					15,000	50,000
					15,000	0
					15,000	0
					20,000	0
					20,000	0
					40,000	76,000
					Missing	Missing
1998-9				1	18,000	12,000
Total	1			19		
No answer	1					
Average		3,000	–		18,882	20,385
N = 21						

At the time of this study, all purchases of houses and plots were illegal. As mentioned in the introduction of this sub-section, 21 buyers of this block were interviewed.

Three respondents bought their plot and house from a buyer, which means that the plot was already sold once (one plot was even sold three times), and ten buyers bought the plot from an allottee.[51] No information is available as to who the eight respondents bought the plot from.

When Table 4.16 is compared to Table 4.14, which shows the prices paid for plots and houses, and the investments made by all the buyers in the sample of Ambedkar Nagar, it becomes clear that the average amount paid per house and the investments made per house in the block are somewhat higher than in the total sample. The average price paid per house is Rs 1,305 more and the average amount invested is Rs 5,000 more in the block sample as compared to the total sample of Ambedkar Nagar. It is not clear where this difference comes from. It might be so that the price paid per house is a bit higher in this part of Ambedkar Nagar due to the active mediation of local leaders, who charge for their 'work', but this does not explain why the average amount of the investments made is also higher.[52]

Thirteen buyers used to be tenants before they bought a house in Ambedkar Nagar, and two couples used to live in with their family but they decided to buy their own house in order to have some more privacy. All but two of the buyers obtained the allotment order from the allottee in the allottee's name. Many said they did try to convert it. Some were told by the allottee that it would be possible to convert it but after the sale it turned out not to be possible. People said that until a few years back, the Slum Board did change names on allotment orders.[53] Two buyers had changed the name on the order, one with the help of an 'educated friend', the other with the help of his employer. Many buyers would very much like to convert the name on the allotment order. Buyers with an allotment order in the allottee's name said that it did not create any problem when they paid their monthly instalment to the Slum Board. Some people paid 'on behalf of', others just signed with their own name. One person had an agreement of the sale on paper, but all others only got the allotment order. The following story illustrates how people can get cheated in this trade.

Seven years ago Lakshmi and her husband bought a house in Ambedkar Nagar. They were living in Swami Thotham, near Indira Slum, in Adyar where they rented a place for Rs 250 a month. Their neighbour from Indira Slum got an allocated plot in Ambedkar Nagar, but as he did not want to shift to the area he sold it to them for Rs 7,500. The allottee kept the allotment order, and Lakshmi and her husband only obtained a document mentioning they had bought the plot from him. When they wanted to occupy their plot in Ambedkar Nagar, someone else claimed their house as he had the allotment order of the plot. It seemed that the allottee had mortgaged it for Rs 10,000 which he had not repaid, so the other person claimed to be the owner of their plot. The case is pending in court and based on a court order they are living in the plot for the present.

The man who has the allotment order has already offered to sell it to them for Rs 10,000 and they will probably accept the offer as 'it is better than waiting for the court to make a decision, money will be wasted and it will take ten years before it will be finished'.

Although many of the buyers paid some amount to the Slum Board in order to get the NOC, they stopped paying after they had obtained the document. Many of the buyers, including the ones whose story is told below, think they have made a good decision in buying a plot.

Ganesan and Devaki have three children, two daughters and one son, all of whom go to a government school in Maduvangarai, which is close to Ambedkar Nagar.[54] Ganesan works night shifts as a mechanic and earns Rs 1,700 a month. His wife does not work outside the house.

This family used to live in Maduvangarai as tenants where they paid Rs 500 a month. Based on the amount of money they had to spend they decided to buy a plot in Ambedkar Nagar in 1992. If they had had more money they would have selected another place. Their friends and relatives had also bought a plot here, and based on their information, they came to Ambedkar Nagar.

Ganesan and Devaki bought the plot from an allottee who had never lived in Ambedkar Nagar. One of their friends mediated the purchase, as he knew the original owner of the plot. The transfer was arranged amongst themselves and the local leaders did not play a role in it. Ganesan himself did not know anything about the original owner. They asked Rs 10,000 for it, but eventually it was bought for Rs 8,000. After the purchase they only received the allotment order, and there was no agreement of the sale on paper. The allotment order was in the name of the allottee, and until then, that had not created any problem. For five years, they paid the monthly instalment to the Slum Board, in the name of the allottee. Two years back they received the NOC with which they applied for an electricity connection. From then onwards they stopped paying to the Slum Board. Ganesan knows that many buyers changed the name on the allotment order three years back and he would like to do the same. But he has been told that it is not possible nowadays and nobody knows when it will be possible again. Besides, he thinks it will also cost at least Rs 5,000. They invested Rs 35,000 in the house to get electricity, for the plastering and extension of the front portion, and they also have a septic tank.

He and his wife think it was a good decision to buy a house in Ambedkar Nagar and are happy about it. Their house is in a blind street and they never interfere in other people's lives, so they have no problems in Ambedkar Nagar. They also never interfere with the local leaders and they never approach them.

Eight buyers said that they never contacted the local leaders and that they had bought their house without the interference of those leaders. Many people said that local leaders were involved in the illegal selling and mediation in selling of plots, with which they made large profits. At the time of the study two leaders were quarrelling about the division of the profit made in one of those transactions. Two local leaders had reconstructed a house they had bought from an allottee and then sold it. In another case, the local leader was involved in the mediation between an allottee and a buyer and had signed the sales deed, for which he had asked Rs 100. Also, local leaders had sold houses illegally after a house had not been inhabited for a couple of years. In those cases they made duplicate allotment orders and sold the house off. One woman said that she approached a local leader to obtain an NOC from the Slum Board as she was a buyer who wanted to apply for an electricity connection. She had paid this leader Rs 2,100, but he gave her a receipt for only Rs 500. She was very angry and tried to get the remaining money back but the leader said she lied about the amount she had given him.

4.3.3 BEFORE AND AFTER RELOCATION: THE PEOPLE FROM CHITRA NAGAR[55]

The following case study investigates whether relocation from the perception of the relocatees can be called a success and whether the life of these people has improved or not. One of the groups that was relocated from an inner city slum in Chennai, the 'Chitra Nagar Group' was studied. This group used to live on both sides of a muddy channel in north Chennai in an old slum dating back to 1961. In 1988, approximately 400 households lived there, or an estimated 2,000 persons.[56] In 1992, the Slum Board shifted 520 households of the Chitra Nagar Group to Ambedkar Nagar.[57] In 1999, nineteen of the 89 respondents of De Wit's research who were now living in Ambedkar Nagar were traced down. They explained how their lives had been affected by the relocation and compared their life in Ambedkar Nagar to that in Chitra Nagar. Furthermore, data were collected on household income and employment, which were compared to data from De Wit's study, in order to determine whether relocation had affected them financially and, if so, in what sense. Table 4.17 lists the types of jobs performed by the heads of the households in Chitra Nagar and compares these with their jobs in Ambedkar Nagar in order to see whether the respondents have changed jobs.

All 19 respondents worked in the informal sector in Chitra

TABLE 4.17: JOB OF HEAD OF HOUSEHOLD IN CHITRA NAGAR AND AMBEDKAR NAGAR

No.	*Job in Chitra Nagar*	*Sex*	*Job in Ambedkar Nagar*	*Sex*	*Extra Wage Earning Household Members*
1	Painter	M	Painter	M	–
2	Auto-driver	M	Working abroad	M	4
3	Helper[58]	M	Helper in travels	M	–
4	Daily servant	F	Too old	F	1
5	Coolie	M	Auto-driver	M	2
6	Helper	M	Travel broker	M	1
7	Old clothes seller	M	Widow, not working	F	2
8	Auto-driver	M	Auto-driver	M	2
9	Auto driver	M	Not working, widows pension	F	1
10	Carpenter	M	Carpenter	M	–
11	Auto-driver	M	Auto driver	M	1
12	Rickshaw puller	M	Travel broker	M	5
13	Rickshaw puller	M	Rickshaw puller	M	–
14	Rickshaw puller	M	Rickshaw puller	M	1

15	Loader (harbour)	M	Coolie	M	2
16	Beggar	F	Not working, widow's pension	F	–
17	Porter	M	Porter	M	2
18	Auto driver	M	Too old	M	1
19	Maistry	M	Maistry	M	2

Notes: * Numbers seven and nine are not the same persons as the male head of the household died after 1988.
* Numbers four and sixteen were already widowed in Chitra Nagar.

Nagar, and they were all paid daily wages. Except for four respondents, who were too old to work in Ambedkar Nagar, all others still work in the informal sector. Ten people still perform the same (type of) job. The other five heads of households did not change their jobs following relocation. Instead, it is because of the informal character of these jobs that people change (or have to change) much more often than in formal jobs.

Except for one old woman who sells flowers in Ambedkar Nagar, another woman who begs and has a widow's pension, and one head of household who has migrated to Malaysia, the place of work for the majority of the respondents has not changed after relocation. Nine persons used to work in Egmore and still do. To reach Egmore they walk to the train station on Saint Thomas Mount, approximately 2 km away, and take a train to Egmore. One person used to work at the Central station and still does. He too walks to Saint Thomas Mount from where he takes a train. No information is available on where the other five people used to work when they lived in Chitra Nagar, but now they work in the city centre, which they reach by bus. None of the respondents of the Chitra Nagar group work in the neighbourhood of Ambedkar Nagar where, according to the Slum Board, many jobs would be available once they were relocated: for men in the industrial zone and for women as day servants.

Comparison of household incomes will tell us whether economic status improved or deteriorated after the relocation. It is very difficult to detect the exact amount of income for each job as they are based on daily wages. Besides, the methods of research used in 1988 and 1999 are different given that two different people conducted them. Nonetheless, an attempt has been made to give an idea of the amount earned by all household members in Chitra Nagar in comparison to those in Ambedkar Nagar.

The average per capita monthly income of the 19 persons for whom data are available was Rs 243 in Chitra Nagar and Rs 327 in Ambedkar Nagar. This means that the average per capita monthly household income increased by Rs 84, which is a significant increase. However, both are still under the poverty line, which stood at Rs 450 in 1999-2000. [59] As Table 4.18 shows, the per capita income of 18 households in Chitra Nagar was below the poverty line, as compared to 16 households in Ambedkar Nagar. [60]

The figures for the total household income per capita per month are given in Table 4.18. In many cases, this figure is different from the amount that is actually spent on the household. In practice, the earners do not give the whole amount they earn

TABLE 4.18: PER CAPITA HOUSEHOLD INCOME PER MONTH IN CHITRA NAGAR, AS COMPARED TO AMBEDKAR NAGAR [61]

Respondent	*Chitra Nagar*	*Ambedkar Nagar*
1	283	400
2	342	489
3	118	333
4	90	240
5	118	343
6	189	267
7	262	163
8	283	400
9	354	400
10	354	800
11	590	271
12	184	470
13	338	314
14	220	250
15	255	363
16	0	150
17	257	246
18	243	56
19	135	264
Average total Rs	243	327
P = 0.044		

to the household, but use part of it for their own spending. For example, men may spend part of their earnings on *arrack* or cigarettes, or lunch bought in a hotel.

As the data of De Wit gave information on the amount that was given to the household, a comparison was made between his data and the data of this study.

The average per capita monthly income given to spend on the household in Chitra Nagar was Rs 177, and for Ambedkar Nagar it Rs 301. Thus means that the average per capita monthly household income increased by Rs 124, which is a significant jump. The per capita monthly household incomes to be spent on the households have increased for 16 households between 1988-9 and 1998-9, and decreased for three households.

TABLE 4.19: PER CAPITA MONTHLY HOUSEHOLD INCOME SPENT ON THE HOUSEHOLD IN CHITRA NAGAR AS COMPARED TO THAT IN AMBEDKAR NAGAR[62]

Respondent	*Chitra Nagar*[63]	*Ambedkar Nagar*
1	107	280
2	107	388
3	89	333
4	38	150
5	50	343
6	142	267
7	262	163
8	260	400
9	265	400
10	295	800
11	236	271
12	184	310
13	338	314
14	220	225
15	225	363
16	0	150
17	215	246
18	236	56
19	101	264
Average total Rs P = 0.002	177	301

Thirty-two per cent of the respondents in Ambedkar Nagar said they could not manage with their household income, 15 per cent said it was difficult for them to do so and 53 per cent replied they were able to manage. These figures are compared with the data from Chitra Nagar, where 26 per cent of the respondents indicated they could not manage, 21 per cent said it was difficult to manage and 53 per cent of the respondents found the household income sufficient to survive. Overall, it can be concluded that the same number of people can manage to survive with the amount of money earned in Ambedkar Nagar as compared to 10 years back in Chitra Nagar and more respondents are not able to manage in Ambedkar Nagar as compared to Chitra Nagar. Six per cent went from having trouble to survive in Chitra Nagar to no longer being able to survive. These findings contradict the fact that there was a significant increase in income after the respondents were relocated, which means that apart from income, other issues play a role given the fact that more respondents in Ambedkar Nagar indicate not being able to manage financially, as compared to the number in Chitra Nagar.[64]

Thirty-seven per cent indicated that they were happy in Ambedkar Nagar whereas only 5 per cent said they were happy in Chitra Nagar at the time of De Wit's study; 26 per cent were partially happy in Ambedkar Nagar as well as in Chitra Nagar; 37 per cent were unhappy in Ambedkar Nagar, against 69 per cent in Chitra Nagar. Overall then, more respondents seem happy, or at least partially happy with their lives in Ambedkar Nagar as compared to Chitra Nagar. Problems that people faced in Chitra Nagar were mainly related to housing. At the time of De Wit's, research there was much uncertainty about whether and when people were going to be relocated, so many of the respondents were very worried. In Ambedkar Nagar, people appreciate the ownership of a house, the improved privacy, and an increased confidence in the future based on the fact that they are not afraid that they will be relocated again. Nonetheless, they are unhappy with the poor condition of services and infrastructure and the lack of employment opportunities.

People were asked to compare the facilities available in Ambedkar Nagar with those in Chitra Nagar. The overall outcome was that people felt that facilities were better in Chitra Nagar. De Wit's research does not substantiate this. He wrote that there was no electricity in Chitra Nagar, that there was only one public convenience unit so people had to resort to defecating on the river banks, that there was no sewage and drainage, that water was provided through lorries and that overall the slum had a 'dirty and disorderly appearance'.[65] Regarding the availability of institutions however, as Chitra Nagar was situated in the inner city, hospitals, schools, bus stations and a train station were within walking distance, as well as market facilities and a ration shop. Employment opportunities also existed there. Overall it can be concluded that more facilities, although not operating fully, are provided in Ambedkar Nagar, but that in regards to the institutions, the situation in Chitra Nagar was better. The scarcity of employment opportunities is a major source of concern for many people in Ambedkar Nagar. Also, people often mentioned that they feel isolated there. Before, when they were living in the inner city, they felt part of the busy life of the city, but now, as one person formulated it, 'we are living in the forest'.

In Ambedkar Nagar many people talk badly about the Chitra Nagar group, referring to them as people having 'bad manners who do not keep their area clean'. That is why one lady explained that she asked the Slum Board officer not to be placed amongst her group after the relocation. Although she lives in another part of Ambedkar Nagar, she still keeps in contact with people from Chitra Nagar and she feels bad when others denigrate them. Many people of the Chitra Nagar group feel very strongly about their group and there is little contact with people of other groups. Besides, people have most contact with people in their own street. Especially in dead-end streets people stick together, help each other and keep their street clean. In the main roads contact between neighbours seems to be less frequent.

4.4 Conclusion

This chapter dealt with the organization of the relocation project by the government; it described the general household characteristics of the respondents and the ways they dealt with their relocation and housing issues. Table 4.20 brings together research questions two, three, and four which focus on perceptions and expectations of the target group, the policies implemented by the government and NGOs, and the accountability, effectiveness, and appropriateness of those policies.[66] A short summary will be provided hereunder.

As can be seen in Table 4.20 for the design and set-up of the whole relocation project, the target groups were not consulted.

As for housing, in the early stages of the construction, relocatees themselves could decide how to spend the loans obtained. From their perspective, this strategy was effective, but from the perspective of the loan providers it was not so they stopped it. One-fourth of the respondents in this study were not relocated, which means that although not planned and approved off by the Slum Board, many people have decided not to live in the relocation site and they have either sold off or rented out their plot to others. This means that from the perspective of the target group, relocation was not an option for many people. Had the target group's perceptions and expectations been taken into account, more people would probably have remained in the relocation area and would have benefited from it. At the time of the field study, there was an active trade in plots in Ambedkar Nagar, often with, but sometimes without, mediation by the local leaders, which was a profitable business for them.

Although the relocation scheme did not envisage cost recovery, the relocatees were meant to pay a monthly instalment. Only one-fourth of the respondents actually do. Some of them paid the full amount once a year, but many people paid nothing. Their argument was that they were forced to live in the area and they therefore felt they did not have to pay for it; others are not able to pay the due amount. Overall, respondents appreciated the (future) ownership of a house, the privacy and security obtained but they felt isolated from the city (especially women which is an aspect explored in the next chapter).

In order to assess the effects of relocation on the employment and income of the target group, data from one group before and after the relocation were compared, namely those of the Chitra Nagar group. Also, their perceptions before and after relocation were compared. We saw that all those who still worked (all but one respondent) used to work and still worked in the informal

TABLE 4.20: ACTORS IN RELOCATION PROJECT: COMPARING ACCOUNTABILITY, EFFECTIVENESS, APPROPRIATENESS AND EXPECTATIONS

Services	*Organizations/ Actors*	*Activities*	*Accountability*	*Effectiveness*	*Appropriateness*	*Expectations*
The whole relocation project	CMDA + TNSCB	Project design	The target group was not consulted on the design of the project and the selection of the area	Effective, the plan was carried out the way it was designed	The target group was not happy to be relocated nor with the isolated location of the relocation site, which is also reflected by the high number of buyers and tenants in the area. However, the perspective of not being relocated again is appreciated	People expect that the area will be improved by the government, and by the fact that more buyers are expected to come to reside in the area. Some people expect that in the long run politicians will give them their plot for free
	Government of India + Tamil Nadu State Government + NGOs	Financiers of the project	No information	No information		
Housing	Relocatees + Tamil Nadu	Construction of houses with	The size of the houses was	Not effective: Loans were not	Appropriate: Houses were	Not applicable

contd.

TABLE 4.20 (contd.)

Services	*Organizations/ Actors*	*Activities*	*Accountability*	*Effectiveness*	*Appropriateness*	*Expectations*
	State Government	loans for relocatees	planned but for the construction, people were free to decide how to construct and which materials to use	used for their intended purpose	constructed of thatch and the rest of the (small) loan was used for more urgent expenses. People appreciate the privacy of the house and the (future) ownership	
	TNSCB (till '96), Chennai City Municipal Corporation (from '96 onwards)	Coordination project	No information	No information	Not applicable	Not applicable

Relocatees + HUDCO	Construction of houses with loans for relocatees	Size of houses was planned but people were free to decide how to construct and which materials to use	Not effective: Loans were not used for the purpose it was meant for Not effective: Loans were not used for the purpose it was meant for	Appropriate: Houses were constructed of thatches and the rest of the loan was used for more urgent expenses + people appreciated the privacy of the house and the (future) ownership	Not applicable
Relocatees + NGO + HUDCO	Construction of houses with loans for relocatees	Target groups were consulted by the NGO to decide on the type of house to be built	From the objective of the NGO: Not effective, although the target group was happy, the NGO had to leave the area before the construction	Appropriate: They were happy with their houses and people appreciate the privacy of the house and the (future) ownership	Not applicable

contd.

TABLE 4.20 (contd.)

Services	*Organizations/ Actors*	*Activities*	*Accountability*	*Effectiveness*	*Appropriateness*	*Expectations*
				was over due to problems; from the objective of HUDCO: Effective, as houses were constructed from the loan assistance, but not effective in so far as the NGO left the area before the project was finished		
	HUDCO + TNSCB + contractors	Construction of houses	Target groups were not consulted on the construction of their houses	Effective: Houses were constructed from the loan assistance	Not appropriate: Houses are too small and built of inferior materials.	Not applicable

				However, people appreciate the privacy of the house and the (future) ownership	
Relocatees	Selecting their neighbours in the relocation site	Overall the target groups were consulted and their wish executed	Effective as people were using the possibility to select their neighbours	Appropriate as people's wishes were executed	Not applicable

sector. Many had not changed jobs or had not changed the location site of their job. Most of them still worked in the city center, and had not become unemployed after they were relocated. The household income of the relocatees had not deteriorated; in fact it had improved a bit. The reasons for this were not clear. Nonetheless, almost the same number of respondents indicated that they could not manage financially in Ambedkar Nagar as compared to Chitra Nagar. However, more people indicated that they were happy in Ambedkar Nagar as compared to Chitra Nagar. This could partly be explained by the privacy they obtained, the prospect of the future ownership of a house, and the increased confidence in the future. As far as basic services, people judged that there were more facilities in Chitra Nagar as compared to Ambedkar Nagar, which partly contradicts the research findings because water and sanitation were better in Ambedkar Nagar. However, the availability of institutions and market facilities was higher in the area they previously lived in.

NOTES

1. De Wit, 1993: 179-80. From now on whenever I refer to the TNSCB in the local context I will use the name 'Slum Board' as this is the name that is locally used.
2. Dattatri, s.a.: 10. Some have argued that by building in and on the borders of these tanks the ecological structure has been destroyed. The Citizen's Report of the Centre for Science and Environment (1997) refers to a document of the Housing Board and the Urban Development Corporation, which shows that lakes have been marked off as 'wastelands'. Because of shortage of land, tanks have been used for housing purposes, which has led to groundwater depletion, thereby reducing the levels of the aquifers (Agarwal and Narain, 1997: 263).
3. De Wit, 1993: 180.
4. Dattatri, s.a.: 11. MMDA is now called Chennai Metropolitan Development Authority (CMDA).
5. Dattatri, s.a.: 11-16, 4-8, 13-14.
6. De Wit, 1993: 195.
7. Besselink (1997: 54) stated that the settlers obtained a loan of Rs 10,000 from the Slum Board, but does not mention the source of this information.

8. Dattatri, s.a.: 24.
9. According to the relocatees, shortly after the construction of the first houses by the NGO, problems started between the NGO, which was quite popular amongst the relocatees, and the TNSCB. Consequently, the NGO left the relocation site. According to Besselink (1997: 60), the implementation of the NGO housing scheme did not work out as expected. They were supposed to build all the 2,640 houses in the Velacheri housing project, but in reality they constructed only 64 houses. Different reasons were given for discontinuation. According to the relocatees, the NGO stopped because of a fight in the area. Rumours were going around that rowdies were paid by the TNSCB to kick the NGO out of the area. It seemed that the TNSCB was annoyed by the presence of the NGO in the project because of its popularity. The TNSCB admitted that there had been an incident with the NGO but denied that this had been the reason for the latter's departure. According to them, the incident took place because beneficiaries considered the building process to be too slow. The NGO also admitted there had been a fight, but it did not wish to say anything more.
10. According to Mr Zafrullah, Community Development Officer of the Slum Board. Another CDO of the Slum Board, Mr Rajendran, stated that after living in the relocation site for 10 years and clearing the due amount, the allottees were allowed to sell. This possibility is also mentioned by Dattatri (s.a.: 15). According to him (p. 26) the monthly repayment ranged from Rs 60 to Rs 85 per beneficiary, depending on the type of dwelling unit.
11. Dattatri, s.a.: 13.
12. Referred to by the Slum Board as 'street margins'.
13. Dattatri, s.a.: 39.
14. A Community Development Officer of the Slum Board said so in June 1998.
15. Dattatri, s.a.: 22.
16. De Wit, 1993: 171-2, 174-6, 185.
17. Besselink, 1997: 51.
18. De Wit, 1993: 178. Female-headed households are single-parent households, nuclear, or extended households, headed by a woman (Moser, 1996: 49).
19. As is shown on the map in Section 2.4.
20. Of those, 43 per cent are Saivites and 57 per cent are Vaishnavites.
21. Of those 3 per cent are Roman Catholic, 3 per cent Protestant and 1 per cent Apostolic.
22. More information on the temples, churches and the mosque will follow in Chapter 6.
23. Srinivas, 1962: 65-9.
24. The Constitution of India of 1950 aimed to do away with the caste

system and outlawed discrimination on the grounds of caste. The Constitution also included clauses allowing affirmative action. These would entail policies of positive discrimination and quotas of seats in Parliament, state legislative assemblies, public sector jobs and educational institutions, and a certain fixed percentage of public funds for targeted groups to improve their welfare (Mengers, 1997: 50-1).

25. Béteille, 1992: 2-3, the author has rounded off the figures.
26. Guhan, 1991: 46, two per cent are missing.
27. The term Adi Dravida 'became popular in the early 20th century to legitimise social protest by assuming that the Aryan conquest reduced the Untouchable [or lower segment of the indigenous population] to a low status' (Zeliot, 1992, as quoted in Deliége, 1997: 66).
28. For definitions on households, head of household, female-headed households, etc., see Chapter 20.
29. Moser, 1993: 17.
30. See map of Chennai in section 4.1.2.
31. A Community Development Officer (CDO) of the Slum Board said so in June 1998.
32. Dattatri, s.a.: 22.
33. De Wit, 1993: 185.
34. Dattatri, s.a.: 37, 39.
35. When we speak of a person being given an allotment order previous to the actual relocation, we only speak of an allottee. After the relocation, the terms allottee and relocatee can be used interchangeably.
36. The latter was stopped after a while. The officers of the Slum Board explained that the reason they stopped providing loans to the beneficiaries was that in their opinion, many people did not use this money to construct a house, but used it for other purposes and constructed thatched huts instead.
37. The slum numbers correspond with the numbers in Map 4.1, where their location in Chennai is shown.
38. As with the household income, these figures must be interpreted with utmost caution; many people may not know the exact amount as the investment was often done a few years prior, and spread out over a couple of years.
39. Whether their per capita income per month is significantly lower than that of relocatees and buyers will be discussed in chapter five (Table 5.4).
40. The differences in income between allottees, tenants, and buyers is shown in Table 5.4.
41. A plastered house for instance is more expensive than a house with only brick walls.
42. As mentioned before, relocatees were offered houses or plots through different means. The first settlers were given a plot and Rs 500 to

construct their own house. Later people received a loan of Rs 8,000 from HUDCO to construct their own dwellings. Other houses were built through the help of an NGO. The Slum Board also built houses. The agreement was that the beneficiaries had to repay Rs 66 on a monthly basis as land cost, and Rs 10 for monthly maintenance to the Slum Board for 21 years. After 21 years, if the full amount had been paid, the dwelling and plot would become privately owned. They could pay off the amount due before those 21 years were over and then they would receive a temporary sale deed for five years. In some individual cases, after those five years they could sell off the plot but only to the Slum Board. In general, however, the allotters were not allowed to sell off the plot at any time. At the time of the research none of the respondents were planning to sell off their house. Plots and houses that were already sold were done so illegally, so the amount due was not paid to the Slum Board. None of the houses were sold back to the Slum Board. In 1996, the maintenance of Ambedkar Nagar became the responsible of the Chennai Corporation, not the Slum Board. The corporation then started to charge the Rs 10 as maintenance costs. The Rs 66 for land cost continued to be charged by the Slum Board.

43. Luz Corner and Muthu Rangam Road fall within the category of miscellaneous in Tables 4.3 and 4.6.
44. The selling of brown sugar (heroin) is known to have continued into 1999 as people complained about it. Besides, I have often seen men hanging around in the area doing some secretive handlings which I suspected were drug deals. Sometimes a policeman would enter the area on his bicycle. This news spread through the area very quickly, and these men would then run off immediately.
45. One respondent paid approximately Rs 75 a month; the amount differed per month as he rented it from his brother to whom he just gave whatever he could spare that month. Eight respondents paid Rs 100 a month, five respondents paid Rs 150 a month and two paid Rs 300 a month.
46. One respondent paid Rs 200, three respondents paid Rs 500, other three respondents paid Rs 1,000 and one respondent paid Rs 1,500.
47. This is a day nursery run by an NGO in Ambedkar Nagar for children between the ages of three and five. For more information, see Chapter 5.
48. See also map of Chennai in Section 4.1.2.
49. Do.
50. Only in some individual cases, when the amount due has been paid to the Slum Board, the Board may, after five years, decide to buy a plot from an allottee. This has occurred only a few times since 1990 and the last few years no approval of the Slum Board has been given to sell off any plot. Mr Zafrullah, CDO of the Slum Board, mentioned in July

2000 that for the last 'few years' no approval had been given, he was not more precise about the dates.

51. Some of these allottees had lived in Ambedkar Nagar for a while. For example, an old woman shifted to Ambedkar Nagar with her husband but when he died she did not want to live there on her own, so she sold off her house and moved in with her daughter. Other allottees have never lived in Ambedkar Nagar, either because they did not like the place or because they have a job in the area where they were to be shifted from and could not commute from Ambedkar Nagar daily. A few allottees had obtained more than one house when the allotment orders were handed over by the Slum Board, so when they were in need of some cash, they sold off one house.
52. The price paid per plot cannot be compared because, as can be seen in Table 4.16, only one respondent bought a plot in the sample block.
53. According to Mr Zafrullah, Community Development Officer of the Slum Board, in some individual cases in the past an allottee has sold off his plot to the Slum Board. In the last few years however, the Slum Board has not allowed allottees to sell off their plot.
54. See also map of Chennai in Section 4.1.2.
55. I was very happy to be allowed to use Joop de Wit's research data, which he collected in Chitra Nagar between 1988-90, in order to track some of his respondents down in Ambedkar Nagar and to investigate the impact of the relocation on their lives. I am aware of the fact that those who were too negatively affected by the relocation might have left the area instantly or in the early years after they were relocated. Still, this case study tries to make a comparison between life prior to and after the relocation to Ambedkar Nagar for those who did stay.
56 De Wit, 1993: 122-3.
57 It is doubtful that in four years time the number of families in this slum has grown to 120 families. It is not clear which figure is the correct one.
58. Directing passengers to buses and trains at stations.
59. Rs 451.19 actually, but the figure has been rounded off to Rs 450.
60. De Wit, in his study on Chitra Nagar, found that of a total of 89 respondents, 9 lived above the poverty line (1993: 150).
61. The income figures given for the Chitra Nagar group of 1988-9 are inflated to the 1999 figures by using the Consumer Price Index (CPI) of 1989 and 1999. The figures calculated using the CPI are rounded off.
62. The figures given for the income of the Chitra Nagar data of 1988-9 are inflated to the 1999 figures by using the CPI of 1989 and 1999. The CPI is divided into three categories: industrial workers, urban non-manual workers and agricultural labourers. I have decided to select the CPI of the agricultural labourers as it might come closest to the incomes earned by slum dwellers given that industrial workers also include the

organized sector (which comes under the Factories Act and therefore implies much higher earnings).

63. The figures calculated using CPI are rounded off.
64. This issue will be discussed further in the following chapters.
65. De Wit, 1993: 123.
66. These concepts have been defined in Chapter 2.

5

Employment, Basic Services, and Social Security: The Government, NGOs, and the Households

This chapter describes the role of the government as provider of employment, basic services, and social security. Initiatives that the inhabitants themselves take up in these fields and the role of the NGOs that are present in the area are also touched upon.

5.1 Provision of Employment and Basic Services by the Government[1]

5.1.1 Employment

The Slum Board recognized that the relocation would severely disrupt employment opportunities. They executed a survey amongst the slum dwellers previous to their relocation and found that the dominant occupations of the men involved construction, fishing, and cycle-rickshaw pulling whereas women mainly worked as domestic servants and vendors. In his report for the TNSCB, Dattatri writes that except for the fishermen and domestic servants, everyone was commuting to their workplace, and he presents this as an argument in favour of the relocation, as if it would make no difference whether one travels for fifteen minutes or for one hour. He also mentions that vendors are not location specific, which is partly true, but business is much better at, for instance, bus and train stations in the city centre than elsewhere. In order to reduce the negative impact on employment opportunities the Slum Board was planning to offer vocational training in the new relocation site. Also, the resettlers were told that jobs were available in the nearby factories and that the Slum Board would mediate for them. Dattatri's report states that fishing accounts for only 4 per cent of the total occupation and that many fishermen were involved in trading and could continue their job at the new site, hereby implying that travelling would not be a problem. Significantly, the people depending on fishing itself were not taken into account.

5.1.2 EDUCATION AND HEALTH CARE

In the neighbourhood close to the relocation site corporation schools were available, and while laying out the site, nursery schools were also built by the Department for Social Welfare and run by NGOs. Sites were also reserved for a primary and a high school. Two NGOs were planning to open health clinics in the area. For the present, the dwellers were dependent on private and public health facilities in the neighbourhood of Velacheri.

5.1.3 WATER AND SANITATION

The provision of piped water was ruled out on the grounds of cost and non availability of supply lines in the vicinity.[2] The Chennai Metropolitan Water Supply and Sewerage Board (CMWSSB),[3] advised that deep bore wells were unsuitable for the area, and therefore the water supply works consisted of open wells at 20 locations for the supply of water for washing purposes. For potable water, containers were installed which would be filled up periodically by Metro Water through water tankers. The Tamil Nadu Pollution Control Board advised against the construction of low-cost individual latrines, as they would pollute the subsoil; the disposal system therefore consisted of 8-16 capacity public convenience units at 10 locations in the area. The sewage would be disposed of in septic tanks. Storm water drains constructed alongside the main roads were designed to carry storm water as well as waste water generated in the households, for disposal in the Velacheri tank.

5.1.4 INFRASTRUCTURE, TRANSPORT AND ELECTRICITY

The roads were constructed by different contractors but under the supervision of the Slum Board. The nearest bus stop was about 50 m from the entrance of the Velacheri site and the distance that people had to walk depended on what side of the area they lived in. The nearest train station was located about 3 km from the border of the relocation site. The Chennai City Municipal Corporation was entrusted with the installation of streetlights in the project.

The sites that were provided with schools, shops, police station, etc., were to be transferred to the responsible agencies and developed under their own budgets.[4] The staff of the Slum Board supervised the development of the whole project, and the various contractors carried out the works.[5] From 1996, when the development works were completed, the Slum Board handed over the relocation site to the Chennai City Municipal Corporation and since then on the Corporation was responsible for the area.[6]

5.2 Obtaining Employment and Basic Services

The way through which the inhabitants of the relocation site obtain employment and basic services is described below. The basic services described in this paragraph include education and health care, water, sanitation, transport and electricity.

5.2.1 Employment

As illustrated in Table 5.1 the majority of the respondents in Ambedkar Nagar work in the informal sector, in a range of jobs. When we look at the job of the head of the households (hh), 152 heads of households are male and a small number, 6 households, are female. As can be seen in Table 5.2, almost all the jobs are seasonal or irregular, with an average of 20 working days a month and workers are paid on a daily basis. Only four jobs pay on a monthly basis, with 24 working days a month.

In 58 of the 158 households, there is at least one more earner in the family, of whom 33 are male and 25 are female. In 15 households, more than two household members work for a salary.

If per capita incomes per household are taken into consideration, the following bar chart emerges (Figure 5.1).

The average per capita monthly household income in Ambedkar Nagar is Rs 552. The All-India poverty line for 1999-2000 is Rs 450,[7] which means that the average per capita household income per month is above the poverty line.[8] But even

TABLE 5.1: TYPE OF JOB OF THE HEAD OF HOUSEHOLD (HH), AND SECOND EARNERS (SE)[9]

Type of Job HH	*Abs. Numbers*	*Rs a Day (Average)*	*Type of Job SE*	*Abs. Numbers*	*Rs a Day (Average)*
MALES			MALES		
Daily wages (informal, 20 days/month)	136	81	Daily wages (informal, 20 days/month)	26	82
Monthly wages (formal, 24 days/month)	4	103			
Monthly wages (informal, 20 days/month)	11	65	Monthly wages (informal, 20 days/month)	7	84
Unemployed	1	0			
FEMALES			FEMALES		
Daily wages (informal, 20 days/month)	3	50	Daily wages (informal, 20 days/month)	10	61
Monthly wages (informal, 20 days/month)	3	20	Monthly wages (informal, 20 days/month)	15	26
Total	158		Total	58	

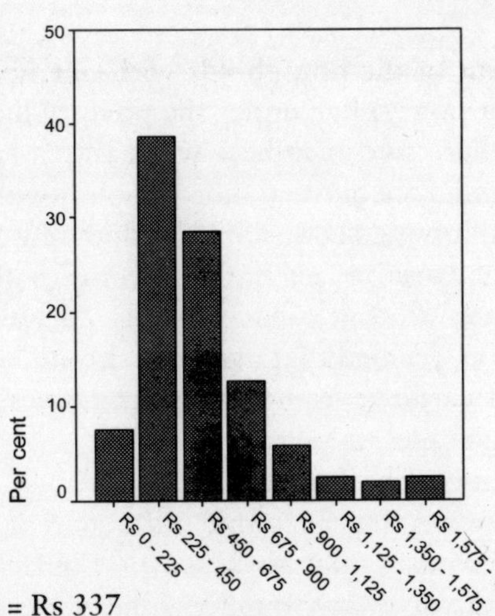

N = 158
Mean = Rs 552
Standard deviation = Rs 337

FIGURE 5.1: PER CAPITA INCOME PER MONTH PER HOUSEHOLD[10]

though the average monthly per capita income is above the poverty line, 47 per cent live below it and have an income between Rs 75 (which is the lowest per capita income found amongst the respondents) and Rs 450. On the other hand, there is a small group of 14 per cent who have a relatively high per capita monthly income of over Rs 900 up to Rs 1,760, which is the highest per capita monthly income found.

Table 5.2 indicates that in more than half of the households, only one household member works. Nonetheless, in 37 per cent of the households, more than one household member works.

TABLE 5.2: NUMBER OF WORKING MEMBERS PER HOUSEHOLD

Number of Working Household Members Per Household	*Abs. Numbers*	*%*
1	100	63
2	43	27
3	9	6
4	5	3
6	1	1
Total	158	100

Sixty per cent of the households with one household member working (for a salary) live under the poverty line, as opposed to households where two members work (for a salary), where 30 per cent live under the poverty line. The following tables analyse whether the following six variables influence per capita income:

Although the variable 'per capita income' is slightly positive it is not so much that it unacceptably influences the mean. Therefore it was decided that averages should be used, as well as the analysis of variance in order to see whether these differences between the averages are significant.

No significance was found, both at the 0.01 and at the 0.05 levels, which means that the found differences in income between the different groups could be based on coincidence only. Even though no significance was found and the group of female-headed

Tables	*Variables*
5.3	Female- or male- headed households
5.4	Whether they are relocated, tenants or buyers
5.5	The year of relocation
5.6	The fact that prior to the relocation they were pavement dwellers or slum dwellers that they lived on the tracks of the MRTS
5.7	The geographical location they were relocated from
5.8	Their caste background

households is too small to compare with the male-headed households, the decision was made to incorporate this table as the group of female-headed households has very specific characteristics and are often poorer than male-headed households. Contrary to expectations however, the female-headed households have an average income that is Rs 54 higher than the income of male-headed households. Again, this can be based on coincidence, or on the fact that these female-headed households have relatively older children who contribute to the household income.

Of the 152 male-headed households, 71 households live under the poverty line. Of the six female-headed households, two households live under the poverty line.

No significant difference was found, both at the 0.01 and at the 0.05 levels, which means that the found differences in income between the different groups could be based on coincidence only. It was expected that the income of buyers would

TABLE 5.3: PER CAPITA INCOME PER MONTH FOR FEMALE-HEADED HOUSEHOLDS IN COMPARISON TO MALE-HEADED HOUSEHOLDS (IN RS)

Group	*Abs. Numbers*	*Mean*	*Std. Deviation*
Female headed households	6	604	292
Male headed households	152	550	340
Total	158		
P = 0.703			

be higher than the income of relocatees and tenants as they had the financial capacity to buy a plot, which means they have to have a relatively secure and well-paying job. Although the average income of buyers was higher than that of the relocatees, remarkably, the income of tenants was even higher, which cannot be explained.[11] However, no significance was found in the difference in income between the three groups, so, as said before, this can be due to coincidence.

TABLE 5.4: PER CAPITA INCOME PER MONTH FOR RELOCATEES, TENANTS, AND BUYERS (IN RS)

Group	*Abs. Numbers*	*Mean*	*Std. Deviation*
Relocatees	120	534	332
Tenants	8	624	393
Buyers	30	604	346
Total	158		
P = 0.492			

A comparison between the average per capita monthly income of the households of relocatees, tenants, and buyers revealed the following: 57 of the relocatee-households, 5 of the tenant-households, and 11 of the buyer-households have a per capita monthly income below the poverty line.

No significance was found, both at the 0.01 and at the 0.05 levels, which means that the found differences in income between the different groups could be based on coincidence only.

The selection by the Slum Board of who is to be relocated when was purely arbitrary. It was thus natural that there would not be any significant difference in the average per capita income between those different groups, which proved to be the case. If there was to be any significant difference in income, it was expected that the group relocated earlier would have a higher per capita income than the groups relocated later as they would have had more time to organize their lives in the relocation site and find suitable jobs. The opposite turned out to be true, although not in a significant manner; the ones relocated later had a higher per capita income than the ones relocated earlier. As indicated earlier, this can be due to coincidence.

TABLE 5.5: PER CAPITA INCOME PER MONTH OF RELOCATEES, BASED ON YEAR OF RELOCATION (IN RS)

Group	*Abs. Numbers*	*Mean*	*Std. Deviation*
Relocated in 1990	21	439	343
Relocated in 1991	20	548	251
Relocated in 1992	23	538	306
Relocated in 1993	10	575	364
Unknown when relocated	46		
Total	120		
P = 0.584			

Of those relocated in 1990, fifteen households have a per capita monthly income below the poverty line; of those relocated in 1991, seven households have a per capita monthly income below the poverty line, of those in 1992, ten households have a per capita monthly income below the poverty line, and of those relocated in 1993, five households have a per capita monthly income below the poverty line.

TABLE 5.6: COMPARISON OF PER CAPITA INCOME PER MONTH OF FORMER PAVEMENT DWELLERS AND HOUSEHOLDS RELOCATED FROM THE TRACK OF THE MRTS (IN RS)

Group	*Abs. Numbers*	*Mean*	*Std. Deviation*
Pavement dwellers	59	568	339
MRTS	52	486	339
Not given	9	611	233
Total	120		
P = 0.351			

No significance was found, both at the 0.01 and at the 0.05 levels, which means that the found differences in income between the different groups could be based on coincidence only.

The selection of pavement dwellers that were to be relocated was purely arbitrary and therefore it was to be expected that there would not be any significant difference in the average per capita income between those two different groups; this turned out to be case.

Of the pavement dwellers, 25 households have a per capita monthly income below the poverty line, and of those relocated

TABLE 5.7: PER CAPITA INCOME PER MONTH FOR HOUSEHOLDS ACCORDING TO PREVIOUS GEOGRAPHICAL LOCATION (IN RS)

Group	*Abs. Numbers*	*Mean*	*Std. Deviation*
Central-North Chennai	32	499	316
Central-East Chennai	32	389	172
Central-South Chennai	20	676	468
Central-West Chennai	27	650	352
South Chennai	8	521	197
Not given	1		
Total	120		
P = 0.008			

from slums that were situated on the tracks of the MRTS, 29 households have a per capita monthly income below the poverty line.

There is a significant difference in per capita income between the different groups as listed in Table 5.7, which is remarkable and there is no reasonable explanation for it.

Of those relocated from Central-North Chennai, 18 households have an income below the poverty line, for those relocated from Central-East Chennai, 19 households have an income below the poverty line, for those relocated from Central-West Chennai, the figure is seven households, for Central-South Chennai, nine households, and for South Chennai, three households.

Though there was no significance found at the 0.05 level, it is close to being significant, so the community background could be a factor that influences the per capita household income. This was to be expected as low caste people have less opportunities than those who have a high(er) caste background. The last group who have no caste and are in fact all Christians with an average per capita household income comparable to the SC/ST group, which is not remarkable, as many conversions have taken place in the group.

Of the SC/ST 44 households have a per capita monthly income below the poverty line; for the Most Backward Castes, the figure is 20, for the Backward Castes, 4 and for the Forward Castes, it is 3 households. Of those who do not belong to a caste group, 2 households have a per capita income below the poverty line.

TABLE 5.8: PER CAPITA INCOME PER MONTH ACCORDING TO DIFFERENT CASTE GROUPS OF ALL THE RESPONDENTS (IN RS)

Group	*Abs. Numbers*	*Mean*	*Std. Deviation*
SC/ST	95	503	265
MBC	41	604	424
BC	8	594	403
FC	11	763	442
No caste (Christian)[12]	3	502	257
Total	158		
P = 0.114			

Notes: SC/ST = Scheduled Castes and Scheduled Tribes; MBC = Most Backward Castes; BC = Backward Castes; FC = Forward Castes

The relocation has had a major effect on the employment opportunities of the relocatees. Most of the respondents work in the informal sector and depend on the city centre for their income. This applies especially to female servants who work in the residential areas close to their former slum location. Once relocated, they were deprived of their source of income. Others commute back and forth, which not only takes time and money, but because of the informal character of many of the jobs performed, is a risky undertaking, as workers may have to travel and not earn anything some days.

To prevent the loss of jobs and give the inhabitants alternative employment opportunities, the Slum Board offered vocational training through the NGOs in Ambedkar Nagar. Typewriting courses, tailoring classes, and paper craft making were offered but only eight respondents joined. Those who joined did not benefit much from it, as they have not been able to set-up their own business. For instance one respondent explained that she had joined the tailoring class offered by the local NGO GEMS but that when she finished it successfully and wanted to start her own business, she was not able to acquire a sewing machine and had given up the effort. Meanwhile in the GEMS hall in Ambedkar Nagar, many sewing machines, paid for through the Nehru Rozgar Yojana scheme by the Slum Board, were left idle at the time of the study. The reasons the 150 respondents gave for not joining one of those training was that they were either not interested, had no time, or were not aware of its existence.

As another alternative to counteract the possible loss of jobs following relocation, the Slum Board informed the relocatees, before the relocation, that in the factories close to the relocation site many jobs were available and that the Board would act as mediator. However, only two respondents actually worked in these factories, and they had obtained those jobs without the intervention of the Slum Board.

Shop Owners

In the original layout of the relocation area there was only one area allocated near the lake for shops, but in 1999 this area was still vacant. Shops were not intended to be located throughout Ambedkar Nagar and besides, plots and houses were not designed to be used as shops. Nonetheless, there are many shops all over Ambedkar Nagar that were selected for this case study, in order to find out whether the shopkeepers/owners are allottees, tenants, or buyers, why they opened up a shop in Ambedkar Nagar, in what way the allottees were affected by the relocation, and what the occupation of the shop-owners was before they shifted to Ambedkar Nagar.

One or two family members, mostly the male head of the household and his wife or one of his children, run most of the shops, though there are a few with employees. In 1999, there were approximately 45 shops in Ambedkar Nagar. In some cases, it was difficult to distinguish whether a house was a shop as some tailors and ironing businesses worked inside their houses. Besides, some shops opened once in a while. In this case study, 42 shop-owners and employees were interviewed; 3 shop-owners did not wish to participate. Table 5.9 shows the different types of shops that were integrated in the study, and the number of persons interviewed from the different types. The definitions used by the sanitary inspectors of the Corporation are used here to define the different types of shops in Ambedkar Nagar. Petty shops only sell cigarettes and betel-nut; provision stores sell groceries and eatables; and teashops sell tea and coffee.

As can be seen in Table 5.9 the majority of shops sell provision or are tea-stalls.

TABLE 5.9: TYPES OF SHOPS AND NUMBER OF PERSONS INTERVIEWED

Types of Shops	*Products Sold (Amongst Others)*	*Abs. Numbers*
Provision-shop	Soaps, *dals*, noodles, vegetables, rice, pickles, tea, sugar, candy, vegetables	20
Petty-shop	*Pan*, *beedies*, cigarettes, betel-nut	1
Tea-stall	Tea, coffee, and sometimes snacks or *tiffin* (*idli* or *dosa*)	12
Tailor-shop	Stitching	4
Ironing-shop	Ironing	3
PCO unit[13]	Phone calls	1
Chicken-stall	Chicken	1
Total		42

The shops in Ambedkar Nagar are located all through the area. Table 5.10 shows that most houses and shops are combined in the same loca tion; some have extended their front portion, others are lucky to have two allocated plots and use one plot for their house and the other for their shop. Some have rented or bought one or two plots. The table also shows the number of plots shop-owners have and whether these plots are bought, rented or allocated.

TABLE 5.10: SPECIFIED NUMBER OF PLOTS PER SHOP-OWNER

Number of Plots	*Specification*	*Abs. Numbers*
House and shop in the same plot in Ambedkar Nagar	Allottees	8
	Tenants	4
	Buyers	4
House outside-, shop inside Ambedkar Nagar	Tenants	5
	Buyers	3
House and shop in two different plots in Ambedkar Nagar	Both plots allotted	3
	Both plots hired	4
	Both plots bought	4
	1 allotted plot, 1 hired plot	5
	1 allotted plot, 1 bought plot	2
Total		42

As can be seen in Table 5.10, of the 42 shop-owners interviewed, 18 respondents are allottees (8 live and work in the same place, 3 have two allotted plots, 5 rented another plot and 2 bought an extra plot) and 24 have either bought or rented a plot, or both. Twenty-six respondents live in one plot and have their shop in another, but 16 respondents live and work in only one plot.

Before these shop-owners shifted to Ambedkar Nagar, 21 of them were already working in a shop. Some were working in a grocery-wholesale business, employed in a shop, or working as a pavement seller. Others were involved in exactly the same business as they are at the new site. The other 21 shop-owners had done all sorts of different jobs before.

The respondents had different reasons to start a shop in Ambedkar Nagar. Some were relocated and continued with the same business. Others were employed before the relocation but were not able to proceed with it as the distance that had to be travelled to the work spot was too much, so they opened a shop in Ambedkar Nagar. Some buyers and tenants thought Ambedkar Nagar was a cheap place in compared to other areas in Chennai and therefore decided to come to Ambedkar Nagar. In some cases family members other than the head of household decided to open a shop to supplement earnings. Others were working in the grocery-wholesale business and saw Ambedkar Nagar as an opportunity to start their own shop.

Only a few shops have employees. One tailor employs four persons on an irregular basis. These employees are paid per piece and they only come when there is enough work to do. Two bigger grocery-shops and one teashop employ people who are paid on a daily basis. In most other shops, more than one family member works.

Many shop-owners mention that a few years back there were many social problems and there was a lot of fighting in Ambedkar Nagar. Theft from shops also occurred regularly. Now, as a police outpost is stationed in Ambedkar Nagar and tension is reduced between the different groups that were relocated, life is better. Others explained that a few years back, when they opened their shop, there was not much competition and earnings were good.

But nowadays the number of shops has increased considerably and therefore earnings are less. One tea-shop owner said that a few years back everyone used to come to buy tea from the tea-shop as milk was hard to get, but since milk sachets are available everywhere, people make their own tea at home nowadays. Many shop-owners do not know exactly how much they earn. Many said that they earn 'enough to survive'; the amount being between Rs 30 and 150 a day, depending on the type and the size of the shop. Many just take from the shop whatever they need, food and money, and the rest is used to buy new stock.

There is no difference in how allottees, tenants and buyers feel about the future of their business in Ambedkar Nagar. Some respondents have clear ideas, and want to expand into a big shop. Others foresee increasing competition in the future and some mention that they are not able to think about the future, as survival today is already hard enough for them. The following story is of a tailor, an allottee who is not happy with the re-location.

From his childhood Kannan has been working as a tailor. After he finished his fifth standard education, the teacher told his father, who was also a tailor, that he could better educate his son in the tailoring business as studying was difficult for him. After he followed tailoring lessons from his father, he started his own business in Mylapore.[14] He was able to build up a profitable business as he stitched garments for big shops. He employed four persons and was earning a good living.

Then in 1993, he and his family were relocated to Ambedkar Nagar. One plot was allocated to his family, where they constructed a small house. Part of the plot was used to construct as a small tailoring shop. His family had been living in Mylapore for generations and they had *patta* land. He and his three brothers were lucky that when they were relocated the government gave them compensation for the land; each of them received Rs 25,000. But still, to construct the house and shop, and to apply for electricity in order to proceed with his business, Kannan had to invest Rs 1 lakh so he had to sell off two stitching machines. Due to the lack of space and because he had to sell his machines he was not able to employ anybody, so he lost big orders, and now he is only able to earn approximately Rs 70 a day. In order to expand his business, Kannan tried to apply for a government loan. He went to the office in Marina Beach,[15] but then elections were held, another party came into power and his application never came through.

Kannan says that due to the relocation, he has lost a big source of income and sometimes he feels very bad about it. Now his only hope is that his two sons will study well in order to find themselves better jobs and they will be able to live a better life, with less worries.

As is clear from the above story, the relocation has impoverished the tailor and his family. The following story is of a former tenant who became a 'house-owner' and who is quite happy with his life and business in Ambedkar Nagar.

Originally Nagappan is from a village in southern Tamil Nadu, but as it was very difficult to earn a living in agriculture, he migrated to Chennai 25 years ago. He left his wife and children in the village and went in search of a better livelihood. Over the years, he has lived and worked in several places in Chennai, and he has done all sorts of jobs. Finally one year ago he heard that Ambedkar Nagar had houses for rent and he could start his own business there, so he decided to move there.

He rented a house for Rs 300 a month and started a teashop. As there was some vacant land near the public convenience units near his house, one month ago he approached Sundaram, a local slum leader, and asked him whether he would allow him to build his hut in that spot. The local leader approved of his plans in return for Rs 4,000. So Nagappan calculated that instead of paying Rs 300 each month for many years, now he only had to pay Rs 400 a month for ten months, after which he would be the owner of the shop. So he constructed a small house annex tea-stall for Rs 2,000, and vacated his old place. Although this is not legal, he feels with the protection of the local leader, no one will tell him to vacate his hut.

Opposite the tea-stall Nagappan has rented a small part of a plot from an old lady and he has used it to start a chicken stall. With both shops, he feels he has a good business. He is able to save Rs 1,000 a month and once in a while he goes to visit his family in the village to give them some of the money. He feels quite happy as in a few months' time he will have his 'own' piece of land and he says his life has improved a lot over the years. His future plans are to improve his shop, and to have a few employees. He likes to imagine himself as an old man sitting behind the counter collecting the money.

In the above story, it is interesting to note the power of a local leader—even though he did not own the land, he sells it off. In other words, Nagappan bought the permission to build a house. What will happen when an official of the Corporation does not agree with him staying there?

5.2.2 EDUCATION AND HEALTH CARE

Education

Some NGOs in Ambedkar Nagar run *balwadis,* but only three of the respondents' children go there, as the number of children that can be admitted is small. Children between the ages of three and five can join the *balwadis*. Education is free but they do not receive the midday meal. Instead, the NGOs themselves provide lunch or snacks. One of the NGOs runs a homework class, where children are helped with their homework. Also, one NGO runs a Transit School for former child labourers, which is sponsored by the Slum Board. There, these children learn the basics and after one year, are admitted to a formal school run by the corporation in the vicinity of Ambedkar Nagar. As mentioned before, the Slum Board initially planned to build a primary school as well as a high school in Ambedkar Nagar, but this was not realized. Table 5.11 indicates the level of education of the respondents and then that of the members of their households.

As can be seen in Table 5.11, 235 respondents in Ambedkar Nagar are not literate or they are literate without formal schooling, 179 respondents have a primary education, and 168 respondents have a middle or secondary education.

Of the children below the age of 18, 52 per cent attend school and 48 per cent do not. Those going to school attend NGO schools, Corporation schools, municipal schools, panchayat schools, or private schools. The only difference between a corporation school, a municipal school and a panchayat school is an administrative one. The Corporation schools are situated within the city limits and fall under the responsibility of the Chennai Corporation, the municipal and panchayat schools come under the responsibility of the municipality and the panchayat respectively. A private school is founded by private initiatives and fees have to be paid there. All these schools are within 2 km of Ambedkar Nagar. Furthermore, NGOs in the area have set-up *balwadis* for children between the ages of three and five.

The NGO-, Corporation-, municipal-, and panchayat schools provide free education in the sense that no fees have to be paid. But they are not free of cost, as parents have to buy uniforms, books, and supplies.[16]

TABLE 5.11: LEVEL OF EDUCATION OF RESPONDENTS AND THE MEMBERS OF THEIR HOUSEHOLD

Sex	*Male*				*Female*				*Total*	
Age	*<18*		*>18*		*<18*		*>18*			
Level of education	*Abs. numbers*	*%*	*Abs. numbers*	*%*	*Abs. numbers*	*%*	*Abs. numbers*	*%*	*Abs. numbers*	*%*
1	2	0	25	4	5	1	46	7	78	11
2	7	1	70	10	0	0	80	11	157	22
3	1	0	1	0	6	1	4	1	12	2
4	61	9	31	4	60	9	27	4	179	25
5	21	3	11	26	17	2	15	2	64	9
6	15	2	49	7	13	2	27	4	104	15
7	0	0	1	0	0	0	0	0	1	0
Sub-total	107	15	188	27	101	14	199	28	595	84
Missing									110	16
N = 705									705	100

Notes: Level of education:
1 = Not literate
2 = Literate without formal schooling
3 = Literate below primary education (*balwadi*)
4 = Primary education (I-V standard)
5 = Middle education (V-VIII standard)
6 = Secondary education (VIII - +2 standard)
7 = Graduate and above

Of the 100 children that do not attend school, 51 are not willing to go to school, sometimes even when the parents insist they go. The parents of 8 children do not themselves see the need to educate their children; the education of 3 children is complete; the parents of 1 child said prefer to send their child to work as they are in need of the extra income; for 37 children, no information was provided by their parents. Although some respondents mention the long distance children have to walk to go to school, many seem to be quite happy with the number of schools in the neighbourhood. Also, people mention that since they are poor they are happy to send their children to a corporation school, where at least education is free.

TABLE 5.12: TYPE OF SCHOOL ATTENDED BY CHILDREN BETWEEN THE AGE OF THREE AND SIXTEEN

Type of school	*Abs. Numbers*	%
1. NGO *balwadi*	3	2
2. Corporation school	75	45
3. Municipal school	60	36
4. Panchayat school	20	12
5. Private school	9	5
Total	167	100

Formal Health Care Practices

Two NGOs in Ambedkar Nagar run a doctor's clinic, once or twice a week, and charge Rs 5 per visit. Furthermore, special health camps are sometimes organized by the NGOs. Respondents also mentioned that they went to a local doctor outside Ambedkar Nagar. One NGO also ran an Integrated Child Development Scheme (ICDS) centre once, but at the time of this research it was no longer functioning. Eighty-nine per cent of the respondents are not happy with the medical facilities in and around Ambedkar Nagar. The nearest government hospital that provides free medical assistance being 5 km away in Saidapet, many complain about the long distance. As many people do not have their own means of transportation and depend on busses and other means of public transport, especially at night, it is very difficult for them to reach a hospital in case of an emergency. In the immediate neighbourhood, there is a private clinic where people go in case of an emergency or for minor treatments, but it expensive. For all other matters, they travel to Saidapet. Many respondents would prefer to have a government hospital in the vicinity of Ambedkar Nagar. Others would prefer to have a dispensary in the neighbourhood. Before relocation many people were living in the city centre where all these facilities used to be right next-door and they feel very unhappy to have lost all that.

The Social Welfare and Nutritious Meal Programme Department runs a scheme that provides poor pregnant women with some extra money to compensate for their wage loss during confinement and to supplement their nutritional needs. When they apply eight to twelve weeks prior to giving birth, they can receive Rs 500. Four respondents have received it through the Corporation hospital where they delivered their baby. Others said they tried to get it but did not receive the money. Many women did not even know about the scheme. All women go to the hospital for child birth. For immunization of the children, they go to the government hospital, where the injections are free of cost. Some people just go to the chemist's and buy whatever the chemist advises them to take.

Informal Health Care Practices

A few people mention they never use traditional health practises as the 'English doctor' had told them it might interfere with the 'English' medicine. Almost all the respondents (96 per cent) use traditional health practices before and after childbirth.

During the first few months of the pregnancy women are not allowed to eat papaya or mango as this can result in a miscarriage, because it 'heats up the body'. A pregnant woman explained that there are many other rules she should obey. She is not allowed to sit in the tailoring seat nor is on the doorstep, as the area is believed to be 'like a god which you should not block'. If she sits with her legs up or crossed, it is believed that the baby will get a big head. For the delivery, many women return to the parents' house and the mothers prepare a special curry called *Marundu Kuzhambu*, a gravy made of drumstick, brinjal, pepper, dry ginger, *dal* powder, and medicinal herbs in order to 'heat up the body' and kill the infections. The first eight days after the delivery, the new mother has to be very strict because if a child falls ill, she will be blamed for not sticking to her diet. At that time, she is not allowed to eat any 'cooling' items. After the birth, the baby is given a special creamy gravy made of garlic, neem leaves, pepper and cumin seeds. Others said that whenever children have a cold, till the age of four years, they are fed the following recipe: turmeric, garlic and pepper, cumin seeds and asafoetida are crushed and turned into a ball which is dried in the sun, and then crushed into small amounts which are given to children; others also feed it to the newly born. In case of disease and during the different seasons, 'hot' and 'cold' food items are recommended or prohibited. One person said that for dysentery, she makes a *rasam* of *drumstick* in order to cure it.

While interviewing, we came across one child infected with chickenpox. Her mother told us that there are three sorts of pox, which they called 'Mariatta' because they believe the goddess Mariyamman comes in this form.[17] The mother believed the pox to be a 'gift' of Mariyamman, and it means that 'the goddess is in her'. To make Mariyamman leave peacefully, the women did not use medicines, but covered her daughter with neem leaves and neem leaf powder and fed her buttermilk and curd. When the disease aggravates it is called 'Pongal in your feet' and then rice, water, and cow-dung cakes are brought to the Mariyamman temple.[18]

Many people, 72 per cent, make use of an astrologer or fortune-teller once in a while. Astrologers are consulted to select an auspicious day for marriages and to select auspicious days and hours of the day for certain activities. Astrologers also visit Ambedkar Nagar regularly. When they arrive, a small crowd usually gathers around them in order to hear what they have to say. The astrologers ask the day and time of birth, and then predict the future. Also, when money is available, people sometimes consult a parrot. The 'parrot man' comes to Ambedkar Nagar once in a while, and with his parrot in a small cage, he walks around and people can consult him. The parrot is then taken out of to cage and asked to select cards from a pile. The 'parrot man' will predict the future according to the type of card selected by the parrot. A few people also believe in the predicting of the future through the interpretation of the form taken on by shells that are thrown on the ground.

5.2.3 WATER AND SANITATION

Water

For washing and cleaning purposes, 20 wells were dug in the area. Some of them are now in a poor state, but are still used, mainly for bathing, washing clothes, and house cleaning.

Drinking water is provided through lorries by Metro Water. It was intended that about a dozen water lorries would provide water in Ambedkar Nagar on a daily basis, but as will be discussed later, this was not always the case. One lorry contains 9,000 litres and each family is given a few pots of water a day, for 25 paisa each. One pot contains on average 15 litres. The remaining water is stored in water containers placed by Metro Water. This water is divided later in the day, or is kept for days the lorry is not coming. There are 16 such water containers in Ambedkar Nagar. Many people complained that they could not get enough water. The following anecdote is a typical example of the officials' lack of knowledge on Ambedkar Nagar: one engineer of Metro Water responsible for the water supply in Ambedkar Nagar, was under the impression that in the whole area there were only 800 households instead of 2,640. A system of auctioning for engaging water distributors was organized by the leaders of the local Ambedkar Makkal Podhu Nala Sangam (Ambedkar People's Social Welfare Association).[19] Women were appointed by them to distribute water in the area.[20]

As Velacheri is a new area under development, the water distribution system was not yet fully operational. Therefore, when the allottees were relocated to Ambedkar Nagar, Metro Water initially provided them with water through water lorries. As this was very expensive, in January 1999 a private company was contracted to provide water to the area for three years. It is obliged to provide 400,000 litres of water a day to the area and Metro Water pays them according to performance and outcome. Whenever the private company is not able to provide service, Metro Water will send lorries, the cost of which will be deducted from the payment to the company. Metro Water has chosen this temporary solution as this is much cheaper than servicing the area by water lorry: a 1,000 litres provided by the private company costs between Rs 36 and 40, whereas water provided by Metro Water with lorries costs between Rs 70 and 90. After three years Metro Water expects that Velacheri will be linked up with the main water system.[21]

Next to Ambedkar Nagar, Metro Water built an expensive desalination plant, which is operated by a private company. Raw water is pumped up and cleansed of bacteria and salt through a system of reverse osmosis and then supplied as drinking water in Ambedkar Nagar through 23 taps. From the start, the company has faced many problems. The yield of water is insufficient, especially during the hot season when there is little rain, it is very difficult to provide enough water to Ambedkar Nagar. The raw water is highly contaminated with bacteria, organic matter, and carbonates which are difficult to filter. Furthermore, due to the contamination, the filters have to be cleaned very often. Another problem is power failure and low voltage, which hamper the supply of water to Ambedkar Nagar. The private company concludes that Metro Water should provide them with an extra generator, which the latter is not willing to do.

When water is provided through the tap, it is only available a few hours a day, early in the morning. But on many days, it is not available at all. Then the 'water women' or the operators of the company have to call Metro Water to send lorries, and on those days the water is again provided through the old system.

As already mentioned, when water lorries provided water, there was a system whereby 'water women' were responsible for its distribution and they received a small amount of money for this task. It was their responsibility to distribute the water evenly amongst all households and whenever the lorry did not come they would contact Metro Water. When tap water was introduced, this system was discontinued, as many felt that tap water was 'free water' and that everyone was allowed to take as many pots as they liked, free of cost. Because water was only available for a few hours a day, and its amount varied per day, some people were able to fetch many pots of water while others could not get anything. This resulted in many quarrels.

When sufficient water comes through the taps, many people take three to six pots daily, which is more than the number of pots they are allowed to take from the lorry. Lorry and tap water is used for drinking purposes, but tap water is also used for cleaning. Many people are not happy with the water provision; they said the water lorry was much better. Since the introduction of tap water, the amount of water is often not sufficient, and they do not like the quarrels that blaze up at the tap. Besides, many worry that during the summer time water provision will even be less. Also they do not like the taste of tap water, as it's 'too soft'.

Sanitation

Public convenience units of either 8 or 14 seats were built in ten locations of Ambedkar Nagar, which averages out to approximately 106 persons per seat. The disposal system consists of a septic tank for each unit. As no water is available in the toilets and cleanliness of these public convenience units was a problem from the start, the leaders of the Ambedkar Makkal Podhu Nala Sangam tried to collect money from all inhabitants to employ some people for cleaning the public convenience units. As it appeared to be too much of a burden on the local people, they went to the Zonal Office of the Chennai Corporation to demand a solution. As a result the Corporation employed 10 persons. Also, a few years back one of the local slum leaders approached the Corporation to install a pay-and-use toilet in his neighbourhood in Ambedkar Nagar. Whenever people use it, they have to pay a small amount, and those who make use of it are very happy with it. Although for its usage they have to pay a small amount, many people, especially women, appreciate that at least these toilets are clean and illuminated. The overall majority, 75 per cent, makes use of the public convenience units, and some make use of the pay-and-use toilet. Others defecate out in the open field.

Ninety-five per cent of the respondents are unhappy with the public convenience units because they are dirty, not maintained, overcrowded, and without water. The situation is particularly difficult for women and children. People also complain that the toilets are not used properly. One person said that because the toilet is free 'no-one knows the value of it so they make it dirty'. Also, as the septic tank is not emptied regularly it overflows, which causes a lot of nuisance. According to many, it would be a major improvement if the public convenience units were cleaned daily and if water was provided. Some also say that one person should be in charge of the maintenance and cleaning of the public convenience units. Two respondents have their own toilet connected with the underground sewage system, which cost one of them Rs 3,000 in 1997. Many other people would also like to have their own connection but for them it is much too expensive.

Others say they would not know where to put the unit, as their plot is much too small.

Storm Water Drains

Storm water drains were constructed alongside the main roads to convey large amounts of water that need to be disposed of quickly, especially during the monsoon, and also wastewater generated from the households. This water is supposed to be disposed into the Velacheri tank, as the underground sewage system is not in operation throughout the whole of Ambedkar Nagar. The problem is that many of these drains are blocked by the garbage thrown into them. Many people complain that they form breeding grounds for mosquitoes. In some parts of the area people have tried to clean the storm water drains, but lack of cooperation among inhabitants poses a problem and leaders do not take any initiative. In parts of Ambedkar Nagar, only a few people cooperated in cleaning the drains, most were not interested. Their response was 'what is the use of keeping the drains clean, while others always throw their garbage in it?' This attitude results in many quarrels, and people who were annoyed often approached me. They told me that their local leader was not taking any initiative and that they had tried to approach the local councillor several times by phone and in person at the Division Office without any result. They asked me whether I could inform the councillor about this problem. The Corporation only reconstructed part of the drains which had collapsed, but still many are constantly blocked. Initially, the Corporation also used to clean up the drains. But in 1999 they never did so. Although one NGO also helped to clean the drains, the overall condition of the storm water drains is bad.

Waste Management

Garbage collection is the responsibility of the Corporation, but there is no regularity in the service. Every street in Ambedkar Nagar has piles of garbage; there are mounds of it in the open areas and in the storm water drains. The accumulation of garbage is a source of irritation for many people in Ambedkar Nagar. According to the local councillor, 'the situation regarding garbage collection could be improved, but total accumulation is not there'. According to many people in Ambedkar Nagar, however, garbage is collected very irregularly. Some people said that for the past half year nobody has come to collect it, so they either throw their garbage in the junctions of their street, in the storm water drain, or in the open spaces, as they do not know where else to put it. People who live near the tank throw their garbage in the water. Sometimes piles are burned in the streets in order to get rid of garbage. Some people complained at the Division Office in Velacheri and talked to their local leaders about this problem. The residents would like the garbage to be cleared regularly and dustbins to be placed in the area. Many people mention that they along with their neighbours keep their own streets clean. Most dead end streets and small lanes are reasonably clean, but an accumulation of waste can be observed in the main roads, as these are wider and there is less social interaction and pressure between people living on either sides who often belong to different groups. One NGO is organizing waste collection in one part of the area, but many people in Ambedkar Nagar do not have too much faith in this initiative.[22]

5.2.4 TRANSPORT AND ELECTRICITY

Transport

Many employees have to travel far to their place of work. The average distance is 6.6 km, so in total employees travel approximately 13 km a day. Thirty-three per cent travel more than 20 km a day. Apart from that, two people work in other cities, one in the south of Tamil Nadu, and one in Bangalore. They live there and come to visit their family in Ambedkar Nagar once in a while. Fourteen per cent work in Ambedkar Nagar itself, mainly women. One woman for instance sells fish, which she buys once a week in Royapuram and sells in a bunk shop in Ambedkar Nagar. Other women go to the wholesale market in Koyambedu to buy flowers or fruit, which they sell on the streets of Ambedkar Nagar. Of the 228 family-members of the sample for whom the mode of travelling is known, 66 per cent go to work by bus, 1 per cent by auto (auto drivers), 10 per cent by cycle, 1 per cent by moped, 5 per cent by train (after first walking approximately 2-3 km to the train station on Saint Thomas Mount), 14 per cent walk to neighbouring areas such as NGO Colony, Alandur and Adambakkam, and 2 per cent go by tricycle. One per cent change their mode of transport once in a while, depending on the amount of household money and the place of work. The average amount that is spent daily on commuting to work is Rs 7.

Many people complain that the bus stop is at a distance of about 1-2 km depending on where they live in Ambedkar Nagar, and that buses all irregular. Many respondents feel that a bus stop nearer to Ambedkar Nagar and an increase in the number of the buses (they are always very crowded, especially in the morning and afternoon when people commute to work) would be an improvement. Apart from travelling to work, people spend about Rs 83 a month on transport in order to visit family, religious places or go to the hospital.

Electricity

The Chennai Corporation was entrusted with the installation of streetlights in Ambedkar Nagar. They provided lights on all the main roads, at a rate of one light per 40 metres. The lights burn irregularly and when they do, they burn at a very low voltage. Toilets have no light, which is a nuisance to many people, especially women.

In order to apply for a private electricity connection, the applicant first needs to get a NOC from the Slum Board, which grants one only after the applicant has paid the outstanding monthly instalment owing to it. Some people have applied for it just after they were relocated and when they received the NOC they stopped paying the monthly instalment. Others were only able to apply for it just recently, and they had to pay a large amount to the Slum Board. The amount of the monthly instalment to be paid to the Slum Board is Rs 76 per household.[23]

Only after they have paid up to the day that they apply for the NOC can they receive it. If, for example they arrived in Ambedkar Nagar in 1990, the amount due to the Slum Board in 1999 is approximately Rs 7,848 and 360 to the Corporation. Buyers face an extra problem in obtaining the NOC, because buying and selling off plots is not allowed, so they usually apply for the NOC in the allottee's name. This worked well as many of the buyers in Ambedkar Nagar have electricity which they themselves have applied for. Many people complain about the amount of 'speed money' that had to be paid in order to receive the NOC and the connection from the Tamil Nadu Electricity Board. Furthermore, it takes a lot of going up and down to the different offices, which is a burden for many people. Almost half of the respondents (47 per cent) have electricity in their homes, and 7 per cent of them tap it either from their neighbours or from the main electricity wires in the streets. When the latter is done, they normally hang the wire up after dark and remove it early in the morning in order not to get caught either by the police or by the employers of the Tamil Nadu Electricity Board, who come to Ambedkar Nagar every two months to collect the electricity bill. The average amount people have paid to the Slum Board in order to get the NOC is Rs 3,800 and the average paid to get the connection from the Electricity Board is Rs 3,600. So in total, these respondents have spent an average of Rs 7,400 to get the connection. The average amount that is spent on the electricity bill every two months is Rs 150. People who tap from their neighbours pay an average of Rs 100 every two months to them, according to the meter. The electricity is used for running radios, fans and even televisions. For the television, a private antenna is usually used, but some houses even have cable connection. People love to watch Tamil movies, especially the classic MGR and Sivaji Ganesan ones, and in some households the television is always on.

5.2.5 MARKET FACILITIES

As already discussed, at the time of the research there were about 45 shops in Ambedkar Nagar itself. In addition, a number of vendors walk around the streets selling a variety of products, snacks like *bonda*, *samosa* and *vada*, cosmetics and bangles, religious articles like small statues of gods, household articles, plastic and clay water pots, cloth and *saris*. Some vendors also sell on an instalment basis, where the advantage for the buyer is that a small amount has to be paid daily or weekly and in the meantime, the product can already be used. Eventually, however, the product is more expensive than if it had been paid for all at once.

A few hundred meters from Ambedkar Nagar is a small post office, and in Kakkan Nagar, 1 km away, is a shopping centre with large provision shops. For additional shopping people have to walk to Alandur, about 2 km from Ambedkar Nagar, where there is a big marketplace.

The respondents are not dissatisfied with the market facilities available in and around Ambedkar Nagar, although many people say that in their previous locality the facilities were better and products were cheaper.

5.3 Obtaining Social Security

5.3.1 The Ration Shop

As explained in Chapter 3, the PDS provides food grains and a few other items through ration shops all over the country. The public can obtain products from these shops through ration cards. Tamil Nadu has different types of cards.[24] Pink cards are issued for persons living under the poverty line. Family size, which is mentioned on the ration card, determines the quantity of products that can be obtained. Different income groups can obtain different products, and people living below the poverty line can obtain more products than higher income groups.

The ration shop that serves the inhabitants of Ambedkar Nagar is close to the area, about 0.5 km away, and is open daily, except Sundays. On a typical day, a big crowd of mainly women can be found queuing there. Products that can be bought from the shop are oil, rice, sugar, wheat, *atta*, and kerosene. During festivals, special products like palm oil are also sold. Once a month all the ration-cardholders can buy the products from the shop, except for rice, which can be bought weekly. The monthly sales are a problem for many people as it is difficult for them to pay the full monthly amount for a product. There are no fixed dates for buying the products as the people go to the ration shop whenever they have the money.

Eighty-three per cent of the respondents have a ration card, all pink cards, and 17 per cent do not have it. There are several reasons for respondents not to have a ration card. It is only issued to people who have a legal ownership or tenancy over the place of their residence and so some tenants in Ambedkar Nagar are not able to apply for the card as the owner of their plot already has a ration card corresponding to his house number. Furthermore, as the renting out of plots is also illegal, tenants do not have a legally valid proof of their tenancy.[25] Others have not yet transferred their ration card from the shop in their former location to the one near Ambedkar Nagar, as they say it is a very difficult procedure which involves a lot of visits to the Civil Supplies Office and also some bribing. Some people have applied for the transfer but are still awaiting the card. Some respondents have just moved out of their parents' home and have to apply for a separate card. Meanwhile, they buy products from the ration shop on their parents' card. Others borrow the card from their neighbours. Some people complain about the quality of the products sold at the ration shop, mentioning, for instance, that the rice is not of a good quality and therefore they only use it to make *idli*, they buy rice from the regular shops for other meals. Many complain that they never obtain the correct weight for which they paid (receiving, for example, 800 gm of rice but paying for 1 kg). According to them, the ration shop employee sells the difference in the open market. The employee himself acknowledged that he sold part of the stock in the open market in order to supplement his salary. He explained that he had already approached his boss several times for a pay raise but as he had not listened, he had decided to take this step.

The pink ration card is not only used to buy products at the ration shop, it is also used as an identification card in absence of other forms of identification, for instance in loan applications.

5.3.2 SAVINGS, LOANS, AND PENSIONS

Savings

The financial status of most of the respondents is such that they are not able to save any money. Eighty-one per cent of the respondents do not save any money due to lack of earnings. Some of these people are repaying debts, and some women mention that their husbands manage the finances so they do not know whether or not he saves money. In other cases, the husband drinks, so there is no money left to save. A minority of the respondents (19 per cent), save some money. Most of the savings is in a chit fund, at home or with a savings group of an NGO. Others go outside Ambedkar Nagar to save money, sometimes by joining a vessel fund where they pay Rs 100 a month for a number of months after which they can obtain bronze vessels. Some have joined a private company fund. Some save in a bank, and several of them buy gold whenever they have some extra money. The average amount respondents save is Rs 200 a month.

Loans

A major problem for many people is the lack of credit opportunities. Especially for self-employed women selling items like flowers, fish, vegetables and fruit. Another serious problem is the lack of access to information about the possibilities of obtaining loans. Those, who are aware of the existence of credit possibilities explained that the application procedures for finance schemes or bank loans are so elaborate and time and money consuming that it is almost impossible to apply. A major problem in applying is that many certificates need to be submitted along with the application form, such as community and income certificates, which in many cases are not easy to obtain. Often, people do not even know where to get them from. Leaders are also not very helpful in these matters. Some people said that they are not interested in helping the poor and needy, but only the ones from whom they can expect something in return. So for more people the only sources of credit are the moneylenders and pawn brokers.[26] In general, the operational features of money-lenders are relative accessibility, convenient opening hours, quick processing, flexible collateral (in the case of pawnbrokers), high interest rates, excellent monitoring systems, and often good recovery records.[27]

There are two types of moneylenders active in Ambedkar Nagar: 'professional moneylenders' who depend on money-lending as their main source of income, or spend most of their time lending it, and part-time moneylenders, who are shop-owners supplementing their income through moneylending. There are some professional moneylenders who come to Ambedkar Nagar daily to lend and collect money. The local leaders also operate as *thandal*.[28] The following anecdote brings out the procedure of borrowing from a moneylender by a self-employed woman who sells fish in Ambedkar Nagar. She has six children, and as her husband has deserted her, she has to support herself and her family.

> Early in the morning Manjula gets Rs 200 daily from a *thandal* in Ambedkar Nagar. With the money, she goes to the Alandur wholesale market to buy fish. She returns to Ambedkar Nagar and during the day, walks around its streets trying to sell off as many fish as possible. The *thandal* charges 10 per cent interest, so she has to repay him Rs 220 every evening. Manjula says that her daily profit, after repaying the moneylender, is approximately Rs 30 or 40, which is not enough for her family.[29]

Some people mentioned that they had given their allotment order as collateral to the local leader from whom they borrowed money.[30] Some people borrow money from the *thandal* in order to visit their family back in the village. One lady said that she borrowed Rs 500 each *Adi* (a Tamil word for July) in order to visit a temple. Afterwards she paid back Rs 25 weekly until the loan was repaid. Many people consider the professional moneylender as their last resort. They prefer to borrow money from elsewhere, as the moneylender charge high interest, are known to be very strict and impose harsh reprisals against defaulters. Some are even said to beat up defaulters. In order to buy the daily groceries, women often borrow small amounts of money from their neighbours, friends and relatives, which they

PAWN TICKET Form F (Sec. 7 & Rule 6)

J. DHAGLARAM CHOUDHARY

Pawn Broker P.B.L. No. 19/96-97

No. 11, KAKKAN NAGAR MAIN ROAD,
ADAMBAKKAM, CHENNAI - 600 088.

No. 5878 DATE 30-10-97

Name of the Pawner ....

Full address ....

.... CHENNAI-600 0 88

Amount of Principal of Loan Rs. 370/-

Rupees in words ....

Rate of interest charged at 18% per annum.

The time agreed upon for redemption of articles ONE YEAR

No.	Full and detailed description of the articles (Weight to be noted in case of jewels)	Gross Weight Kg. Gm. Mg.
1	One pair silver	87

Present Value

Rs. 370/- Rs. 375/-

I declare that the above mentioned gold ornaments are my own and were manufactured before 10-1-1963 my monthly income Rs. ....

Signature of Pawn Broker or his Agent

Signature or left thumb impression of the Agent

FIGURE 5.2: PAWNBROKER'S CERTIFICATE

normally return in the evening when the income earning family members return home with their daily wages.

A moneylender who lends while taking physical possession of the collateral is called a pawnbroker. Pawning involves the surrender of the asset being pawned to the lender until the loan plus interest is repaid. If the loan, or at least the interest, is not repaid during the specified time, the pawned item is forfeited to the lender. The articles that people in Ambedkar Nagar normally give as a collateral are their ration card, jewellery, and bronze vessels. Some people have also given their allotment order as collateral. In 1989-99, these pawnbrokers were only located in the neighbourhood surrounding Ambedkar Nagar, but when I returned to Ambedkar Nagar in 2001, a few pawnbrokers had made their appearance in the area.

Pensions

The government ruled that the minimum age for pension eligibility for persons who are unable to work due to leprosy, insanity, paralysis or loss of limb is 60 years, and for severe cases 45 years. For other persons, the minimum age to apply for an old age pension is 65 years. Destitute widows of all ages can also apply for a pension, as well as deserted wives over the age of 30 years. The money is paid through the Tahsildar Office (Distress Relief Scheme Office) and the amount is Rs 150 a month.

Of the 158 households that were interviewed through the use of the questionnaire, 21 people were eligible under the scheme—one male above the age of 65 and 20 widows. The man did not receive the pension as he was not aware of the existence of the scheme and no one had told him about it. Of the 20 widows, 11 received a widow's pension and the majority had only been receiving it for a few months. Only one woman had been receiving it for the past 10 years. Two women had applied for a pension a few months back but they were still waiting for a reply and seven persons did not receive a pension, either because they did not know how to apply for it, or they had applied but for reasons not known to them they did not get it.

A local leader had approached some of the widows and handed them application forms for widows' pension. He told them to fill them in and return the papers to him, along with two photographs, and he would apply for the widows' pension at the Tahsildar's Office. They had complied, and a few months later, they received the pension for the first time. One woman said that along with seven other widows she approached another local leader and he helped them to apply. Six out of seven now receive the pension. For his help, they paid him Rs 10 each. Others said that for the mediation of the local leader, they paid Rs 150. One woman was told by her employer to approach the Tahsildar's Office on her own so she did. She paid Rs 300 and was admitted into the scheme immediately. All of these women are happy with the pension they receive. Although the majority of them live with their children, the pension makes them feel less of a burden to their family.

5.3.3 NOON MEAL SCHEME

In the Corporation-, municipal-, and panchayat schools children receive a free midday meal provided under the Noon Meal Scheme. De Wit reported that for many poor parents this is a reason for sending their children to those schools.[31] Many people in Ambedkar Nagar are also happy that a free meal is given with the Noon Meal Scheme, but complain about the quality of the food and would appreciate if it could be improved. Therefore some mothers pack a lunch for their children.

5.4 NON-GOVERNMENTAL ORGANIZATIONS

5.4.1 NGOs IN THE AREA

Initially, many problems existed in Velacheri. Social problems arose from the fact that people from different communities and different backgrounds were now close neighbours. Furthermore, there were many fights between different 'gangs' in Ambedkar Nagar about the illegal selling of *arrack* and drugs.[32] Also, the area lacked many facilities that the Slum Board had promised, like sufficient water supply, public convenience units, and electricity. As the new residents of Velacheri became increasingly dissatisfied with the relocation and crime increased, NGOs were approached by the Slum Board to assist in setting up projects in Velacheri. Another reason for approaching the NGOs was financial. The Slum Board hoped extra funds would become available for the community of Velacheri through these organizations.[33]

The two major NGOs operating in Ambedkar Nagar are GEMS and World Vision. There are also a few smaller NGOs active in area and their activities will also be looked at. Lastly, the opinion of the respondents regarding these NGOs will be discussed.

George Educational, Medical and Charitable Society, or GEMS, was set-up by a Keralite businessman towards the end of the 1970s. The NGO has been active in Tamil Nadu since the early 1990s. As explained before, in the early years, when the relocatees were newly moved Ambedkar Nagar, there were many social problems. Therefore the Slum Board asked the NGO to start working in the area, which GEMS did in 1993. It built two community halls and started a local office in one of the halls. In the past, GEMS had organized vocational training classes like tailoring, typewriting and paper craft making. The Slum Board, the Nehru Rozgar Yojana Scheme and some private funds sponsored these programmes. Furthermore, they organized a women's savings group, which was rather popular, but all these activities stopped after a while. At the time of this research, GEMS ran a doctor's clinic one evening a week in one of the halls, three *balwadis* and a child labourers' class where former child labourers were educated for one year before they were sent to corporation schools. For a short while GEMS also organized a day-care centre for old people that looked rather depressing as these old men and women just sat there all day, some days watching television, other days doing nothing as they had nowhere else to go and nothing to do. However, they could at least enjoy each other's company there. Again, lack of interest made this a very short-lived project.[34]

World Vision is an international Christian NGO set-up in 1947. Since 1976 it has been operating in Tamil Nadu. This NGO paid for all its projects through its own means and did not receive any money from the Slum Board or the government. It came to Ambedkar Nagar in 1990, when the inhabitants were affected by the monsoon and the Slum Board asked if World Vision could provide the people in the relocation site with food, medicines and drinking water. The NGO was involved in community development. They ran a homework class for school-going children, a *balwadi,* and training courses like typewriting and tailoring. They also ran a doctor's clinic once a week, which cost Rs 5 per visit. Moreover, they had set-up a popular women's savings group with 70 to 80 members. Weekly, the members saved Rs 10, which was collected by the supervisor, who put all the money in a joint bank account. For every five members one leader and one supervisor were appointed. They coordinated the savings group. The members jointly decided who was eligible to receive a loan from the savings. The maximum that could be obtained was Rs 3,000 and this had to be repaid within five months, with an interest rate of 2 per cent. To become a member of the women's savings group a subscription of Rs 10 a month had to be paid. The members themselves decided who was allowed to join the group.

In addition, there were a few small NGOs active in Ambedkar Nagar, such as Youth with a Mission, New Life, and Compassion for India. These were small Christian organizations who provided, among other things, loans for hut improvements and financing a *balwadi*. World Vision tried to coordinate its work with these small NGOs. For instance, in May 1999, they organized an eye camp together, at the World Vision centre in the area.

The following story is about Mary, a retired teacher who lives outside Ambedkar Nagar and who has set-up a *balwadi* in the area, in cooperation with Youth with a Mission.

Mary is an elderly Roman Catholic woman who lives outside Ambedkar Nagar. She is very energetic, and comes to Ambedkar Nagar daily to run a *balwadi*. She is a retired Lower Kinder Garten (LKG) teacher trained at the teacher's college in Saidapet, and she has worked for nearly 40 years. Twenty-five years ago she suffered a heart attack. The doctors did not think she would survive and at that time she explained that she had made 'a vow to God' that, if she recovered, she would, after retirement, dedicate her life to working for the poor. After she retired, she came in contact with the NGO Youth with a Mission who were working in Ambedkar Nagar and she decided to help them. That is how she started her work in Ambedkar Nagar.

Five years ago Youth with a Mission opened a school in Ambedkar Nagar in a small hut and a year later, Mary joined them. Soon she had the idea of buying a piece of land to build a school and approached the Slum Board. Officers of the Slum Board told her they could not help her, as they could not give land to an individual. They advised her to set-up a trust to improve her chances of obtaining a piece of land. So she set-up the Joseph Welfare Trust, which she registered at the Tahsildar's office. This took a very long time and cost her Rs 3,000. However, the Slum Board still did not help her with a piece of land, so she illegally bought two plots for Rs 20,000, all private money, from some allottees who lived outside Ambedkar Nagar, in order to construct a school. As the allottees did not have a photo-pass, only a written piece of paper with a stamp, after she bought these plots she received official papers along with the plots. The purchase was approved by the local slum organization Ambedkar Makkal Podhu Nala Sangam and put on paper. In January 1998, construction of the school, for which she had collected Rs 50,000 from a Tamil church and some money from friends and relatives, began. In total, the cost was Rs 175,000 for the construction and Rs 20,000 for the plots. According to Mary, the Slum Board knows that she has bought the land illegally but because social work is involved, and the land was bought in the name of the trust, and there was no other way the Board can legally transfer ownership, it allows the situation to exist. Mary paid for the building, and all the other costs like books, uniforms, play materials and food are paid by Youth with Mission.

Children from all the relocation groups go to this school and many people are interested in sending their child to it, but there is place for only 40 children every year. After they turn five, they are sent to the municipal school in Alandur where the education is free and they are provided with the Noon Meal Scheme.

Youth with a Mission employs four people, one teacher and one helper who come from outside Ambedkar Nagar, and one cook and one helper who both live in Ambedkar Nagar. Mary is planning to buy two houses opposite the school that she rents at the moment and uses as kitchen and playground for the smaller children. The owner of these two plots told her he wanted to sell them for Rs 75,000. Although this is very expensive and Mary doesn't know from where to get the money, she has decided to buy these two plots as they are just in front of the school and she will never find such good spots in the future. She paid Rs 1,000 in advance, which again is all private money. As Mary's husband died 15 years back she said that she is 'as free as a bird'. Besides, her children all have good jobs, and she says she can decide on her own to spend her private money on the poor.

5.4.2 THE ROLE OF NGOs ACCORDING TO THE INHABITANTS

The main problem with GEMS was that the staff changed often, and many of them were not really interested in working in the area. They had preconceived ideas about the inhabitants of Ambedkar Nagar. Some even made very provocative comments against them. These ideas were reflected in one of the staff papers, which discussed their role in Ambedkar Nagar:

> Having worked for more than 2,000 families for four years at the Velacheri Rehabilitation Centre, a few revelations have given unpleasant surprise to our workers, they are: most residents are lazy and will never do a clean job (. . .), and many of them have no difficulty in telling lies.[35]

Also, GEMS did not adapt its programmes and initiatives to the needs and wishes of the people in Ambedkar Nagar. The voices of the inhabitants themselves were not listened to. Many people complained about GEMS, especially its leader Mr George. According to Govindan, a local leader:

> GEMS is not good as George dominates. He is a millionnaire, instead of drinking coffee with us he goes to the US to drink a cup of coffee, he only comes here in his big *Tata* to tell people what to do. He does not listen to people, and he does not even speak proper Tamil.

According to many people Mr George only comes to Ambedkar Nagar when there is a big event and politicians are invited, in order to get publicity. During the research period of about 1, 5 years, he never visited Ambedkar Nagar, and whenever I visited the GEMS head office in Chennai he was always abroad. Only two persons of the local staff were in the area on a daily basis.

In the second phase of the Sustainable Chennai Project, Ambedkar Nagar was chosen as one of the pilot project areas and GEMS was selected to coordinate the project in cooperation with Chennai Metropolitan Development Authority (CMDA), the implementers of the Sustainable Chennai Project. The pilot project was initiated amongst 300 households in Ambedkar Nagar selected by GEMS from near the community hall. They all belonged to the Chitra Nagar group who normally also join all the other activities initiated by GEMS. The project focused mainly on the improvement of water and sanitation facilities, garbage collection and infrastructure. It was stated that the project should be carried out through a committee with representatives from the community, the Slum Board, Metro Water and GEMS, but the selected households were not involved in the formulation of the goals and strategies of the project. The main problem was that the NGO did not trust the community and the project was never discussed properly within the community itself. It was even mentioned by the NGO staff that the project had to be formulated from outside as the local inhabitants of Ambedkar Nagar 'only come up with funny ideas'. Only minor adaptations would be made in consultation with the people. Obviously, no full cooperation and participation could be expected when the opinion and experience of the inhabitants themselves are not taken seriously. Another problem was that the local GEMS staff running the project was discharged. At the time of this research, Manju was in charge of the project in the area. A Catholic woman who was relocated from Krishnamurthy Colony, she lived in Ambedkar Nagar with her children. As her husband left her for another woman, Manju had to work to provide for the family. For many years, she had worked for GEMS as a leader of one of the women's groups. She used to like her work and because she was from Ambedkar Nagar itself she knew most people, she understood their needs, and spoke their language. She was instrumental in helping some people apply for and obtain a ration card. When GEMS was selected for the pilot project under the Sustainable Chennai Programme, Manju was asked to head it in Ambedkar Nagar. Critical GEMS supervising staff member, Manju one day was fired because according to her she was very critical towards GEMS staff. According to the GEMS staff she had practised fraud with shopping lists, but it is more likely that she was fired because she was openly criticizing the people in charge of the NGO.

For the garbage collection, composting, and sweeping of the area, two women were appointed, who, besides other work had to collect garbage from every house to door on a daily basis. To make it easier these women were given tri-cycles, but because the roads were so bad it was difficult for them to pull the cycles through the area. People were asked to put their garbage in a bucket provided by GEMS and to hand it over to these women. Instead, in many cases these buckets were used for other purposes like storing water and not for throwing garbage, as people did not like to keep the garbage in their house. Every day, only a few people handed their garbage over to these women. These 'garbage women' were also meant to separate the organic from the in-organic, burn the inorganic and use the organic for composting—tasks for which these women had joined a training course. This composting was a complete failure due to the unsuitable construction of the pit the organic waste had to be dropped in; the structure was too high so the women could not turn over the waste properly. Moreover, the location of the pit was near the Public Convenience (PC) units where it was very dirty and they did not want to work there. They had informed GEMS about these problems but the supervising staff had not listened. Another part of the project involved the planting of samplings. This also failed as these plants were not protected, and no one in the area was informed about this initiative, nor about the reasons these samplings were planted; so in a few weeks time they were all damaged. As was to be expected, the outcome was that the project was not functioning at all; it turned out to be a complete failure and a waste of money.

Five per cent of the respondents were either joining a women's savings group or another activity organized by World Vision, or were participating in the activities of Youth with a Mission. Five per cent were members of the local Ambedkar Makkal Podhu Nala Sangam, members of a political party, members of the local Indira Panchayat or of the local mosque committee. But 90 per cent were not involved in any of these organizations, either because they were not interested or because they were not aware of their existence. Those who were aware of the organizations and their activities were asked their opinion about them. Six per cent of them replied that whenever these organizations arrange something, they should approach the inhabitants. Eighteen per cent replied that in the early days of Ambedkar Nagar, there were many social problems and at that time the NGOs did a good job in easing the tension. Fifty-two per cent said that although they did not join any activity yet they were happy that these organizations were situated in Ambedkar Nagar. Typically, the group nearest to the NGO building joined in their activities more than others living further away. Many people did not like to mingle with other groups. Therefore, 14 per cent said that they did not join any activity of the NGOs as they only worked with other groups. Four per cent said that they normally joined the meetings organized by the NGOs and 6 per cent were very negative about all the organizations in Ambedkar Nagar and did not want to have anything to do with them. Respondents complained that GEMS used to organize many things like, for instance women's savings groups, but they explained that these activities were mainly the work of one enthusiastic local staff member who worked for GEMS. When she left, all the activities just stopped.

5.5 Conclusion

Table 5.13 brings together research questions two, three and four which focus on perceptions and expectations of the target group, policies implemented by the government and NGOs, and the accountability, effectiveness, and appropriateness of those policies.[36] A short summary of what was actually found will follow.

As can be concluded from the Chitra Nagar case study in Chapter 4, the financial status of the relocatees has not deteriorated due to the relocation; in fact, it has even improved a bit. However, more people judge that for them it is more difficult to manage since they were relocated. This might partly be explained by life in Ambedkar Nagar being much more expensive than life in Chitra Nagar. People have to pay for many facilities. Although in Chitra Nagar people also had to pay for drinking water,[37] many other facilities were free. For housing, people in Ambedkar Nagar have to pay Rs 76 a month; PC units are for free but whenever they want to make use of the pay-and-use toilet, they have to pay a small amount; when they have to visit a doctor, they can get free treatment from a government hospital but they have to take a bus, or visit the NGO clinic, which costs Rs 5. Moreover, when they have to commute to work, it costs on average Rs 7 a day.[38] So although on paper there is on the average a slight improvement in the per capita income, due to all the extra expenditure on basic facilities it can be concluded that the financial situation of the respondents after the relocation has deteriorated.

An additional comment should be made on the role of NGOs. The success of both major NGOs that are active in the area (meaning that the local community values and appreciates their work) depends upon the enthusiasm of their local staff and their attitude towards their target group. One NGO has a professional

TABLE 5.13: OVERVIEW OF ACCOUNTABILITY, EFFECTIVENESS, APPROPRIATENESS, AND EXPECTATIONS OF EMPLOYMENT AND BASIC SERVICES

Provided	*Organizations/ actors*	*Activities*	*Accountability*	*Effectiveness*	*Appropriateness*	*Expectations*
Basic services	Contractors	Construction of roads, *PC units*, storm water drains, wells	No accountability	Roads: Not effective as they are of bad quality; PC units: Effective as the number of PC units planned were constructed; Storm water drains: Effective as they were constructed the way they were designed; Wells: Effective as they were constructed the way they were designed	Roads: Very bad, the area is almost inaccessible during monsoon, and rickshaws, handcarts and water tankers, etc., almost cannot enter the area and they were not constructed up to corporation standards, which resulted in a delay in the handing over of the area from the	Roads: Black top roads should be provided; PC units: More PC units should be provided and lights and water should be installed in the PC units; Storm water drains: Not applicable; Wells: Not applicable

contd.

TABLE 5.13 (contd.)

Provided	*Organizations/ actors*	*Activities*	*Accountability*	*Effectiveness*	*Appropriateness*	*Expectations*
					Slum Board to the corporation; PC units: There are not enough PC units and there is no light or water in them; Storm water drains: Appropriately constructed; Wells: Not appropriate as the quality of water is not good	
Employment and maintenance of	TNSCB (till '96)/ Chennai City Municipal	Maintenance of roads, *PCs*, storm water	No information	No information	PCs: Not appropriate as they are not	Roads: (see provision); PCs: Should be

basic services	Corporation (from '96 onwards)	drains, wells, waste management	maintained and septic tanks are not emptied regularly; Storm water drains: Not appropriate as they are not maintained and emptied regularly so unable to convey storm water; Wells: Not appropriate as the area around the wells is not maintained; Waste management: Not appropriate as waste is not	cleaned more regularly and septic tanks should be cleared more regularly; Storm water drains: Should be maintained and cleaned; Wells: The construction should be maintained; Waste management: Garbage bins should be provided and garbage should be cleared regularly

contd.

TABLE 5.13 (contd.)

Provided	Organizations/ actors	Activities	Accountability	Effectiveness	Appropriateness	Expectations
					collected and there is no place to dump it.	
Employment and maintenance of basic services	Metro Water	Provision of water through tankers	No accountability	Not effective as it is too expensive	Before the collective action started: Not appropriate as tankers came irregularly; After the collective initiative started: Appropriate as tankers came regularly and distribution was organized	After the start of the collective initiative: Everyone was happy
	Partnership (Metro Water -	Provision of water through taps	No accountability	Metro Water: Effective as it	Provision is not appropriate as	The provision of water will

private company)			cuts down their costs; Private company: Not effective as the quality of raw water is very bad leading to blockage of the filter and problems with the electricity making regular water provision difficult and leading to cuts in their payment from Metro Water and problems with the community	it is not regular; often not enough; respondents do not like the taste of it; Fights blazing up at the taps as no-one is in charge of its distribution	have to become regular and its distribution has to be organized

contd.

TABLE 5.13 (contd.)

Provided	*Organizations/ actors*	*Activities*	*Accountability*	*Effectiveness*	*Appropriateness*	*Expectations*
	TNSCB	Mediation for jobs	No accountability	Not effective: No jobs were found for the relocatees	Not appropriate: No action was undertaken	More jobs should be created in the neighbourhood of the area, especially for women
	Chennai City Municipal Corporation, municipalities, panchayat and private organizations	Education	No accountability	Effective; Many types of schools are available	Appropriate: There are public schools free of cost closeby	The standard of education should improve
	Government of Tamil Nadu	Health care (hospital)	No accountability	Effective as there is a government hospital closeby	Inappropriate: The government hospital is too far	A government hospital should be built closeby
	Chennai Transportation Corporation	Bus service	No accountability	No information	Not appropriate: Buses are not regular and overcrowded.	More regular bus services should be provided

					Train station is not connected by bus	
	Chennai City Municipal Corporation	Electricity (public and private)	No accountability	Public: Effective as it is provided; Private: Effective as anyone who pays the instalment can apply	Public: Not appropriate as they burn at a low voltage and irregularly; Private: Expensive and elaborate application procedures	Public: Should burn more regularly and at higher voltage; Private: Application procedures should be simplified
Social security	Tamil Nadu State Government	Public distribution system, loans and pensions and Noon Meal Scheme	No accountability	PDS: Effective as the ration card is used by almost everyone; Loans: Not effective as	PDS: Appropriate as it is used by almost everyone but not appropriate in	PDS: Weekly sales are preferred and the application and transfer procedure should be

contd.

TABLE 5.13 (contd.)

Provided	*Organizations/ actors*	*Activities*	*Accountability*	*Effectiveness*	*Appropriateness*	*Expectations*
				they do not reach the target group; Pensions: Not effective as they do not reach the target group completely; Noon Meal Scheme: Effective as many children make use of it	the sense that the problem is the monthly sales and the elaborate bureaucratic procedures for application and change of address; Loans: Not effective as it is very difficult to apply due to elaborate bureaucratic procedures and ignorance/ unawareness of the target group; Pensions: Not appropriate as	simplified; Loans and Pensions: More facilities should be provided, especially for self-employed women, target groups should be informed better, application procedures should be simplified; Noon Meal Scheme: The quality of the food provided should be improved

				they reach only half of the target group due to elaborate bureaucratic procedures and unawareness of the target group; Noon Meal Scheme: Appropriate as many children benefit from it	
NGOs	Provision of health clinics, vocational training, education, savings groups, waste management	No accountability, although for some initiatives, community meetings were organized. In practice the	Health clinics: Effective as many people make use of them; Vocational training, education and savings groups:	Health clinics: Not appropriate, only for minor health problems and not free; vocational training: Not	NGOs should listen and adapt their policies and programmes more and better to the wishes of the local

contd.

TABLE 5.13 (contd.)

Provided	*Organizations/ actors*	*Activities*	*Accountability*	*Effectiveness*	*Appropriateness*	*Expectations*
			target group had no influence at all in the selection and implementation of the programmes	Effective as many people join; Waste management (experimental): Not effective as only a few people co-operate	appropriate as it does not lead to improved employment opportunities; Education: Appropriate but the capacity is too small; Savings groups: Appropriate but the capacity is too small; Waste management from the perspective of the whole community:	community and not impose their programmes on them

Not appropriate, people do not want to keep their waste in their house, it serves only a small group, people are not interested in composting, from the perspective of the waste collectors employed local staff including inhabitants of the area itself; the other has had many staff changes over the years, and therefore less contact with their target group. Whenever they take up a project, it is developed and implemented in a top down manner, i.e. they impose their programmes on the target group. Consequently, these often fail, as they are not designed according to the perceptions and expectations of the local community. The other NGO is more successful as it works in close cooperation with the inhabitants. Many inhabitants regret that they have a limited capacity and therefore work only with a small percentage of the community. Many more women for instance are interested in joining the savings group but the capacity is limited.

NOTES

1. The information on basic services is obtained from Dattatri, s.a., and Besselink, 1997: 38.
2. Dattatri, s.a.: 18.
3. Also locally referred to as Metro Water and therefore from here onwards I will also use this name.
4. But in practice this did not happen.
5. Dattatri, s.a.: 17-21.
6. The handing over of the site from the Slum Board to the Corporation was delayed for a while because the latter refused to take it over due to the very bad state of the roads in the area. According to an officer of the Corporation, they were not constructed according to their standards.
7. Rs 451.19 actually, but as mentioned in the previous chapter, it has been rounded off to Rs 450.
8. A number of remarks must be placed here: first it is very difficult to get an exact idea of the amount of income per household and per head because of the type of jobs that are performed. As already mentioned, the majority of the people in Ambedkar Nagar work in the informal sector, where jobs are not regular, and some jobs are even highly seasonal. In construction for instance, during the monsoon no work is done, so construction labourers do not have an income. Besides, many are hired for a certain job, during which they work rather regularly, but when the job is finished, it can take a while before a new job is found. Because of this irregularity, it is very difficult for people to give an exact estimate of their income. Whenever the respondents could not give the exact number of days they work, an average of 20 days a month was

used, which in some cases may be too high, while in others too low. Another reason why the figures may not be completely correct is that some people might want to hide their poverty, while others may want to hide certain sources of income. For that reason, though the interviews were conducted with much caution, the figures may be somewhat misleading. Also, as can be seen in the case study on Chitra Nagar, the per capita household income is in some cases higher than the per capita income that is actually spent on the households, as in some cases not all that is earned is given to the household but spent for individual purposes.

9. For a more detailed version of this table, see Appendix I.
10. Daily wages are multiplied by 20, which is the average number of working days, as discussed above.
11. Nonetheless, as is discussed in Chapter 4, tenants are the most vulnerable group. Also, tenants cannot apply for a ration card, as their status is not legalized. Although the status of buyers is also not legalized, they normally use the relocatees' allotment order to apply.
12. Although Muslims theoretically also do not belong to any caste group, the six Muslims in this study indicated they belong to a caste group.
13. PCO means Public Call Office, which is a public telephone booth.
14. See also map of Chennai in Section 4.1.2.
15. Do.
16. For information on the Noon Meal Scheme, see Section 5.3.3.
17. Mariyamman is the goddess of smallpox, as well as cholera and other epidemic diseases (Fuller, 1992: 45). As smallpox has been eradicated in India and chickenpox has a similar appearance to smallpox, it is now also believed to be a curse of Mariyamman. For more information on Mariatta, see Appendix II.
18. For more information on Mariyamman, see Section 6.1.3.
19. More information on this local slum organization will follow in Chapter 6.
20. This system will be described in more detail in chapter six.
21. Mr C.P. Singh, managing director of CMWSSB told me so in July 2001.
22. More information on this initiative can be found later in this chapter.
23. In 1996, Ambedkar Nagar was handed over to the Corporation and the Rs 10 maintenance cost had to be paid to the corporation. The remaining Rs 66 for land costs still had to be paid to the Slum Board.
24. According to the head of the Civil Supplies Office with whom I had a conversation in July 2001, as of 1999, only pink cards have been issued to everyone, so no difference is made anymore between people below and above the poverty line. However, the *Hindu* of 2 January 2002 speaks of a three-card system. This three-card system, according to the *Hindu*, will be replaced by a two-card system, a green card will be issued for families below the poverty line, and those above the poverty line

will get a blue card. The government has fixed Rs 2,000 per month as the eligibility clause for below poverty line families, but it has seven other parameters to identify them including ownership of a house, nature of construction, possession of scooters, tractors or other vehicles, and telephone and power consumption. According to website of the Tamil Nadu Government there are only pink and yellow cards, the pink cardholders are entitled to rice and other essential commodities at prices fixed by the government from time to time. The yellow cardholders can draw their rations other than rice based on options. Those who opt out of rice can draw an additional quantity of sugar or kerosene as the case may be, in lieu of rice as fixed by the government from time to time (<www.tn.gov.in, 2002>[accessed in February 2002]).

25. Buyers who have obtained the allotment order from the relocatee have ration cards in the name of that person.
26. Smets (2002: 93) calls both types moneylenders and makes a distinction between the different types by looking, amongst others, at the type of relation between the borrower and the lender and the type of collateral used. He states that a moneylender who takes physical possession of the collateral, a pawnbroker, has a more economic rather than personal relation with his client as compared to the moneylender who does not take physical possession of the collateral. This is also found to be the case in this study. Moneylenders provide their clientele with predominantly small loans for a short period, which can even be for a day or a week.
27. Different authors as quoted by Smets, 2002: 93.
28. All these moneylenders are unregistered and unlicensed.
29. In this study, it was found that the 10 per cent interest was charged for small amounts of money, up to approximately Rs 500. It is not clear whether a higher interest rate is charged for larger amounts of money and if the loan term varies for different amounts of money. Smets (2002: 93) found that in Hyderabad, the size of the loan from moneylenders for shelter improvement varied from Rs 2,000 to the 30,000, with the loan term varying between six months to four years. The maximum interest rate reported was 20 per cent.
30. As he takes a physical possession of the allotment order, the local leader operates as a pawnbroker.
31. De Wit, 1993: 129.
32. This is also underlined by Besselink (1997: 58) who writes about the problems in Ambedkar Nagar like social problems, selling of *arrack* and the rowdies who were manipulating people in the area in 1997. At that time there was no police outpost and many women complained about it.
33. A Community Development Officer of the Slum Board told this to me.

34. When I returned to the area in 2001, GEMS had stopped their work at the site. I was told by a former social worker of GEMS who lives in Ambedkar Nagar that there were problems between the staff of GEMS and the inhabitants of Ambedkar Nagar and Mr George had decided to stop working in the area.
35. GEMS Foundation 2, s.a.: 14.
36. These concepts have been defined in Chapter 2.
37. Twenty paisa a pot: De Wit, 1993: 123.
38. Obtained from the complete survey.

6

Local Collective Initiatives in Ambedkar Nagar

This chapter discusses the theoretical findings in the data analysis. It also provides insight into what are known as local initiatives and local knowledge. A general introduction will be given on the concept of local or grassroots initiatives, after which the case studies (chit funds, water distribution, and temple festivals) will be described. These case studies will be introduced through a theoretical overview. The temples, a mosque, and the position of local leaders in the area will also be described.

6.1 Collective Action and Local Knowledge: The Issues

Attention has already been drawn to the fact that much of the policy focussing on the poor has yielded mixed results. This is due in part to the formal and institutional constraints encountered in the formulation and implementation phases, including financial, coordinative and logistic problems. Another reason which will be highlighted in this study is the top-down approach used in the formulation and implementation of policies. Policies did not take into consideration the perceptions and expectations of the target group. The message Chambers (1998) delivered was that 'to develop relevant and sustainable policies require local voices to be heard'.[1] This seems evident but is actually a new approach in development thinking. Epstein argues that 'a full understanding of cultural factors, and grassroots level problems in all their full economic, political, and social dimensions is a necessary precondition of any successful development plan and activity'. [2] The question that immediately arises is what should be done with the information collected from the grassroots, or, as preferred the 'local communities'? Is it important to only listen to local people, or should the information also be transformed into the adjustment or redefinition of policy, or should a completely new approach be developed? More importantly, who should formulate these policies, the policy makers after consulting the target groups or the target groups themselves?

In his analysis of the crisis of capacity building in Africa, Dia (1996) states that there is a 'structural and functional disconnection between formal institutions (including the entire government machinery with all ministries down to officials in deconcentrated offices, but also banks, financial institutions and development agencies) that are mostly transplanted and informal institutions (including informal savings groups, microenterprises, village-level indigenous groups, councils or committees) that are rooted in African history, tradition and culture'. Dia argues that neither institution is adequate in itself: formal institutions should become more responsive and marked by more legitimacy and accountability; informal institutions have to renovate, be flexible, and adjust to challenges and changes. The key word he uses is 'reconciliation'. He states that reconciliation between indigenous and formal institutions brings together 'dominant societal values of indigenous cultures on the one hand and technical and organizational ideologies supporting modern institutions on the other'. He also argues that government and NGO programmes have to rely more on methods and approaches that 'take into account' the incentives and constraints that are specific to the local context. They must also 'consider' societal attitudes, organizational and leadership.[3] It should be stressed that these issues are central to my research. The question, that arises here however, is what is meant by 'to take into account' and 'consider' and who decides what should be taken into account and considered, and to what level and degree of detail? Equally important is the question of who is in control—the bureaucrats or the autonomous players.

There have been very few studies undertaken on the developmental perceptions and expectations of the local communities. One of the targets of this study is to explore and analyse local initiatives and forms of organization and how and why these initiatives are developed and maintained. The local community develops these initiatives based on local knowledge and local experience. A definition of local knowledge is that it is the sum total of the knowledge and skills that people in a particular geographic area possess and which enables them to make the most of their environment. Much of this knowledge and these skills have been passed down from earlier generations, but individual men and women in each generation adapt and add to this body of knowledge in a constant adjustment to changing circumstances and environmental conditions. They in turn pass on the body of knowledge intact to the next generation, in an effort to provide them with some material on which to build their own survival strategies.[4]

Indigenous knowledge is not only related to the environment and rural areas, but it is also applicable to the urban areas. In this research, indigenous forms of organization are studied that encompass more than only the physical environment. These organizations and initiatives are also based on skills such as how to organize a group of people, how to negotiate and reach an agreement, and how to deal with scarcity. In this study, I prefer to use the term 'local knowledge' instead of 'indigenous knowledge' as I have already explained in Chapter 2.

In the urban context, there are initiatives that are developed locally, in a particular area (like temple festivals) or in reaction to the absence or inaccessibility of government programmes and facilities (like chit funds). In the following sections, local initiatives and organizations that play a major role in the location under study will be discussed in a general manner. Later in this chapter, we will turn to the local initiatives in Ambedkar Nagar, which are of a collective as well as individual nature.

6.1.1 CHIT FUNDS: THE ISSUES AND THE LOCAL PRAXIS

As the world of formal finance is very difficult for poor people to access, several forms of informal finance structures exist. There are four types of informal credit:

1. Direct but intermittent lending by individuals or institutions with a temporary surplus of funds.
2. Lending by specialized individuals or institutions, whether from their own funds or from those of others they have access to.
3. Lending by those whose main activity lies in markets other than credit but who combine credit transactions with transactions in these other markets.
4. Group finance.[5]

The fourth category, group finance, specifically chit funds, will be studied in detail. Chit funds are indigenous financial institutions peculiar to south India, particularly Tamil Nadu and Kerala. They developed at a time when banking and credit facilities were inadequate and people in general had to rely to a large measure on indigenous sources for their many productive and consumption needs.[6] These chit funds have the advantage of accessibility, flexibility and adaptability, ranging from small neighbourhood or workplace-based institutions whose primary attraction is that they are a vehicle for savings, to larger, more impersonal organizations, which offer a quick means of raising funds urgently needed for production or consumption.[7] A chit fund represents a very important livelihood strategy, as it is the main way of saving for poor households.[8]

Chit funds are a very popular finance system used by large parts of the population for a great variety of reasons. There are both registered (formal) chit funds, which are either registered under the All India Chit Funds Act 1982, or under one of the state Acts, as well as a large number of unregistered (informal) chit funds. A survey amongst members of registered chit funds revealed the major drawing points of chit funds as a means of savings:

1. The element of reciprocity, or the inbuilt provision for borrowing at short notice, a sort of guarantee of access to liquidity especially important to business people.
2. The possibility to save in instalments.
3. The compulsory nature of having to do so once the initial decision to join is made, which may defer other consumption expenditures.
4. The convenience and the absence of formalities.[9]

Whether this is also applicable to the informal, unregistered chit funds will be examined later. In chit funds, people pool money and deposit their savings in a relatively safe place and gain access to a lump sum. Reciprocal relations are important for the proper functioning of such financial self-help groups.[10] Dia has studied tontines, the African form of chit funds, and concluded that the success of these indigenous organizations lies in the fact that they are more flexible than banks and that there is mutual dependence, which puts pressure on the members not to default.[11] Smets (1996) in a study undertaken in India argues that social control can be an important barrier against fraud and defaulting, and he found that in extreme cases the social pressure to ensure the payment of contributions has resulted in suicide.[12]

It bears repeating that, as formal finance is very difficult for poor people to access, an alternative source of finance is chit funds. Twelve per cent of the respondents in Ambedkar Nagar were part of a chit fund.[13] This section will provide insight into the different chit funds organized in the area. An explanation will be given as to the procedure involved, the organization, and the purposes to which the money obtained from the chit funds are put to.[14] In Ambedkar Nagar, chit funds differ in system, the number of days between the auctions or draws, the amount of money paid by the participants, and the number of people joining them.[15]

The two types of systems are the auction system and the lot system. The auction system, which will be described below, was introduced because many participants in a group were in need of money at the same time. The lot system gave the amount to a person who might not be in need of it.[16] For this case study, information was collected from five different chit funds organized by seven agents (two chit funds were organized by a couple, one by a married couple and the other by two neighbours).[17] In the past, one of the agents had organized two more chit funds, one of the lot system and one of the auction system but at the time of the research only chit funds of the auction system were found operating. These auction chit funds are organized weekly and monthly, and involve 10-14 participants. The chit funds covered in this case study are the following: one weekly chit fund of

Rs 1,000 in which 10 participants have to pay Rs 100 a week for a period of 10 weeks, and six monthly chits. The latter, in ascending order are: two chit funds of Rs 2,000 a month, where 10 participants have to pay Rs 200 a month for a period of 10 months; three chit funds of Rs 5,000 a month, where 10 members have to pay Rs 500 a month for a period of 10 months; and one chit fund of Rs 1,400, where 14 participants have to pay Rs 1,000 a month for 10 months.

The following is the description of the usual procedure used for of an auction chit fund. Suppose an auction chit fund of Rs 1,000 a month is started where 10 participants, including the agent, have to pay Rs 100 a month for 10 months. The first month each member pays Rs 100 and so the total reaches Rs 1,000. Of this Rs 1,000, Rs 30 is deducted as commission money for the agent, who normally charges 3 per cent commission. In total then, there is Rs 970 in cash. Then the bidding starts. Depending on how many members are in urgent need of cash the bidding goes up and the person who places the highest bid gets the fund. Suppose the highest bid is Rs 550. This Rs 550 is called the *thallu*, or dividend, and this amount is commonly distributed amongst all the participants. This means they all get Rs 55, which is subtracted from their subscription money of Rs 100. That means each participant has to pay Rs 45 in the first round. The remaining Rs 420 goes to the person who had placed highest bid, plus the Rs 55 dividend, minus the monthly subscription money of Rs 100, so this person gets Rs 375. The agent receives Rs 30 commission, plus Rs 55 dividend, so in total she gets Rs 85. During the second round in the second month, all participants have to pay the subscription but no auction is organized as the full amount goes to the agent and kept aside as 'rotation money' for emergencies. The agent has to guarantee that in every round, the full amount of the chit fund is collected. In case of a defaulter or when a participant is not able to pay in time, the agent has to fill in the amount. From the third until the tenth round, the total amount of Rs 970 is auctioned again every month. Persons who have placed a bid and obtained the money once have to pay the subscription money of Rs 100 but they are not allowed to join the meetings any more. In the last round, there is no auction as there is only one participant left, and she will get the full amount of Rs 970, minus the subscription money of Rs 100, so in total she receives Rs 870. In the early rounds of the auction chit fund, many members are competing for the fund, so the dividend goes up, which is profitable for the participants but not for the person placing the bid. In the last rounds there are only a few participants left so competition is less and the last bid is normally low which is profitable for the person placing the bid, but the dividend is low. Although all the participants are very keen on ending last, many are forced to bid in earlier rounds due to urgent need of cash. For some participating in a chit fund can be very profitable, for others less so.

We mentioned that in an auction chit fund, the agent keeps the full amount of the second round as 'rotation money' to be used as a reserve. When a participant is not able to pay in time or when they default and leave, the agent has to pay instead. One of the agents of the case study said that in those cases, she charges 3 per cent interest. In some cases, when a member is not able to pay for a round in time but expects money in a few days, she will borrow the money from a moneylender. As participants are all from the same neighbourhood and know each other well, social pressure plays a major role in pressuring participants not to default. The stronger and well-organized an agent is and the better she knows the participants, the more chance she has to save the rotation money for her own benefit. So normally these agents allow only well-known people to join their chit funds. Participants too select the agent on the basis of her strength and good name, as the stricter an agent is, the more chance there is the chit fund will be a success. On the other hand, when members lose faith in their agent, they may stop paying their contribution, which happened in one of the chit funds described in Chapter 4. All the chit funds covered in this case study were organized amongst neighbours and friends, all belonging to the same relocation group, and often living on the same street or block. Sometimes, members introduce a guest, mainly friends or family, but normally it is very difficult for new members to join a chit fund group. Whenever a participant, due to an acute financial crisis, is not able to proceed with a chit fund, someone else can, with the approval of the agent, be introduced to take her place. These two persons have to arrange the financial procedure amongst them.

The agent is the main decision maker in the chit fund. She decides who is allowed to join, she sets the amount of the chit fund and the number of days between each auction, where the auction is held and when, when participants should pay and how much is to be charged when members are not able to pay on time and there is need to borrow from the rotation money. In addition, the agent decides whether members are allowed to be replaced by someone else and by whom in case of financial problems. Also, the agent normally leads the auction. If she is not able to read and write she may appoint one of the participants to keep the accounts. Depending on these conditions and the credibility of the agent, people may decide to join or not.

Although I was told there were chit funds organized and joined by men (and where much larger amount of money were pooled) I did not come across them. The majority of the chit funds found in the study were organized and joined by women only. In many cases the husband did not even know his wife had joined or organized a chit fund. One of the agents explained that she organized the auction when her husband was asleep or out. As all the participants live close by, they can contact each other very fast and organize the auction in a short time. She has informed all the members that her husband is not allowed to know, so they all keep it a secret. She has been doing this for many years. Her husband is not allowed to know as he is a drunkard and she is afraid that he will use the rotation money for his own purposes. As he does not give her enough money to run the household and to send their children to school, and he does not allow her to get herself a job, organizing the chit fund is a way for her to earn some extras. In cases where a husband knows his wife joins or organizes a chit fund, she is only allowed to do so if all members are women (or, as in one of the chit funds, when a married man is joined by his wife).

Several participants and agents of chit funds explained that they used the money obtained by the chit fund for household purposes like the plastering of the house, applying for an electricity connection, school fees and uniforms, ceremonies and festivals and weddings and deaths. During some periods like the start of the new school year, and the festival and marriage season, many participants are in need of cash so the bidding goes up very high. This is profitable for the other participants as then the dividend is high, but it is not very profitable for the bidder. The advantage of a chit fund as compared to a bank account, according to participants, is that money is easily accessible without any formalities.[18]

6.1.2 WATER DISTRIBUTION: ISSUES AND THE LOCAL PRAXIS

As the provision of water for the urban poor is often insufficient, local initiatives are frequently developed to meet with these shortages.

In India, most of the urban poor draw their water from the public stand post managed by the local bodies. In cities where no taps are provided, tankers distribute water.[19] Rao (1990) mentions the initiatives of water vending that have been developed by slum dwellers who depend on tankers for water delivery. He has observed that in Chennai,[20] the slum communities elect a representative who is responsible for ensuring water is delivered by a truck of Metro Water. The representative collects 10-15 paisa per pot from the people and ensures equitable distribution. From the amount collected, around Rs 10 is paid for every trip the trucks make. In this way, people's own efforts and arrangements have ensured them a regular and adequate water distribution.[21]

These systems also existed in villages. The following anecdote is interesting in that it illustrates what can happen when a 'modern' tube replaces a traditional, indigenous water distribution system.

> Originally water in the village was provided through a well. Villagers employed two to three persons each year to draw water and distribute it among village families. Each household paid the persons drawing the water a fixed amount. Rights to draw water were auctioned each year; the winning bid went to whoever was willing to draw the water for the lowest amount. For the last few years, water has been provided through a tube well by the government, which has resulted in an uneven water supply: some days, more water than needed is distributed, other days no water at all is distributed. The villagers are unwilling to pay for the appointment of someone to look after the water supply and to contact the government office when water is not provided. A possible explanation for the unwillingness to pay is that households that have their own tank store water in times of abundance, so that when no water is provided through the tap, they can still make use of their stored water. Since non-payers cannot be excluded from getting water, such a system leads to more inequality. People who do not have their own tank, probably the poorer households, are dependent on the provision of water from the tube wells and therefore on a person looking after the supply of water from which the non-paying households

also benefit. Before the introduction of the tube, water was available only after expending considerable effort, and persons not paying their share could be deprived of water. This punishment for free-riding is extremely effective as there are no conveniently located alternative sources of water.[22]

Agrawal (1993) concludes from this that indigenous institutions effectively deal with problems faced by people as regards resource needs until governments intervene and 'develop' people. The benefits from a seemingly equitable intervention like the provision of tube wells may lead to inequality. Although it is clear that the introduction of government provided services might lead to inequality, Agrawal's view on indigenous institutions is in my opinion too romantic, because indigenous institutions are not always based on principles of equality. As mentioned earlier, in some cases indigenous institutions in fact reinforce patterns of inequality and social exclusion.[23]

As noted in Chapter 5, until the end of 1998 Metro Water provided water in Ambedkar Nagar. At that time, a system existed whereby 'water women' were responsible for water distribution in Ambedkar Nagar. From January 1999 onwards, the Board leased out the water supply to a private company that provided water through taps. First the situation existing prior to December 1998 will be described followed by an account of the water distribution system in operation as of January 1999.

An auction was organized by the leaders of the local slum organization Ambedkar Makkal Podhu Nala Sangam[24] and women were appointed to distribute the water in the area. In the early years, the water distribution in Ambedkar Nagar was not at all organized, and there was no regularity in its supply. One 'water woman' responsible for water distribution in the Chitra Nagar area explained that in 1992 she and others of her group approached their local leader and took him along to the Metro Water office to request water lorries to be sent to Ambedkar Nagar on a daily basis. From then onwards, the water supply was more regular. Since 1996, whenever there are problems with the water supply, the local councillor responsible for Ambedkar Nagar is also approached.

Accurate data on the number of water lorries that provided water in Ambedkar Nagar are not available. Even officials from the Metro Water office gave contradictory information. Approximately 10-14 lorries drove to Ambedkar Nagar almost every day to supply its inhabitants with drinking water. Each lorry contained 9,000 litres and approximately 200 to 300 households were supplied by one lorry. The water from each lorry was distributed by the 'water woman'. The area had six 'water women'.[25] The distribution took place near the water tanks that were placed by Metro Water at different spots throughout the relocation site. Early in the morning broken pots were lined up in a row in order to reserve a place in case the lorry would arrive. As soon as the water lorry arrived large crowds, mostly women, gathered around the lorry, and usable water pots replaced the broken pots. The 'water woman' sat on a crutch underneath the lorry and handled the water pipe with which the pots were filled from which the water was until everyone was provided. The remaining water was stored in a water-tank from which it was distributed later in the day to those who were not able to get it from the truck.

In order to have a well-organized distribution system, a few years back the Ambedkar Makkal Podhu Nala Sangam decided to auction the right to distribute the water from the lorries. People from all the different areas gathered in the local *Sangam* hall where the auction was organized, and the one person placing the highest bid was entitled to be in charge of the water distribution in one of the distribution points for a whole year. The auction money was paid to the local leaders who said that they would spend it on the different local temples.[26] The local leaders decided that only women would be entitled to apply for the distribution. According to some respondents, handicapped ladies and widows were selected to become the water distributors because the job was their only source of income. It is a stressful job and sometimes quarrels blaze up during the water distribution, so these women needed to be strong. Although some of the elected women were actually widowed or handicapped persons, majority of the 'water women' were those who bid the highest. The actual auctioning was only held once; afterwards, the people themselves decided who would distribute the water, and how much should be paid to the temple by the distributor. Amounts of Rs 600 to Rs 1,500 were mentioned as auction money. In some cases, the

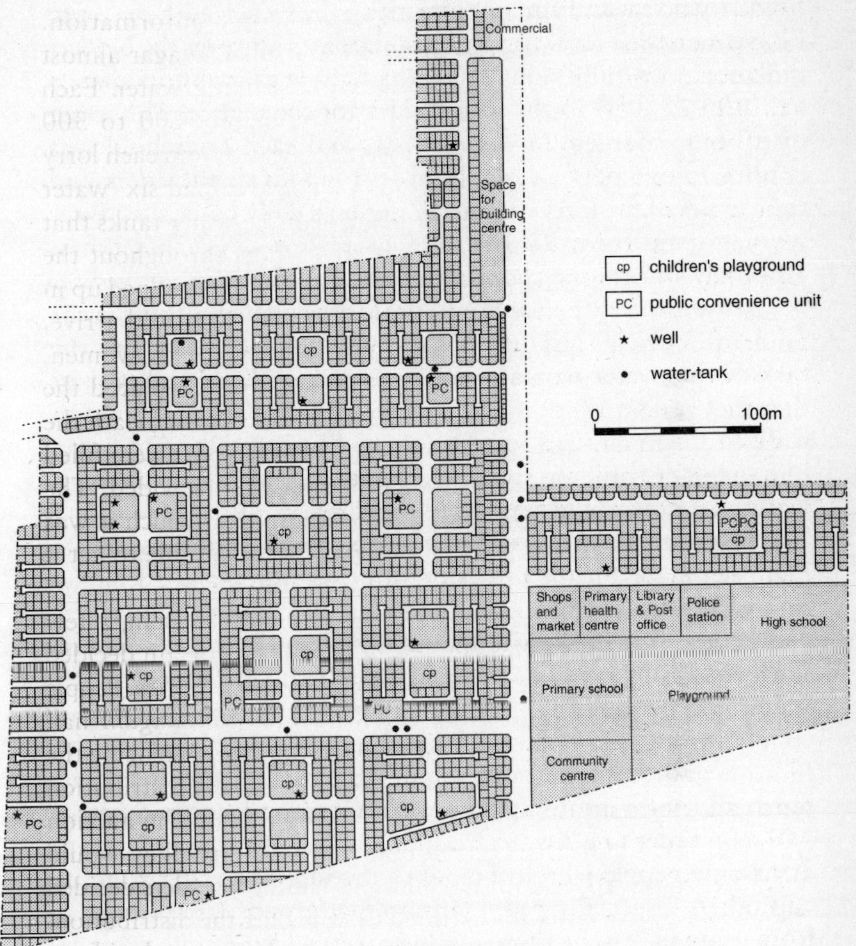

MAP 6.1: LOCATION OF WATER-TANKS AND WELLS IN AMBEDKAR NAGAR

bidders paid the full amount directly to the local leader, meant to be spent on their local temple. In some parts however the bidders did not pay the full amount immediately, but gave approximately Rs 10 to 15 daily to the local leader for the temple. The water distributor charged 25 *paisa* a pot, and each household was entitled to two pots a day.[27] In order to motivate the driver and the cleaner of the lorry to bring water on a daily basis, the 'water woman' paid them Rs 10 to 15 every few days. Sometimes, especially during the monsoon when the roads in Ambedkar Nagar were barely passable and the lorries often got stuck in the mud, truck drivers just did not show up. In those cases, it was the task of the 'water woman' to phone Metro Water and request that they send a water lorry. One woman said that she used to walk to the main road to wait for the lorry to come and direct him to her distribution spot, as in some cases he used to drop his water in a tank at the main road and drive away.

When Ambedkar Nagar was designed and built, arrangements had been made for the provision of piped water, and 23 public taps were installed throughout the area. In January 1999, water provision by lorries was stopped and replaced by water supplied through taps by a private company (described in Chapter 5).

Ambedkar Nagar has faced many problems even since water supply through taps started. First, there is a problem with the location of the taps. In some ends of Ambedkar Nagar there is no tap at all, which means that women have to walk approximately 160 m in order to get water, resulting in physical strain. In some areas only people who live close to the tap take water from it, and others, especially people from other groups, are prevented from using the tap by those living near it, which results in many quarrels. Sometimes these women are even compelled to get water from outside Ambedkar Nagar. Another problem is low water pressure. The residents approached the private company several times to resolve this low pressure problem, but without any result. People then started to dig pits near the taps. This way, the water does not need to be pumped up into the tap but can be tapped from the underground water pipe itself. In some parts of Ambedkar Nagar, people have taken it upon themselves to make a cement structure in the ground around the underground water pipe. These 'entrepreneurs' collected money from all the tap users

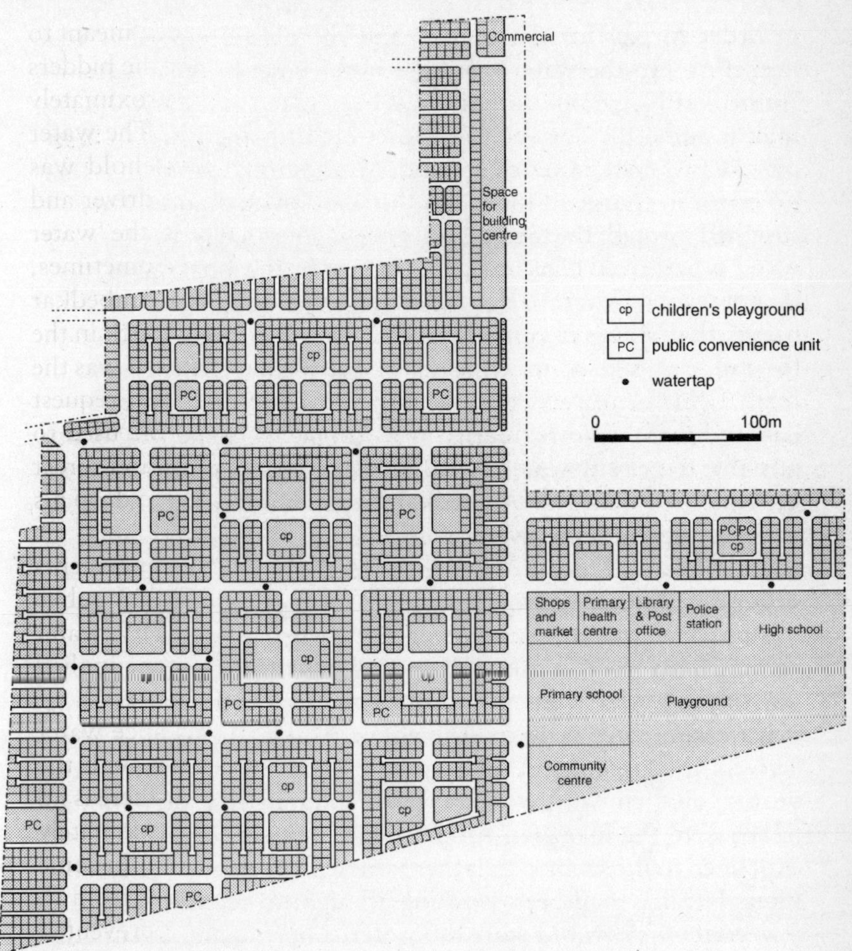

MAP 6.2: LOCATION OF WATER TAPS IN AMBEDKAR NAGAR

in order to pay for the cement and the plastic pipe that was needed to tap the water from the water pipe. In other parts of Ambedkar Nagar, no initiative has been taken and the holes are muddy and difficult to access. Moreover, drinking water in these pits is easily contaminated by mud. An additional problem is that no one is in charge of the water distribution any more. Water is supplied through the taps for only a few hours a day. Because tap water is perceived of as being free of cost by the inhabitants, they do not want to revert to the system of lorries bringing water. This means that whoever comes first once water is running through the tap, can take as much as he or she pleases. This results in many fights because as water is only provided for a few hours a day and there is no regularity in its supply, so some people are not able to get any water at all. This also forces some people to get water from outside Ambedkar Nagar. On the days when no water is supplied, the 'water women' take up their old task and contact Metro Water to have them send a water lorry. The old water distribution system then comes into operation once again.

One day, during the summer of 1999, when no water had been coming for a week, a group of approximately 30 women, led by one of the 'water women' went to complain at the plant of the private company next to Ambedkar Nagar. As soon as they arrived, the large metal doors were closed. The women started beating on them with wooden sticks, shouting that they wanted to speak to the manager. After a while, someone came out and explained to the women that there was a problem with one of the filters but they had been working all night to repair it and in a few hours they would start the water supply again. Eventually the women went home and water came later that day.

The engineers at the plant complained that the inhabitants of Ambedkar Nagar did not properly use the expensive water they provided. As the water comes through the tap free of cost, and people are not informed about the real costs, respondents use the water provided for cleaning and washing, while they used Metro water only for drinking purposes as they had to pay for it. Besides, many people complained that they did not like the taste of the tap water—they found it 'too soft' and therefore not fit for washing. The private company claimed the water they provided was of much better quality than the chlorinated water provided by the Metro.

6.1.3 TEMPLE FESTIVALS: ISSUES AND THE LOCAL PRAXIS

The Mariyamman festival is part of the Dravidian heritage.[28] It is one of the major temple festivals of the Scheduled Castes in Tamil Nadu and is in honour of the Mariyamman, a Kali-like goddess. Mariyamman means the 'goddess who changes'. She is also locally known as Mareyamman, the goddess of rain.[29] According to Arunachalam (1980) the festivals of Tamil Nadu are of a socialistic pattern because 'there is always thought of the poor and less gifted and provisions are made for them'.[30] The origin of Mariyamman is described below:

> Once Siva took the form of the great Brahmin Rishi Nilakandar, and Parvati took the form of his wife Renukai. They had four sons. Every morning Renukai would go to a pond, swirl her fingers in the water, and a mud pot full of water and flowers would emerge from the pond. This she would carry to Nilakandar for his morning *pooja*. One morning, however, as she was leaning over the pond, she saw the reflection of a divine messenger of the gods passing overhead, and admired his figure. Because of this mere thought, she lost her chastity and she was unable to make the pot and the flowers emerge from the pond. When she returned home to Nilakandar and told him what happened Nilakandar cursed her and sent her away from his house. Nilakandar then called his four sons to him and asked, 'which one of you will behead your mother?' Three refused, but the fourth, Parasaraman, agreed to do so, saying 'you are my father, and there is nothing above a father's word'. Parasaraman then chased his mother with a long knife until he caught her at a Chakkiliyan house. Out of fear, Renukai embraced the Chakkiliyan woman, and at that moment Parasaraman swung his knife and beheaded both women. Parasaraman carried his mother's severed head back to his father, and told him, 'now that I have fulfilled your desire, I request a boon from you'. Nilakandar agreed and Parasaraman said he wanted his mother brought back to life. Nilakandar gave him a magic stick to do it, and his mother would be returned to life. Parasaraman went to do so, but in his confusion he put his mother's head on the Chakkiliyan woman's body, and the Chakkiliyan woman's head on his mother's body, and restored them both to life. When he returned with the former being, Nilakandar saw what had happened, and told Renukai, 'your body has changed and you are no longer welcome here. Go out as a changed body. Sprinkle and remove pearls (the reference is to smallpox, whose

pustules are compared to pearls). Earn your food from *pooja* offerings. Since you have the head of a Brahmin and the stomach of a Chakkiliyan, you may receive both vegetarian and meat offerings.' So Renukai went about changing forms as Mutalamman, Mariyamman, Periyapalaiyattar, Sengeniyamman, Kaliyamman, Selliyamman and Dandumariyamman.[31]

Not much has been written about the organizational aspects of the festival and the influence it has on social cohesion within a community. In order to get more insight into the way local communities organize themselves and how consensus is obtained and maintained, the local temple festival is selected as one of the case studies. These festivals require the support, including financial, and consensus of the entire multi-caste community. Moreover, the festivals are deeply rooted in local culture and are ascribed to and performed by persons with expertise and knowledge.[32] Even though in the countryside the Mariyamman festival is a festival for all castes and it reflects the unity in the village, there are stringent rules as to which castes are allowed in which parts of the temple.[33] And although persons from different castes who share the same territory like a hamlet or a village worship the goddess Mariyamman, some worshippers are more equal than others.[34] In rituals, members of the higher castes take precedence over members of the lower castes, and the high caste persons perform specialized ritual roles of a higher nature than do lower caste persons. Beck (1972) found that in Konku, Tamil Nadu, there is a sharp division between right-hand and left-hand sub-castes and that at left-hand caste festivals, all devotees are treated as equals and no formalized ranking is observed, but at right-hand caste festivals, the hierarchical relationship among participants is emphasized in the ceremonies that are performed.[35] Thus the unity of a major section of the village, rather than the whole settlement, is ritually expressed at these festivals.[36] The essence of the right-left dichotomy lies in the rivalry for status of two sets of sub-castes that operate with fundamentally different criteria. The first set—the right-hand one—takes pride in its right to land management and in its concomitant political power in a local territory. The opposite set attempts to minimize its involvement in a particular place, especially where this entails relations of long-term economic dependence on other groups. This group stresses its non-agrarian wealth, its ritual purity and its connection with south Indian scholarly and philosophical tradition. In the celebration of the *Mariyamman* festival only the right sub-castes are vital. Beck mentions that in the past, left-division women were probably excluded from the festival activities.[37]

For this case study, one temple is being studied. It is dedicated to *Karu Mariyamman*, which is one form of the mother goddess Kali,[38] and is maintained and visited by the people relocated from Shanti Nagar and Adyar, who live close to this temple. The temple is constructed of hollow bricks and has a thatched roof. The construction is incomplete due to lack of finances.

The temple was built a few years back and started with a few bricks representing the goddess. One person donated a statue of *Karu Mariyamman*, another donated the bricks with which the structure of the temple was built. In first few years, the festival was organized by a few men of the Shanti Nagar group who collected money from the people. After a few years however rumour spread that these men swallowed half of the amount that was collected, using it for their own purposes instead of spending it on the festival. Unhappy with this, many people stopped donating, and therefore these men stopped organizing the festival from 1996. One day, a woman from their group went into a trance and was brought to the temple where Mariyamman instructed through her that if the temple festival was not organized their whole group would be cursed. Consequently, three women of the Shanti Nagar group felt obliged to organize the festival. They first sought the approval of their local leader Sundaram and his wife before starting the organizing. From 1997 onward these women have been organizing the Naga Shakti Karu Mariyamman Festival every year. Normally it is held in the seventh or the eight organize it in the 7th or 8th week of the Tamil month of *Adi*, depending on the amount of money they collect.[39] They start the organization on the first day of *Adi* with Jaya, one of the women, going to a printer to order a receipt book and pamphlets announcing the organization of the temple festival. The pamphlets also give an overview of the amount of money collected the year before and the expenses. The printer prints it for free, after which the actual money collection starts.

ஓம் சக்தி
ஓம் நாகசக்தி கருமாரியம்மன் துணை

ஓம் நாகசக்தி கருமாரியம்மன் ஆலயம்

டாக்டர் அம்பேத்கர் நகர், ஆதம்பாக்கம், சென்னை-88.

8-ம் ஆண்டு உற்சவ கைங்கர்ய பத்திரிகை

தேனினும் இனிய தமிழ் தெய்வமே ஸ்ரீ நாகசக்தி கருமாரி அம்மனே
தேடிவரும் பக்தர்கள் வினைதீர்க்கும் ஸ்ரீ நாகசக்தி கருமாரி அம்மனே
ஆயிரம் கண்கள் கொண்டவளே ஸ்ரீ நாகசக்தி கருமாரி அம்மனே
அகிலத்தை ஆளுகின்ற ஸ்ரீ நாகசக்தி கருமாரி அம்மனே
மனதார வணங்குகின்றோம் ஸ்ரீ நாகசக்தி கருமாரி அம்மனே
இன்னும் உன்னை புகழ எங்களுக்கு விலையில்லை ஸ்ரீ நாகசக்தி கருமாரி அம்மனே.

அன்புடையீர், வணக்கம்!

நிகழும் மங்களகரமான ஆடி மாதம் 14-ம் தேதி (30-7-99) வெள்ளிக்கிழமை 5-வது வாரம் மாலை 6 மணியளவில் காப்பு கட்டுதலும் மறுநாள் 15-ந்தேதி (31-7-99) சனிக்கிழமை 7 மணியளவில் சத்திய கரகம் ஊர்வலம் நடைபெறும். மற்றும் 16ம் தேதி (1-8-99) ஞாயிற்றுக்கிழமை அன்று பகல் 12 மணியளவில் கூழ் ஊற்றல் விழாவும் நடைபெற உள்ளது. இதைக் காணும் பெரியோர்களும் தாய்மார்களும், இளைஞர்களும், வியாபாரம் பெருங்குடி மக்களும் தங்களால் இயன்ற நிதி உதவியும், பொருள் உதவியும், வழங்கி, ஸ்ரீ நாகசக்தி கருமாரி அம்மன் அருளைப் பெற்று இவ்விழாவை சிறப்புடன் நடத்தி ஒத்துழைக்குமாறு உங்கள் அனைவரையும் கேட்டுக் கொள்கிறோம்.

உள்ளூர்	- 2015	கோயில் செலவு	- 1771
வெளியூர்	- 3696	பந்தல்	- 1410
தனி	- 3000	ரேடியோ	- 2500
		பம்பை	- 2700
	8711		8381

இப்படிக்கு,
கோயில் நிர்வாகிகள்
டாக்டர் அம்பேத்கர் நகர், பொதுமக்கள்

ஸ்ரீ சிங்காரவேலன் பிரஸ், கிண்டி, சென்னை-32.

FIGURE 6.1: FESTIVAL PAMPHLET

The three women are helped by local boys, who go door to door in Ambedkar Nagar to collect money. They cover the whole of Ambedkar Nagar, but they are most successful in their own group, as these are the people who will also visit the festival. Jaya maintains that it is very difficult to collect money in Ambedkar Nagar as people are poor. Besides many say that they would prefer that the money be invested in the improvement of the area instead of a festival. Consequently, they have to keep convincing people and visiting them often in order to receive small amounts of money. They also approach the shopkeepers but they have an agreement amongst each other that together they would only donate Rs 200 for every group organizing a festival, so not much is collected from them either. Relatives and acquaintances outside Ambedkar Nagar also contribute for the festivals.[40] According to Jaya the men were able to collect much more as they had better contacts with rich and politically powerful people outside Ambedkar Nagar, but nowadays they were just not interested in helping the women with the collection. Also, when water was still provided through the water lorries, Jaya was distributing it, and the money that she earned was spent on the temple. Since 1999, water has been coming through the tap for free, so this source of income has also stopped. Still these three women continue, as they feel obliged to the goddess to organize the festival. Jaya, who also looks after the administration, keeps the collected amount. In 1998 they collected Rs 8,711, Rs 2,015 of which was collected from inside Ambedkar Nagar, Rs 3,000 from one individual, and Rs 3,696 from outside Ambedkar Nagar. They spent in total Rs 8,381: Rs 1,771 on temple decoration: flowers, turmeric, kumkum, camphor and a sari for Mariyamman, Rs 1,410 for a thatch roof over the festival ground, Rs 2,500 for the hiring of a radio and VCR[41] and Rs 2,700 on the rituals performed by a *gurukkal*, or priest. The festival lasted for three days, from Friday till Sunday. Before the festival started, the local leader Sundaram and his wife were invited and after the initiators of the festival blessed them, the festival took off. There were performances such as body piercing and fire walking.[42] The statue of Mariyamman was carried through the area on a chariot. Gruel was distributed and on the evening of the second day, Tamil movies were shown.

6.1.4 TEMPLES AND MOSQUE IN AMBEDKAR NAGAR

As noted earlier, there were 16 temples in Ambedkar Nagar, both private and owned by groups. They differed in size; some were very small private shrines, others were bigger community temples. The majority of them were dedicated to the goddess Mariyamman. There was also one big recently constructed mosque.

Almost 93 per cent respondents visited the local religious places. Hindus visited the temples, the small minority of Muslims visited the local mosque and the Apostolics visited their local church. Since there is no Roman Catholic church inside Ambedkar Nagar, Roman Catholics go to the churches in the surrounding neighbourhood of Ambedkar Nagar. Some Hindus do not visit the local temples. A family who had bought a plot and had just recently moved to Ambedkar Nagar for instance explained that they did not feel attached to their new environment and therefore they still visited the temple in their former neighbourhood.

Besides visiting the local religious sites, the overall majority, 86 per cent, also goes to religious places outside Ambedkar Nagar. They either visit the Vadapalani Murugan temple in Chennai or Thiruverkadu, a temple in the vicinity of Chennai dedicated to Karu Mariyamman, or both.[43] Some people also went to Tirupathi, a pilgrimage site dedicated to Venkateswara, Andhra Pradesh. Some men went on a yearly pilgrimage to the temple of Aiyappan in Sabarimalai in Kerala.[44] One Muslim mentioned that besides the local mosque in Ambedkar Nagar, he visited a mosque in Egmore, but all others only visited their local mosque. The Roman Catholics go to church in the neighbourhood of Ambedkar Nagar, either in Adambakkam or Kakkan Nagar.[45]

Most respondents (83 per cent) donate money to the temple (festival), church or mosque. Besides donating for the Mariyamman or Vinayagar festival, some Hindus also donate to a church. Some Christians and Muslims also donate money for the local Mariyamman festival. Seventeen per cent of the respondents do not donate anything, 32 per cent donate between Rs 21 and Rs 41 a year for religious festivities, and 51 per cent donate between Rs 41 and Rs 61.[46] Besides donating, 4 per cent help during the yearly Mariyamman festival. They either collect money for the festival, cook, or organize the festivities. Of these, two women sweep the church and the temple the whole year

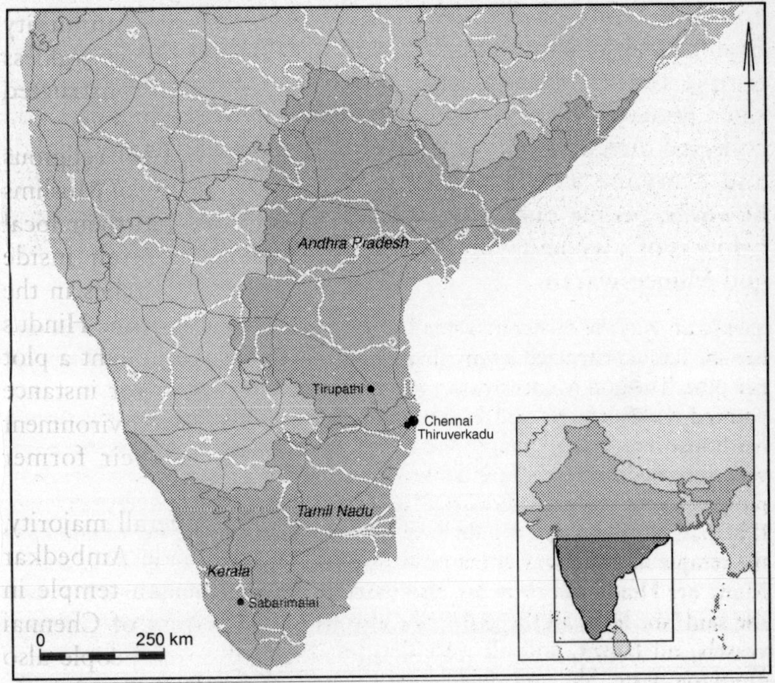

MAP 6.3: SOUTH INDIA

through. The overwhelming majority, 96 per cent, are not involved in any of these activities.

Some of the temples are constructed on land that was allocated by the Slum Board for community purposes. Although this initiative shows the importance for the local community of having its own temple, which obviously has a community function, the Slum Board speaks of illegal occupation. Nonetheless, they will not take any action against it as they fear it would create serious problems. Some smaller temples are constructed near the main road and one temple is constructed on land allocated for housing. These are all group temples, i.e. financed by a group of people and maintained by it. Some are only partly finished; construction will proceed when money is available. One of these temples is the temple of the Chitra Nagar group. Initially constructed of thatches but over the years its construction has been improved and now it has a brick wall and an asbestos roof, which was paid from money generated by the water distribution and the annual temple festival. Because the water distribution has stopped since January 1999, money for temple improvements had to be collected directly from the residents. The temples are open to all and everyone who wants to do *pooja* can come. Normally, however, people only visit their own group temple. The story below is of a woman who owns a private temple dedicated to the god Muneeswaran.

Saraswati was the owner of a small Muneeswaran temple. When I first met her she had constructed a very small temple in the compound wall around her plot. The god Muneeswaran was represented by three bricks that were painted with turmeric and *kumkum* paste. A few months later she turned her house into a small temple and rented the house next door, as she felt 'it was not good to have a family life in front of the gods'. She has been very pious since the day she was married and her husband was also very religious. If he had not liked it, it would have been very difficult for her to maintain the temple like she was doing now. She has a wall full of godly pictures. Many are Hindu but there are also paintings of the Buddha and Mary, as she said 'she liked all the gods'. She also had a collection of small bronze vessels, oil lamps, and all were decorated with flowers, turmeric and *kumkum* paste. She said that during the festival of *Muneeswaran*, in the month of *Chittirai*,[47] she did special *poojas*. Every night from the fifth day of *Amavasya*, new moon, until the fifteenth day, *Poornima*, or full moon day, she did a special *pooja* with milk, normally after 7 p.m. Friends could also come but she did the *pooja* herself, and no money was collected from other people.[48] Sometimes people brought cigarettes and liquor to the god Muneeswaran, as she said 'he is like a man and is fond of these items'.

When I returned to Ambedkar Nagar in 2001 and visited Saraswati she had constructed a big Muneeswaran temple in front of her house. She said that she was obliged to build it because in a dream, Muneeswaran had instructed her to do so. Consequently, she and her husband fasted for two years; eating only vegetarian meals and not having sex. She had to keep everything very clean and her husband did not shave himself before and during the construction. To pay for the construction, she tried to collect money from the people in Ambedkar Nagar but not many were forthcoming as 'they all prefer Mariyamman'. Saraswati had pamphlets printed to inform the people about their plans but she still had to strain herself a lot and visit people many times. Even then many of them only gave very small amounts (between Rs 3 and 11). She also collected money outside Ambedkar Nagar. To raise the needed amount, she mortgaged most of her jewellery and bronze vessels. The construction cost Rs 2.5 lakh and now she has a debt Rs 60,000, mostly with friends outside Ambedkar Nagar who only charge her a minimum amount of interest; some have even given it without charging interest. Although happy to have constructed the temple and done something for the god, Saraswati at the same time feels her life is in shambles as now she has nothing left; all her money has been absorbed by the temple.

The construction of the temple was completed in early 2001, and a big opening ceremony was held in the Tamil month of *Chittirai,* which is the main festival month for Muneeswaran. Saraswati again had pamphlets printed and distributed to the people in Ambedkar Nagar, outlining the programme and requesting financial help. She also invited people to register themselves if they wanted to participate in the *poojas*. The festival lasted for three days and started with a big procession where the statue of Muneeswaran was picked up from the station and carried to Ambedkar Nagar. After that, the 108 milk *abhishekam* started. For the *poojas*, 21 *gurukkals* or priests were invited. During the entire festival period, free food was distributed. On the invitation letter for the opening ceremony, Saraswati had named all the 'important persons' of Ambedkar Nagar, including Sundaram, local leader and president of the Ambedkar Makkal Podhu Nala Sangam, and Krishnan, local leader of the Chitra Nagar group. She said she had done this out of respect for these people but they never even came once to see her temple. It is likely also the case that if she did not invite them, they could have created problems. The opening ceremony cost Rs 20,000, which is included in the total cost of Rs 2.5 lakh.

A very large mosque had recently been constructed in Ambedkar Nagar by a committee of 11 members elected from amongst the Muslim community in the area, numbering approximately 50 families. The total cost of construction was Rs 8 lakh to 10 lakh, which was collected from amongst the Muslim community in Ambedkar Nagar and from donations from family and friends outside. In addition, Rs 150,000 was borrowed from shop owners. An *imam* and a helper are employed in the mosque, and they are paid from the subscription money, which is Rs 20 a person a month, and through donations from outside Ambedkar Nagar.

6.1.5 SLUM LEADERS AND THE LOCAL SANGAM: ISSUES AND THE LOCAL PRAXIS

As indicated, slums are not homogeneous communities: there are the poor and the less poor. Some people have more access to the outside world than others. Those who lack access to, for instance, employment, loans from banks, and information, need relations with persons outside the household in order to survive. They are often dependent on the patronage of one or more social networks (like the patronage of local leaders) for their survival and improvement of economic status.[49] Such networks, which often differ between men and women, can extend beyond the border of the neighbourhood all the way to settler's village of origin. A distinction can be made between horizontal and vertical networks. According to Smets (1996) who did research in different slums in Hyderabad, an example of a horizontal organization is a slum dwellers' association.[50] Examples of vertical relations are the relations between a local leader and the inhabitants of a popular neighbourhood, which is of a patron-client nature. Such a relation is based on expected advantages for both parties involved. A patron (also referred to as a broker) expects respect, support, and services, and in some cases, votes in return for the goods and services he promises and also sometimes actually delivers to his clients.[51] Entering a patronage relationship, even if it is a coercive one, or if the patron or broker is exploitative, can be seen as a rational choice, as a survival strategy to gain access to scarce resources.[52] Given the close co-operation between the government apparatus and local leaders/politicians, patronage is, mostly, the only channel through which residents of illegal (or slum) colonies can get access to public and other goods and services.

Though residents may be helped by the system of patronage, Van der Linden (1997) found that patronage stands in the way of a permanent solution to problems, as the interests of the patrons often do not coincide with those of the clients whose interests they are supposedly serving. Also, the patrons strive for ad hoc solutions to parts of problems only. They cannot afford to solve problems in the long term or in a structural way since, by doing so, they would undermine their own usefulness: the problems are the basis of their income and/or their power.[53]

However, it is now being recognized that slum leaders play a crucial role in low-income urban settlements. They are the mediators between local residents and supra-local institutions, be they governmental, political, or private. Local leaders are important political agents and influence the implementation of development or community participation schemes. As De Wit has vividly described it, slum leaders are the chief slum brokers, 'moving like spiders in the city web of networks they have carefully spun'. He mentions that in the two slums he studied, the leaders, from the slum dwellers' point of view, were very important mediators. The leaders in those two slums were all involved in 'good' and 'bad' activities, being more or less exploitative. Their activities may or may not contribute to an improved position of the urban poor.[54] The popularity of local leaders in the contexts of scarcity depends on their capacity to get things done. A person with power in the local context often has direct access to leaders at higher levels and, through this access, is sometimes able to channel advantages into the local setting. While caste and extended family networks remain important in the definition of local power, political connections outside of the local context are less and less influenced by such considerations. They often lead to the 'top', enabling particular people to achieve very much.[55]

Four per cent of the respondents in Ambedkar Nagar were active in politics, either as a member of the local slum organization Ambedkar Makkal Podhu Nala Sangam (Ambedkar Peoples' Social Welfare Association) or a political party. Eighteen per cent approached the slum leaders to complain about the state of the facilities in Ambedkar Nagar or whenever they needed help in applying for a pension or a loan. Seventy-eight per cent said they tried to stay away from the leaders, as they would only 'create problems'. It was also said that often these leaders expect something in return. Though some leaders in Ambedkar Nagar are more popular than others, in general the inhabitants are not very happy with them as 'they only help people from whom they can receive something in return and they are not interested in helping the really needy and poor ones'.

Each relocation group had its own local leader; some had more than one leader. In the early years, there were many fights between local leaders of the different relocation groups for a variety of reasons including the illegal sale of *arrack* and drugs. This situation led one of the local leaders of the Chitra Nagar group to leave Ambedkar Nagar and return to his home village. Discussions were held with respondents about the role of the local leader of the Chitra Nagar group. De Wit (1993) found that in Chitra Nagar there were two local leaders—Krishnan was linked to the Dravida Munnetra Kazhagam (DMK) party, and Murugavel to the Congress party, and there was great animosity between them. His daughter explained that when they were relocated to Ambedkar Nagar, the older Congress leader Murugavel left for his home village because he did not want to get involved in the many fights between the local leaders of the different groups. In Chitra Nagar, Subramaniam, a younger man who was also a member of the Congress party and who, according to De Wit, had leadership aspirations, assisted the old Congress leader, Murugavel. So when the old men left, the DMK leader and the young Subramaniam were the two influential men in the community. Subramaniam was helpful to his neighbours and others who came to him for help. In 1998, for instance, he arranged for a water tank to be placed in the main road. The people who lived close to his water tank were very happy with it, but Krishnan was not, as he probably saw a threat to his leadership from Subramaniam. This resulted in several fights over the years. For instance one night, four months after the tank was put in place, a son of Krishnan and a few women came to Subramaniam's house, drunk, and started to create problems, banging on the door and starting to fight. Only when the police eventually arrived did the fighting stop. Another woman said that in order to apply for a widow's pension she first approached Krishnan for help, but he could not get it for her. Afterwards she approached Subramaniam, and he eventually arranged for a pension for her and nine other widows. Many Chitra Nagar people tried to ignore Krishnan as they felt he did not do anything for them, 'he always asks something in return and he is not interested in helping the poor people.' Some people were afraid to talk about the local DMK leader as he was an influential person because of his party membership and they just accepted his leadership, believing that otherwise it would be impossible to survive in Ambedkar Nagar. Two women belonging to the Chitra Nagar group approached a leader from another group to apply for a pension, as Krishnan did not want to help them. One woman said, 'when these leaders do a good thing, we can accept them as leaders, but when they don't do anything, how can they expect us to call them leaders?' I also found out that Krishnan was involved in the illegal selling of plots as he offered me one near the main road for Rs 65,000.

Young people mentioned that the local leaders did not do anything for them. In 1999 one young man was trying to start his own football team in Ambedkar Nagar. Earlier he used to play with a team at Anna University, thanks to the NGO GEMS that had put him in contact with its members. Many others wanted to play football in Ambedkar Nagar, so the young man was planning on setting up his own team. He had tried playing in the neighbouring NGO Colony but the locals there did not want them to play there. Since they have nowhere else to play, the young man thought of joining a football tournament with his friends. In July 1999, he still had to get the information on how to register.

There were many problems with the organization of the Mariyamman festival at the local Chitra Nagar temple. As Krishnan was not organizing anything, a few years back a group of young people organized a big festival, which according to them was a huge success. When they tried again to organize the festival the next year, Krishnan, out of jealousy, did not approve of it. Since then, nothing has been organized and many people are disappointed.

The local organization Ambedkar Makkal Podhu Nala Sangam was founded in 1995 in order 'to create unity in the area'. The Sangam was not linked to any political party as members with different political backgrounds were part of it, but the majority of the members of the board were DMK supporters.[56] Before 1995, local leaders were in charge of their own local group and there was hardly any inter-group contact, only conflicts. So in 1995, Das from the Krishnamurthy Colony group and Murthy, both DMK members, took the initiative of setting up an organization for the whole of Ambedkar Nagar. Elections were organized and a president and board were chosen. This organization was meant to be a way of rallying the forces in order to negotiate with the Slum Board and the corporation to improve the facilities in Ambedkar Nagar. Furthermore, when the water lorry was still providing water to Ambedkar Nagar, the Sangam organized the auctions for the distribution. In the first year, amounts between Rs 2,000 and Rs 3,000 were bid. These amounts had to be paid to the organization, but according to the president, they were never paid. Every year, the Sangam organized a big ceremony on Dr Ambedkar's birthday (14 April) and on Independence Day (15 August), when they donated free uniforms and books to school children and hoisted the flag. The members of the board belonged to different groups in Ambedkar Nagar and they were influential men in the area. A number of them were local leaders, but no Muslims had joined. The Sangam also had a women's wing, of which Manju was the leader. She used to be a social worker for GEMS. Her tasks as president of the women's wing were merely to intermediate in family problems and to help people to apply for loans at the Tahsildars's Office and ration cards at the Civil Supplies Office, for which she charged 'a minor amount'. She was quite a strong character and could definitely earn her living from that as she had nothing else to survive on; her husband had left her many years ago, she has two children and for the past half year she was not working as GEMS had fired her. The following story is of a local leader in Ambedkar Nagar.

Sundaram is a local leader in Ambedkar Nagar and member of the AIADMK.[57] He seems to be an influential man in the area and has a big house with an upper floor, which he rents out to three different families. He was elected president of the Ambedkar Makkal Podhu Nala Sangam a few years back. Before that he was the leader of the youth wing of the Sangam for two years. Before Das and Murthy asked him to join the Sangam, Sundaram was involved in fights with the neighbouring areas of Ambedkar Nagar, including NGO Colony. He was also involved in illegal activities like the selling of *arrack*. One day Das and Murthy asked him to stop all his illegal business and become the president of the Sangam. He agreed and was elected. He told me that the first thing he organized after becoming president was the improvement of the PC units. Rs 5 was collected from every household and people were hired to do the cleaning. As many people in the area could not afford to give Rs 5, they went to the Zonal Office of the corporation where they held a demonstration. It worked and the corporation soon sent municipal workers to clean the PC units. Later, their auction for water distribution was a big success. Now Sundaram is trying to get a free *patta* for the people of Ambedkar Nagar. Sundaram he said that three years back the mayor of Chennai, Mr Stalin, had told him to come back in 10 years and then they would speak about the free *patta* distribution.[58]

The Sangam had 530 members who do not pay contribution but are invited to join the monthly meetings and also vote. But in practice only a few join these meetings, which take place in the Sangam hall. Das, the founder of the Sangam, sets the agenda, in consultation with the members who also approach him whenever they want something to be discussed. Before every meeting Das distributes the agenda amongst the members. Officially elections are organized for the board of the Sangam once a year, but in practice not many changes have taken place since 1995. Some people in minor positions have changed but the powerful positions are still occupied by the same persons. They say that everyone who wants to stand for elections can do so on paying Rs 101 to the Sangam. But in practise people are afraid to challenge important persons like the local leaders Sundaram and Krishnan in the Sangam because they are powerful and have many contacts with politicians from outside. Besides they are rude and intimidating. That Sundaram is not afraid to use violence whenever he is challenged became very clear in early 2001 when he murdered two people in Ambedkar Nagar: a man and his son. This man, like Sundaram, was a moneylender in the area and earned a lot of money as he charged 5 per cent less interest than Sundaram. Since then Sundaram has been in jail for the double murder. It is significant that many people did not tell me this had happened; they are afraid even to discuss the subject.

Another way the Sangam earns money is by approaching all the new buyers in the area and asking them to pay Rs 101. Most of them pay, for if they do not, 'they won't be protected whenever there is a problem' explains Das.

6.2 Conclusion

Table 6.1 summarizes and brings together research questions one and four, which focus on initiatives and forms of collective action of the poor and their accountability, effectiveness, and appropriateness.[59] A short summary of what I actually found is provided afterwards.

Chit Funds

Chit funds are organized in the context of a need for credit facilities. Poor people have no access to formal credit facilities, and in Ambedkar Nagar almost only woman can join. Chit funds represent an opportunity to earn some extra cash in times of need, especially for women who are not working for a salary.

Ghate et al. (1992) mention that one of the advantages of chit funds is their easy accessibility, flexibility and adaptability.[60] This needs to be analysed. In Ambedkar Nagar chit funds are only accessible for the (relatively) richer households within the community and the poorer households are excluded as they represent a risk for the agent and therefore for the whole chit fund in that they may not be in a position to complete a chit fund round in case of sudden financial crisis. Chit funds are flexible in the sense that all the procedures are locally based and agents can be approached in order to organize a meeting on a certain day. In practice however, the agent herself sets that date and often does not change it; in that sense, the funds are not accountable to their members. The most important advantage that is identified by the participants is that in order to save and earn some money, they do not have to undertake difficult and time-consuming procedures because all arrangements are made within the settlement. For those who join the chit fund, as well as for the agent, the fund is very effective, but this depends upon the managing capacities of the agent. Those who join are mainly members of the same social group, community, and relocation

TABLE 6.1: OVERVIEW OF ACCOUNTABILITY, EFFECTIVENESS, AND APPROPRIATENESS OF LOCAL COLLECTIVE INITIATIVES

Collective Initiative	*Actors/initiators*	*Activities*	*Accountability*	*Effectiveness*	*Appropriateness*
Chit funds	Relatively richer, stronger women	Deciding which type of chit fund and the amount of money, selecting the participants, organizing and managing the meetings, ensuring no one is defaulting and everyone pays their due amount, keeping the rotation money in custody	No accountability, the agent makes all the decisions	Depends on the managing capacity of the agent, but most chit funds are (very) profitable for the agent	Appropriate for those who are allowed to join; the richer, reliable persons who belong to the same group/street and who are well known to the agent (or to other members of the group), those who are not allowed to join feel excluded and without access to some extra money
Water	Relatively richer, stronger women	Contacting Metro Water, distributing the water evenly amongst the	No accountability	Very effective: water is brought	Very appropriate: Water is

contd.

TABLE 6.1 (contd.)

Collective Initiative	*Actors/initiators*	*Activities*	*Accountability*	*Effectiveness*	*Appropriateness*
		community and collecting the money		to the area and is accessible for everyone	distributed evenly amongst the community, without fights
Temple festival	A small group of religious women	Get pamphlets printed, door-to-door collection of money, keep administration and collected money in custody; based on the amount collected, decide which activities will be organized during the festival	Accountable: Everyone (belonging to the same group) is informed and can join in the organization of the festival	Depending on the amount of money collected the festival is smaller or larger	Normally almost all group member join the festival at their local temple as they feel it is very important
Private temple	One religious couple	Collect money, construct temple, organize an opening ceremony and do *pooja*	Private initiative where others do not join and do not visit the temple, except for some close friends and family	Very effective as a large private temple is constructed	Appropriate: Although it has impoverished the initiators financially, socially they have gained a lot of respect (and

					power) within the community (and probably they will enrich themselves through the temple as well)
The local slum party	Local leaders of different groups in the area	Strive for physical improvement of the area and for free *pattas*, help with application procedures and carry out illegal activities like extortion)	Physical improvement benefits all but help with applications, etc., benefits only the relatively richer households	Very effective: Local leaders earn money and gain power through the organization	Mixed: The physical improvement has had some effect on the whole community but mediation by the local slum party/ local leaders benefits only the relatively richer ones and although they are happy that they are helped, they are not happy with the fact that something is expected in return (money)

background. As mentioned in the literature, social control forms a barrier against fraud and defaulting.

Water Distribution

Water distribution was organized locally because of the Water Board's inefficient provision system. The water is now distributed by relatively rich entrepreneurial women in the area who see it as a means to earn some extra money as well as gain power and respect, given the importance of the role in the area. The distributor makes all the decisions. The system is very effective as everyone is entitled to a certain amount of water, and it is appropriate in that water is distributed regularly and without fights.

As water is a basic need for all, the need to organize it in a suitable matter is shared by all within the community, and community or relocation background is not an issue in this matter.

Religious Activities

Temple festivals and other religious activities were inspired by religious aspirations and to a lesser degree, to earn power and respect. Relatively large sums of money can be collected if the activity is carried out well and it is all spent on the festival itself. The festival and its organization are very accountable and appropriate, but in practice limited to members of the same primary group.

Local Slum Party

The local slum party was initially set-up to lobby for the physical improvement of the area, and as a means for the local leaders to join forces and to hold their power over the inhabitants in the area, as well as to earn money and prestige.

Overall, it can be concluded that whenever money is invested, whenever there are financial risks for the initiator/actor, or there is money to be earned, there is no accountability as to who can join the initiative, but the effectiveness is normally high, as well as the appropriateness (for those who join and for the actors/initiators). The decision of the actor/initiator to start a certain project is based on rationality—the investment will be profitable in the sense of money, and/or power, and/or prestige.

NOTES

1. Chambers, 1998: 1.
2. Epstein et al., 1998: 82.
3. Dia, 1996: 118, 241-2.
4. This is an adapted version of the definition on indigenous knowledge from: Indigenous Knowledge and Development Monitor, 1998: 1.
5. Ghate et al., 1992: 23.
6. Radhakrishnan, 1975: 1.
7. Ghate et al., 1992: 41.
8. De Wit, 1993: 159.
9. Ghate et al., 1992: 91-3.
10. Smets, 1996: 46.
11. Dia, 1996: 199
12. Smets, 1992 as quoted by Smets, 1996: 55.
13. According to Smets (2002: 112), among policy-makers and scientists, chit funds are generally known as rotating credit associations (RCAs) or rotating savings and credit associations (ROSCAs) and he uses the latter term. In this study I will stick to the term chit fund, as this is the term that is, when translated, locally used.
14. When referring to the participants and agents of chit funds, the female form is used, as the overall majority of them are females.
15. Smets (2002: 110) makes another distinction based on the way the finance is allocated to the participants, which can take place in a democratic or authoritarian fashion. In a democratic chit fund, the allocation of the fund is in hands of the chit fund participants, and they form a collective that is also responsible for dealing with the risk of default, while in the authoritarian chit fund it is the organizer who makes the decisions and is also responsible for any default. In my study area only authoritarian chit funds are operating.
16. These terms are used by Radhakrishnan, 1975: 6.
17. The term agent was used by one of the respondents to denote the person organizing the chit fund, and it was decided to also use this term for the study.
18. Interestingly, in De Wit's PhD study (1993), in one of the slums that

was later relocated to Ambedkar Nagar, chit funds were organized, and in this study, agents relocated from that slum explained that they had proceeded to organize chit funds right after they were relocated.

19. Kundu, 1993: 77.
20. Still called Madras at that time.
21. Rao, 1990: 65.
22. Agrawal, 1993: 1-5.
23. Devas et al., 2001: 30.
24. This organization will be described later in the chapter.
25. I have only come across six 'water women', whether there were more 'water women' active in the area, or whether the six known women were distributing in more than one spot, did not become clear to me.
26. Whether this actually happened is, in the least, very doubtful.
27. De Wit (1993) also describes the existence of a water distribution system in his slum before it was relocated to Ambedkar Nagar.
28. Matthews, 1979: 75.
29. Moffatt, 1979: 247. Arunachalam (1980: 296) speaks of the 'Mari cult'. The following are some of the different names he found: Selli, Kurumari, Mahamayi, Maha Mari, Sitala Devi, Kannudaiyal, Kathayi, Ponni, Nagammal, Nadi, and Modi.
30. As examples he mentions that all food offered to the deities on the various festive occasions like Chitrapournami, Pongal, Mattuppongal, Sarasvati Pooja, etc., are distributed to the working class; distribution of slates or pencils on the occasion of the initiation of a child from a well-to-do or average family into the school; distribution of clothes to teachers on this day and on Deepavali day; distribution of oil and powder and eatables on Deepavali day; jaggery, fruits and the like on the Pongal and *Mattuppongal* day (Arunachalam, 1980: 50). Whether the care for the poor can be called socialistic or a form of welfare which is not typical to temple festivals in Tamil Nadu but is a highly valued aspect in many religions like Islam and Christianity is a discussion which I will not go into.
31. Moffatt, 1979: 248.
32. De Wit and de Bruin, 1994: 3.
33. Den Ouden, 1975: 93.
34. Moffatt, 1979: 246.
35. Beck, 1972.
36. Fuller, 1992: 135.
37. Beck, 1972: 121.
38. De Wit, 1993: 127, but according to Arunachalam (1980: 296), Kali is not Mari.
39. In 1999, *Adi* lasted from the 15th of July until the 14th of August, but each year this differs based on the moon.
40. De Wit (1993: 127) found that temple festivals were organized in the

slum that was relocated to Ambedkar Nagar. He describes that the external contacts were such that during the festival there was a procession from the outside temple to the local temple. These external contacts do not exist in Ambedkar Nagar. Here the external contacts exist in the collection of money for the festival, and the hiring of attributes and so on.

41. This is a video recorder.
42. Arunachalam (1980: 298) has described the fire-walking ceremony as follows: the fire-walking ceremony is generally on the last day of the Mariyamman temple festival of ten days, which culminates on *Panguni uttiram*. During all the ten days, the *pujari* goes round the streets carrying a *Karaham*, a brass pot decorated with flowers and woven round with thread and filled with scented water which represents Mari. He stops in front of each house where they organize a special ceremony. On the last day the fire walking is organized. The arrangement of the pit is said to require expert skill and is about ten feet in length and three feet wide, with a depth of nine inches. Good logs of the black babul, acacia, are burned in the pit. The fire walking generally takes place in the afternoon. The *karaham* goes round the temple itself and the firewalkers follow it. They are generally in clothes dyed yellow in turmeric water and carry in their hands, or around their neck, margosa leaves. Some even have a large mud bowl of fire in their hand, placed over some margosa leaves. Just at the end of the pit there is a pit of water, about three feet wide and two feet long. The first walker *pujari* walks over the fire with the *karaham*, and then the others follow. The firewalkers have been on a strict diet the day previous to the firewalking and on the day of the ceremony they have an early morning bath and fast till the ritual is over.
43. For the location of Vadapalani see the map of Chennai in Section 4.1.2, and for the location of Thiruverkadu, see the next map of south India.
44. At Sabarimalai (for its location, see the Figure 6.3) the principal temple for Aiyappan, the son of Siva and Mohini, a female form of Vishnu, Aiyappan is represented as an unmarried god. For Tamils he is the lord of celibacy *par excellence*. The pilgrimage of Tamils to Sabarimalai occurs annually during *Margali* (mid-December to mid-January). Only males, prepubesent girls, and post-menopausal women are allowed to participate, but the overwhelming majority of pilgrims are men. Up to 60 days—but traditionally 41—before the start of the journey, prospective pilgrims begin to observe extensive restrictions, such as no sexual activity, not eating meat or eggs, and sleeping on the floor. The men must wear only the traditional Tamil males' waistcloth, but dyed black, dark blue or ochre. In some places, this collective identity is reinforced by nightly gatherings to sing hymns praising Aiyappan. On the eve of the pilgrimage, each man is initiated in his local temple where

he accepts a special bag containing the items to be offered to Aiyappan, and a miniature funeral is held. The pilgrim as a renouncer cuts his ties with the world and society by becoming dead to it. After that, the journey to the temple, which is travelled by foot starts (Fuller, 1992: 214-15).

45. For the location of Egmore, Adambakkam, and Kakkan Nagar see the map of Chennai in section 4.1.2.
46. Normally they donate a whole (or even) amount plus one extra rupee for luck.
47. In 1999, *Chittirai* was from the 15th of April until the 14th of May, but these dates change every year according to the moon.
48. The new moon day and the full moon day have their own importance. A large number of people observe these days as days of special dedication to the departed ancestors. Particularly on the *Amavasya* day the householder performs the *tarpana* or offering of oblation to the departed souls of the family. The *Amavasya* days in the month of *Adi* and *Tai* are considered especially important in this regard (Arunachalam, 1980: 37-8).
49. Baken, 1990, as quoted by Smets, 1996: 6. Patronage is defined as face-to-face relationships between actors of unequal status and power that persist over time, and which involve the exchange of valued resources (Ward, 1989, as quoted by J. de Wit, 1993: 30). It is distinguished from political patronage or clientelism, which is defined as the dispensing of public resources (or the promise to do so) by political power-holders/seekers and their respective parties, in exchange for votes and other forms of popular political support (De Wit, 1993: 31).
50. I doubt whether these associations are completely horizontal as within these organizations there will always be more and less leading figures, people with more power and better networks than others.
51. Smets, 1996: 7.
52. De Wit, 1993: 30.
53. Van der Linden, 1997: 84, 83. He even wrote that often patrons monopolize information, pass on incorrect or partial information to their clients and try to inhibit the realization of a policy directed at fundamental improvements in order to maintain their position within a community.
54. De Wit, 1993: 290; Ward, 1989, as quoted by De Wit, 1993: 27.
55. Wiebe, 1981: 119, 121-2.
56. At the time of the fieldwork in 1998-9 the DMK was the ruling party in the Tamil Nadu government and therefore the local leaders connected to that party were able to benefit from their political contacts. This did not, however, mean that local leaders who were connected to other political parties were without any influence and power in the area at that time. They were either powerful due to the respect they had

obtained for the role they had played in the area earlier or due to the fact that they did not hesitate to use violence or their contacts in the criminal circuit, as is the case with Sundaram.

57. All India Anna Dravida Munnetra Kazhagam.
58. According to Mr Zafrullah, Community Development Officer of the Slum Board, that will never happen.
59. These concepts have been defined in Chapter 2.
60. Ghate et al., 1992: 23.

7

Conclusion

To recapitulate, the objectives of this study were to investigate how 'policy target groups' perceive development policies, their goals, and their implementation. The study took place in a relocation site at Velacheri, located 15 km from the Chennai city centre and where the TNSCB forcibly relocated 2,640 families between 1990 and 1993.

The goals of the study were: to investigate which initiatives were developed by the local community in the study area; to investigate the perceptions and expectations of the local community regarding relocation, the provision of employment facilities and social security schemes, and the provision and maintenance of basic services; to study which policies were developed by the government and NGOs for the relocated groups and; to assess whether the government and NGO policies and local initiatives were accountable, effective, and appropriate. The overall question that needs to be answered based on the outcome of these research questions is whether these local community initiatives can be matched more effectively with the implementation of development programmes by the government and NGOs.

These questions reveal potential conflict. On the one hand, it is being suggested that until now development policies and programmes have had too much of a top-down character and that they do not incorporate the needs, expectations and expertise of the policy target groups; hence the need to study local initiatives. Eventually though, because fieldwork was done in light of an IDPAD project (as discussed in Chapter 2) and designed to link research to policy and programme making, it was hoped that government and NGO policy makers would heed the outcome of the study. And although there are variations, we have to recognize that in the end, all policy and programmes are top-down. However, the formulation and implementation of policy and programmes can be more successful if the policy target groups are involved in the process.

This concluding chapter draws some theoretical and empirical conclusions and suggests new areas for research on the basis of the study findings.

7.1 Local Collective Initiatives

Several studies have shown that in many low-income urban settlements, there are forms of collective organization such as savings groups, religious organizations, and local slum parties.[1] The World Bank study 'Voices of the Poor' found that in the absence of state resources, the poor themselves view the role of these informal networks and associations as critical for their survival.[2] Numerous authors (a.o. Baud, 2000; de Wit, 1993) have pointed out however, that many local communities face the problem of not being homogeneous entities and being prone to social divisions and conflicting interests. It was hypothesized that collective action occurs at different levels and that it will emerge beyond local divisions like kinship and caste when, within a community, people identify strong common interests.

According to Eckstein (1990), collective action of the poor is predominantly based on organizing basic services, employment, and security. It occurs without government assistance, and is more likely to achieve goals when people have a 'sharpened sense of a shared destiny'. First, I will comment on the second part of the statement, namely that collective action is more likely to achieve goals when people have a sense of shared destiny, and then on the first part, namely that collective action is predominantly based on organizing basic services, employment and security.

Many forms of organization were found in Ambedkar Nagar. Some groups were active right after the relocation, others started later. The activities that existed right after the relocation were chit funds and the construction of temples. Almost all the local leaders active in the slum areas before they were moved continued as leaders in the new area. These initiatives were based on caste and relocation background, indicating that this is the most basic form of collective organization. After a few years, when the community had had time to develop, and in the absence of suitable basic services, different communities started to develop initiatives together to fight for better basic services. A local slum organization was founded through which the local slum leaders joined forces to (among other things) strive for better basic services. Water distributors responsible for better functioning of the water distribution system were selected through the party. These initiatives rose above kinship, caste, and relocation background, thereby confirming the hypothesis that whenever people within a community identify with strong common interests, collective action will emerge beyond local divisions.

As already mentioned, according to Eckstein (1990), collective action of the poor is mostly oriented to organizing basic services, employment and security. I do not agree with this. There are many more types of collective action that are oriented towards a much broader scale of activities. Ambedkar Nagar itself has many forms of small-scale collective action like chit funds (partly based on organizing a form of security), and religious activities like the construction of temples and organization of temple festivals. This suggests that local communities can prioritize different types of collective action, not necessarily limited to basic services, but also based on building up social capital.

Another aspect highlighted by Mitlin (2001) is that the impact of local organizations is not always positive as they do not necessarily assist in the reduction of poverty nor in the consolidation of social capital, they do not always represent the local community as a whole, and do not always make decisions according to consensus. This was found to be true. Grassroots organizations do not always represent the local community as a whole; local collective initiatives based on caste and relocation background only represent particular caste and relocation groups. In Ambedkar Nagar, these initiatives include the chit funds and the temple festival groups. The collective initiatives that emerged beyond local divisions in order to obtain basic services for the community as a whole were the water distribution groups and the local slum organization. In all cases, decisions were not made by consensus but by the initiators. Most of the initiators of these organizations are the 'stronger' and relatively 'less poor' people from the community. The poorest from the community do not even have access to some of the local organizations. Furthermore, some of the organizations do not promote the interests of the poorest people within the community, who are actually the most needy ones. This means that local initiatives are not necessarily inclusive, in that they enhance social stratification, are not necessarily based on democratic principles and equity, and do not strive to provide for the poorest within the community. Furthermore, local organizations can also be involved in illegal activities as is the case with the local slum organization in Ambedkar Nagar, which is involved in the illegal selling of plots, charging inhabitants for acting as mediators in obtaining government services like loans, and extortion practices.

Dia (1996) has stated that 'grassroots organizations' are often inflexible to changes, but in order maintain their relevance, they have to adapt to the changing outside world. What I suspect is that he speaks of different types of local organizations at a more 'meso' or 'macro' level than the ones that were the object of this study. What was found in this study is that in Ambedkar Nagar local organizations are very flexible and adapt quickly to outside changes. This means that local organizations do have the capacity to adapt to change and to react quickly to changing environments and conditions.

7.2 Perceptions and Expectations of Poor Urban Households Regarding Policy and Implementation with Regard to their Habitat

The second research question concerned the perceptions and expectations of poor urban households regarding policy and implementation with regard to their habitat. Little attention has been paid to the urban poors' perceptions and expectations regarding specific housing and basic service policies and their implementation. According to several studies, the urban poors' reactions can be summarized as follows:

1. Government support has been concentrated in the area of infrastructure provision, but maintenance of services

remains poor. Moreover, the poor have hardly any role or inclination in the maintenance of those services.[3]

2. The urban poor feel excluded from participating in decision-making. They believe they are unequally sharing in the benefits of government programmes and NGO initiatives.[4]
3. They have poor access to the government and that the government and NGOs need to be more accountable to them.
4. The oppressiveness of public officials and the corruption of the government are problems; in order to get things done, people have to pay bribes.[5]

Given that not many studies have induced the poor themselves to formulate what their perceptions and expectations of the government are, these need to be interpreted on the basis of my own analyses of studies that focus on perceptions. From the above statements, it can be concluded that the poor experience the government as being far removed from their everyday reality. They do not view the government as a positive institution but as one that fails them in its provision. The poor indicated that they depend more on their own organizations than on the government for their survival.[6]

In Ambedkar Nagar, government service could be subdivided into the provision of housing, employment, basic services and social security. The perception[7] of the local community regarding government and NGO policies in their area is as follows: in terms of housing in Ambedkar Nagar, the relocatees did not want to be relocated in the first place but they had no say in the matter and did not participate in the decisison making. Nonetheless, many people appreciated the fact that now they will have their own house, more security, and increased privacy. In housing issues, the corruption of public officials played a role: in order to obtain an electricity connection within a reasonable time span, the relocatees need to bribe officials. Also, the transfer of names on allotment orders used to be done illegally by officials the relocatees had to bribe. With regards to the provision of employment, the services offered by the government were poor. The inhabitants of Ambedkar Nagar were promised that the Slum Board would mediate in the provision of employment near the relocation site but nothing of the sort was done. Therefore many people have to commute to the city centre to find work. The inhabitants regard employment as a major issue facing them. They often remark that without a suitable job, the ownership of a house was useless. Women especially were affected by the relocation, as in many cases they could not continue with their job in the city centre. They would like the government to provide for alternative jobs near Ambedkar Nagar. With regard to the provision and maintenance of basic services, the inhabitants of Ambedkar Nagar state that it used to be poor in the early days, but has gradually improved. The opinions about maintenance are more negative, as many services are poorly maintained; for instance, waste collection is lacking, storm water drains are blocked, PC units are in a sorry state, and the water supply is scarce. In spite of some critical remarks many people were happy with the PDS and Noon Meal Scheme, and many people made use of these services. On the other hand, the provision of loans was very problematic. Many people, especially self-employed women, were in need of loans, but the government and NGOs were not helpful in this regard. Another major issue was access to facilities once they were established. In the first place, there was lack of information on the availability of schemes, and officials needed to be bribed. Also, it took a lot of time, energy, and political contacts to get something done. Therefore, in order to apply for a certain scheme, a social security programme like a widow's pension, for instance, people depended on the local leaders, who had the information and the political contacts. In exchange, poor people had to pay.

While the poor viewed the government as being far removed from their everyday life in Ambedkar Nagar, their expectations of the government were quite high. They felt that the government should provide them with sufficient housing, employment opportunities, basic services, and social security facilities. They did not expect that all these services would be provided however; they felt that a good government should be obliged to provide them with all the possibilities others in society have, and to lift them out of their poverty. Mostly people were very cynical about the accuracy of facts provided and the moral intentions of the government.

In conclusion, it can be said that the study suggests that government support has been concentrated in the area of service provision but that its maintenance is poor. Also, participation of target groups in design and implementation of programmes is low to non-existent. Furthermore, employment provision, and the access to government schemes like loan facilities, is poor. There is also lack of communication and information provision on the part of the government.

7.3 Government and NGO Policies for the Relocated Urban Poor

We now turn to the policies the government and the NGOs had developed and implemented for the relocated urban poor.

As described in Chapter 1, in the 1950s and 1960s the government's reaction to the emerging problem of slums was to remove them and construct new houses.[8] From the 1970s onwards, self-help became the accepted government approach, with Sites and Services and Slum Upgrading schemes. The problem with this approach was that in many cases, the land issues were not taken into account, so that many improved settlements were still illegal, and Sites and Services Schemes were often situated in remote areas.[9] Starting in 1986, a fundamental review of housing and urban policy took place, where self-help became just a part of a more complex package of policies in land development, finance, and economic development.[10] Housing was no longer seen as an isolated matter but as one that encompassed broader issues like infrastructure, water, sanitation, and transport.[11] Also, the opinion on the role of the government changed. Enablement was understood to mean retaining government responsibilities for the performance of the housing sector, but its provision was to be taken over by NGOs, CBOs, and household self-help.[12]

7.3.1 Relocation Processes

Over the last two decades, the state rationale for slum relocation and the approaches to the issue have changed repeatedly. In the 1940s and 1950s, in order to get rid of slums, crews often brutally removed them from the city centre. During the 1960s, the prevailing attitude was not that slum dwellers needed to be relocated because they had no rights, but more that they occupied valuable land that was needed for city development. It became more usual for public agencies to make provisions for relocation when they proposed to remove a squatter community. During the 1970s and 1980s, the urban renewal programmes gradually moved away from indiscriminate slum displacements and towards reducing the number of displacements. This meant more slums were upgraded, with only partial relocation in order to lower population density.[13]

Internationally, the present attitude towards involuntary resettlement is that it must be avoided or minimized, and that alternative development solutions must be explored. When there is no other option available however, the people affected, mostly the urban poor, should not suffer from the process and they should not be relocated to far-off places.[14] Also, the relocatees and CBOs and NGOs should participate in the relocation process in order to make sure that the urban poor do not suffer.[15]

In India, soon after Independence, the policy was one of clearance and resettlement, and it was implemented on a limited scale. From the Fourth Plan (1969-74) onwards, the policy shifted from clearance and resettlement to on-site improvement of slums.[16] As of 1992, the approach was that forcible relocation was to be avoided wherever possible, but where unavoidable, the community and voluntary agencies should be involved.[17] The major causes of displacement in India are urban economic growth, environmental improvement, slum upgrading, and non-urban programmes, or a combination of causes. The Government of India has finally realized the need for a rehabilitation policy for displaced persons 'because they pay the price for development', but in practice, this most often does not happen.[18] In Tamil Nadu, for instance, there is no state policy for resettlement and rehabilitation.[19] According to Cernea (2000), the vast majority of development resettlers in India have become impoverished. Also, social conflicts may arise from relocation.

Whether Chennai had no option other than relocation is not a question that is studied here, but most of the relocatees were moved due to development projects that were started in their former living area. Internationally, it is agreed that people should not be relocated to far-off places. What this means is not clear, but if we turn to Ambedkar Nagar, apart from the effect of the relocation site's distance from the former location, on the employment opportunities, especially for women, the relocation constituted a big change at a mental level. This was especially true for women who were now going out of the area much less. Before, all facilities were at a short distance, whereas in Ambedkar Nagar, the women felt they were 'living in the forest'. Also, people had to travel much more, which was costly, time-consuming, and problematic especially since, according to the relocatees, transport facilities were not sufficient. Also, there was not much room for the participation of the relocatees, CBOs, and NGOs in the relocation process. People were informed through their leaders of the plans of the Slum Board, and later the Slum Board came to the slum areas to inform groups of people who happened to be there at that time, but no one had any say in the process or as to the locality to which they were to be relocated. The only involvement on the part of the relocatees consisted in the selection of their neighbours in the new locality. After the relocatees were moved to Ambedkar Nagar, one NGO was involved in the construction of some of the houses in the area, and after a few years, one NGO was approached by the Slum Board to start a project in the area. Another NGO came of its own accord.

There are eight major impoverishment risks related to displacement/relocation recognized in several studies on relocation,[20] as discussed in the following paragraphs.

Landlessness is often mentioned in discussions on relocation, but mostly relates to relocation in rural areas. In this study on urban relocation, the opposite happened. In the study area, the relocatees were illegally occupying land (and pavement) in the inner city of Chennai prior to their relocation. After the relocation, they became, in time, the owners of their own plot, so in this sense they gained land. In other words, through the relocation, natural assets were created for the relocatees. This is an important aspect, which until now has not been studied in the literature focussing on relocation. In my opinion, future researchers should pay more attention to how relocatees are able to improve their lives and build up their assets through more secure land tenure resulting from relocation.

With regard to *joblessness*, we need to make a distinction between male and female employment. For men, relocation has had a major effect on the transaction cost of employment in terms of time, money, and job regularity. They were working mainly in the informal sector in the city centre and after they were relocated, no jobs were available in the neighbourhood of the relocation site, so they had to proceed with their jobs in the city centre, which meant they had to start commuting. As these jobs were informal, it meant that often they were not sure whether they would find work everyday after having commuted to the job sites. Travel was not only costly in monetary terms, it was also time-consuming. If we look at the Chitra Nagar case study covering 19 households, we see that ten heads of household had proceeded with the same job after they were relocated, four had retired, and five had changed jobs, but this was not due to the relocation.[21] Women who were working as servants in the middle-class localities near their houses had to give up their jobs after they were relocated, as it was not possible for them to combine their jobs with their household responsibilities. As there were not many jobs available near the relocation site, this meant that many women became jobless. Others who worked in the construction had to commute further than before they were relocated.

Homelessness relates to relocation or displacement with no alternative housing. Although in this study, people were offered new houses/plots, some people were not able to obtain an allotment order and became homeless. Some were not in the area when the Slum Board came to distribute the allotment orders; others were tenants and were not eligible for an allotment order. These tenants are very vulnerable and more research needs to be undertaken on how this particular group can build assets. On the other hand, some people were able to obtain more than one allotment order.

Marginalization can be subdivided into economic marginalization and social and psychological marginalization. As far as ownership of land is concerned, the relocatees, after paying a monthly instalment for many years, would become the owners of their own plot. In this part of the city, where land prices were increasing rapidly, this meant that in the end, if they decided to wait to sell, they would have a very valuable piece of land. So in that sense, instead of what is normally associated with relocation (marginalization), the opposite is true in that natural assets are being created.

With regard to income, if we look at the Chitra Nagar case study, we see that contrary to what earlier studies seem to suggest as to the effects of relocation (a decline in income after relocation), there was a significant increase in income. It is important to mention however that life in Ambedkar Nagar was much more expensive than in the former locality given that people had to pay for many basic services, as well as for increased transport costs. Generally speaking then, it can be concluded that although the actual income improved significantly after relocation, after subtracting the prices paid for basic services and transport, the actual income left for food and other expenses may have decreased. As for social and psychological marginalization, the loss of confidence in society cannot be compared before and after the relocation. Yet, as discussed earlier, most people in the area were very cynical about the State. Nevertheless, they appreciated the fact that they were not to be relocated once more, which gave them a sense of security, something many of them had never experienced before. Women, especially, felt marginalized in the sense that before, when they lived in the city centre, they had felt part of the busy city life, and now they felt very isolated. Also, as many groups with different backgrounds were relocated to the same locality, social problems were initially an issue. Local leaders were fighting over hegemony in the area and there were many fights between different gangs over the selling of drugs and *arrack*. Again, the women especially felt unsafe. When the police outpost was placed in the area the situation improved, although drug trafficking and the illegal selling of *arrack* was still taking place and after dark many people did not dare to leave their houses.

The issue of *food insecurity* is more applicable to rural relocation than to Ambedkar Nagar. Whether there was a *decline in health* cannot be ascertained as it was not studied, but if we look at the Chitra Nagar case study, the basic facilities provided there were less than in Ambedkar Nagar. For instance, people had to defecate at the riverbank, and there was no sewerage and drainage, which would have had some effect on health. While government hospitals were close by, this does not necessarily translate into major effects on the health status.

Loss of access to common property is more related to rural areas and not applicable to the study area. *Basic services* like water, sanitation, and electricity, although not operating very well, were better than in the former location. Access to education remained comparable, but health care, market facilities, and employment deteriorated, and transport was not an issue in the former locality as everything was within a short distance.

Finally, *social disarticulation* did not play a major role in the study area as whole communities were relocated and people were able to select their neighbours. It only played a role for those who were not able to obtain an allotment order.

The *risk to host populations* was not studied in this research.

The overall conclusion is that discussions on relocation and its effects on the relocatees have been much too general. The Ambedkar Nagar study shows that the relocatees were able to build up particular assets, instead of being more marginalized. The effects of relocation on the relocatees depend completely on the facilities provided to the relocatees after they are relocated, and therefore no general assessment can be made on the issue, as has been done until now. Also, there is a big difference in the effects of relocation in rural areas and in urban areas. It is evident that relocation should be avoided whenever possible, but in some cases, governments have no other options. If the site is selected carefully with the cooperation of the target group and employment and facilities are provided in a good manner, relocatees find themselves in a position to build up their assets. More research needs to be undertaken on how the negative effects of relocation can be minimized and how relocatees can be provided with more opportunities to increase their assets.

7.3.2 BASIC SERVICES AND SOCIAL SECURITY

As described above, between 1986-96, a fundamental review of housing and urban policy operated in India. It was emphasized that the review should not only encompass housing policies but also the provision of basic services, transport facilities, employment opportunities, and improvement of the physical environment.[22] In other words, an integrated approach was encouraged.[23] The opinion on the role of the government changed from being that of a 'provider' to an 'enabler' and it was believed that community-based organizations, non-governmental organizations, self-help, and the private sector would have to start playing an important role in the provision of housing and basic services. The new approach implied that the private sector would implement urban development policies more efficiently and effectively than the public sector. Development thinkers now see public-private partnerships as one of the most promising forms of collaboration.[24]

From the 1990s India saw a shift in the financial responsibility for providing basic services from the central to the state government and local bodies.[25] This has had an adverse effect on the availability of basic services because the funds made available to these agencies are meagre.[26] Partnerships for service delivery have also been established. In some cases, local governments are not able to provide many of the services for all their citizens. In such a case partnership arrangements with NGOs or the private sector might improve the coverage or effectiveness of those services.[27] The main points of criticism regarding government programmes and schemes of the Central, state and local governments for shelter and basic services are that they do not reach the target groups due to ineffective targeting and inflexibility.[28] Also, target groups are not informed about the existence of schemes, and there is no co-ordination between the different agencies focussing on the same target groups.[29]

Special programmes for the provision of basic services to the urban poor were not implemented in Chennai in 1999-2000 due to lack of budgetary support. Therefore, their provision fell under the general programmes of the state. NGOs were also involved in providing services in slum areas. Social security programmes existed that specifically focused on the poor, like the PDS, the Noon Meal Scheme, and old age pension schemes. Some of them were efficient, although better targeting could improve their impact. Except for the Noon Meal Scheme, the bureaucratic procedures to be undertaken by the target group in applying or changing conditions are elaborate, complex, and expensive.

Whether the integrated approach of providing housing, basic services, and social security is implemented in the whole of Chennai as a 'new approach' cannot be answered because the relocation site (Ambedkar Nagar) constituted a special case where housing and basic services were all to be provided by the government. Partnerships in the delivery of housing, basic services, and social security were developed in several ways. An NGO was approached by the Slum Board to construct houses in Ambedkar Nagar. For the provision of water, partnership with a private company was established and for the delivery of, among other things, training programmes, health facilities, and educational services, one NGO was asked to start working in the relocation site. The effectiveness of the provision of housing, basic services, and social security in Ambedkar Nagar will be discussed in Section 7.4. The provision of housing and basic services was, until 1996, the responsibility of one agency, namely the Slum Board. Only when the Board wanted to hand over responsibility to the Corporation of Chennai, did it become clear that it had not developed the area (the roads) up to the Corporation standards. This caused a delay in the handing-over process, which says something about the coordination and contact between the two agencies. Whether the provision of basic services has really stopped in Chennai cannot be ascertained as this study only focuses on one area, where provision has been terminated. Social security programmes however continue to be offered.

Overall, it can be concluded that it was difficult to obtain information on the different schemes focussing on the poor in Tamil Nadu, Chennai, and in particular in the relocation site of Ambedkar Nagar. Whenever information was available, there was no general outline or description of the programmes, which made it very complex to compare the different schemes. Often information was incomplete—questions like who the target groups are, where the grants come from, is the programme still proceeding or when and why did it stop remain unanswered. Often schemes are renamed and conditions changed with a change in government, or they were stopped and taken over by others without informing the public. Also, government publications are unclear or incomplete and incorrect, which is even more confusing. Such information is impossible for the target groups to understand, let alone to get access to, as they are often illiterate and uneducated. Furthermore, the situation is also very confusing for the different branches of the bureaucracy itself.

7.3.3 NGO POLICIES FOR THE URBAN POOR

In most developing countries there are dozens of NGOs involved in urban projects; in many, there are hundreds. With regard to cities, three roles have been identified for NGOs: enablers (i.e. community developers, organizers or consultants) alongside community-based organizations; mediators between the people and the authorities who control access to resources, goods and services, and; advisers to consult on policy changes, increase local access to resources, and augment the freedom to use them in locally determined ways (UNCHS, 1996). NGOs have emerged as critical intermediary institutions supporting citizens' organizations in obtaining access to resources and negotiating with the local government and other institutions. Devas et al. (2001) and Mitlin (2001) have listed the major problems of working with NGOs:[30] NGOs did not emerge as being of major significance in poverty reduction due to the fact that some of them are simply business ventures with no real interest in working for the poor; many of the NGOs are too small; the opportunities for policy change are often passed by because there is poor link between operational activities and advocacy; NGOs themselves may have poor links with the community, tense relations with community leaders, and little capacity to organize and support the poorest citizens; NGOs impose their agendas on some of the self-help organizations; NGOs are insensitive to political power structures within the communities and therefore fail to work effectively with existing organizations or fail to transform them into more representative organizations, and; NGOs are sometimes overactive and do not leave space for local organizations to develop their skills and abilities.

In India, many NGOs are active in the poor urban areas. Their main activities, according to Desai (1999), revolve around welfare, providing services, and creating access. Most NGOs have linkages with municipal departments although interaction with state and Central Government departments seems less prevalent and occurs only when they come up against particular problems.[31]

In Ambedkar Nagar, several NGOs were active, of which two were major ones. We will discuss them according to the points raised. Whether they were really significant in achieving a reduction in poverty is hard to say, but at least some of them (one large and the smaller NGOs) were very active and honestly working hard to improve the lives of the inhabitants of the area, so the point made by Devas et al. (2001) does not apply to them. Their programmes were popular and many people visited their health clinic. However, the point made by Devas et al. certainly applies to the other large NGO. Its leader seemed more interested in presenting himself as a benefactor to the outside world than in actually improving the lives of the poor in the area. He looked down on the inhabitants, and whether they actually developed useful projects depended entirely upon the enthusiasm of the local staff. Local expectations and perceptions were not taken into account for the development and implementation of their programmes. Training programmes achieved no results in the sense of creating useful employment opportunities for their participants. During the fieldwork period, there were many staff changes and in 2001 all activities stopped.

The capacity of the NGOs in Ambedkar Nagar is indeed too small. The two major NGOs worked in a scattered area with a limited number of people living in the immediate neighbourhood of their offices. One (major) NGO in particular had programmes that many people wanted to join but its capacity was very limited. Other smaller NGOs worked with very few people. Also, they often did not cooperate with one another.

Although advocacy of NGOs was not a topic of this study, something can be said about it. As NGOs often are dependent on government funding for their projects, it is very difficult for them to be critical towards the government. Of the two larger NGOs that were active in Ambedkar Nagar, one was independent of the government as it financed its projects through its own means; the other depended on the Corporation and the TNSCB for funding, and therefore had to maintain a good relationship with these institutions.

Some NGOs in Ambedkar Nagar had poor links with the community, while others had more contact and were more appreciated. Whether they had tense relations with community leaders needs to be elaborated upon, as there were different types of community leaders in the area. Some leaders had a strong personal agenda and therefore saw the NGOs, who helped inhabitants in obtaining government loans and ration cards, as a threat. Their perception of the situation was that NGOs took over their role and the possibility for them to earn some extra money, and diminished their power in the area. Other community leaders appreciated the fact that NGOs at least were doing something for the community, and therefore they did not create any problem. None of the NGOs reached the poorest in the area. The latter were often not even aware of the existence of the NGOs and their work, as they were so busy just trying to survive. An extra issue, which does not seem to have been noted before, is that there was no coordination between the activities of the different NGOs in the area. The two major NGOs in particular, did not communicate; worse, there was a sense of animosity and competition between them. Had they coordinated their activities, it is likely they could have achieved more.

In Ambedkar Nagar, the NGOs did not specifically impose their agendas on self-help organizations but more on the local community and individuals. Target groups were not listened to, not asked about their wishes and expectations. The NGOs defined their programmes without even consulting their target group and simply imposed their programmes on them. There was no room for evaluation during or after the programme. Some NGOs did not have very high expectations of their target group in terms of their capability to define their own needs.

I cannot say that the NGOs were insensitive to the power structures that were present in Ambedkar Nagar, but they succeeded in finding a way to cope with them, without threatening the leaders, who were very powerful. They definitely failed to transform the political power structures in the area, though it is only fair to add that this is not their goal and is perhaps unrealistic to expect this from NGOs.

When we discuss whether NGOs were overactive in the sense that they did not leave any room for the local communities to develop skills and abilities, we need to make a distinction between different NGOs that were active in the area. One (major) NGO organized a savings group, which was run and organized by the local women. The NGO provided them with a meeting place, and the women themselves dealt with all other matters. The other NGOs were not trying to develop the skills and abilities of local organizations (CBOs), not because they were overactive but because they did not believe in the capabilities of the community. Another issue on local initiatives that has not been noted before is that in Ambedkar Nagar, there was a total lack of knowledge and interest on the part of NGOs regarding the local initiatives that were developed by the community and there were no links between NGOs and such local initiatives. The NGOs did not see the value of these initiatives, did not stimulate them, and did not support them in any sense, which in my opinion is a major shortcoming.

In line with what is mentioned by Desai (1999), the NGOs in Ambedkar Nagar were involved in welfare activities, providing basic services, and creating access to government programmes/ facilities. They had linkages with municipal departments to obtain funding but did not approach the government to try to change or adapt policies.

An additional comment should be made with reference to the poorest inhabitants of Ambedkar Nagar. As mentioned earlier, they were rarely reached by NGOs. The NGOs were not even aware of their existence. The poor had to struggle hard to survive. Besides, they had no access to government policies, were not aware of existing schemes and even when they were, they did not know how to approach the government. Moreover, they were not helped by local slum leaders who always charged a fee that the poor could not pay.

It can be concluded that there are many types of NGOs, differing in size and in approach. They are mainly involved in welfare activities and their commitment often depends upon the enthusiasm of the local staff. They do not take into account local perceptions and expectations. When NGOs receive funds from the government it is very difficult for them to be critical towards it. NGOs are not insensitive to power structures within a community but they do not strive intentionally for changes in the power balance within those communities, although that may indirectly be an outcome of their work. The type of relationship the NGOs have with community leaders depends on the NGOs' approach and on the character of the community leader. Some leaders may regret seeing their influence diminish; others may appreciate the work the NGOs undertake for their community. NGOs often do not reach the poorest and weakest within the community, and do not allow target groups to be involved in the formulation and implementation of programmes. Moreover, they lack interest in local initiatives, and do not try to develop links with these initiatives.

7.4 Accountability, Effectiveness and Appropriateness of Collective Action, and Government and NGO Programmes

The earlier section feeds into the question of whether current initiatives of collective action, government and NGO programmes, were accountable, effective, and appropriate.[32]

Accountability of the Government, NGOs, and Collective Action

Internationally from the 1990s onwards, the role of the government shifted more from being a provider to being an enabler. The provision of housing, for instance, was increasingly left to the market, NGOs and CBOs, and household self-help. Whether this has actually happened in the local context of Ambedkar Nagar will be described below. Put (1998) states that in his research in a rural setting in India, the government's policies were not successful as they were top-down,[33] which means that policies were formulated and implemented without consulting the target group; in other words, there was no accountability. According to the World Bank, the poor feel they are excluded from participation in decision-making, that they share unequally in government policies, and they feel the government and NGOs should be more accountable to them.[34] Regarding the accountability of NGOs, Devas et al. (2001) think that NGOs are not held responsible for their bad performance, in other words they are not held accountable for their actions. As mentioned in Chapter 1, the World Bank study 'Voices of the Poor' on how the poor perceive poverty and development, showed that they feel excluded from participating in decision-making, and that government institutions and NGOs need to be more accountable to them. Whether self-help organizations or collective action groups at the local level are accountable to their members and their community is the last question in this sub-section. A self-help organization is a membership organization, which implies that the risks, costs, and benefits are shared by the members on an equitable basis and that the leadership and/or manager are liable to be called to account by the member for their deeds,[35] a point which is not sufficiently highlighted in the literature on these organizations. It is debatable whether a local organization always represents the local community, or whether it represents only a minority. Such organizations do not always make decisions according to consensus, or in conformity with principles of democratic and equity-oriented decision-making.[36]

In the study area, the target group did not influence the plans and implementation of the relocation project in general. There were two exceptions: the members of the target group were allowed to select their neighbours and they had influence on the construction of (some of) the houses. In the provision (and maintenance) of basic and social services (social security), they had no influence at all. Regarding the accountability of NGOs in Ambedkar Nagar, it can be concluded that the target group of those NGOs had no influence on projects the latter developed and implemented. Although community meetings were organized and people were given the impression that their voice was listened to, it was only for the sake of appearance. Almost all collective initiatives in Ambedkar Nagar were not accountable to their participants. Especially when the initiator invested money, and money could be earned, there was no accountability for those who joined as the initiators made all the decisions themselves.

The literature on self-help organizations tends to romanticize these organizations as entities where costs and benefits are shared among members on an equitable basis and where the leadership and/or manager are liable to be called to account by the membership for their deeds. As stated above, it is clear that this does not apply to the reality in Ambedkar Nagar.

It can be concluded that the accountability of both local initiatives as well as of the government and NGOs in general is low.

Effectiveness of the Government, NGOs, and Collective Action[37]

In India, according to Kundu, government programmes and schemes do not reach their target groups due to ineffective targeting and inflexibility.[38] This is also underlined by Put, who says that policies are not successful in reaching their target group.[39] Furthermore, the urban poor have an unequal share in the benefits of government as well as NGO programmes.[40] According to the World Bank, the poor feel they are excluded from participation in decision-making and that they unequally share in government policies;[41] in that sense, from the perspective of the poor themselves, government policies are not effective.

There are high expectations regarding the effectiveness of partnership arrangements between the government and, amongst others, NGOs and the private sector, in the delivery of housing and basic services,[42] but as this is a recent phenomenon, not much has been published on their effectiveness. Until now, many poor people have relied on informal networks and local institutions for their survival.[43] However, the effectiveness of these organizations depends on the homogeneous character of a community or whether within a community, people identify strong common interests.[44]

Looking at the project plan of the relocation site in Velacheri, we see that it was constructed according to the design, so from the governments' perspective, it was effective. The government, with some exceptions, was content with the way the project was constructed and with the provision of basic services. Also, the prime goal of the government relocation scheme was obtaining land that was illegally occupied by slum and pavement dwellers and using it for infrastructural improvement; in this, they succeeded. However, when the project was transferred from the Slum Board to the Chennai Corporation, the process did not go smoothly as, according to the Corporation, the roads were not constructed up to its standards. Regarding the effectiveness of the NGO programmes, from the perspective of the NGOs in Ambedkar Nagar, excepting the waste management experiment, all other initiatives were effective as many people cooperated in their programmes. In the study area, the effectiveness of collective action depended upon the managing capacities of the initiator, but all (except one) collective initiatives undertaken in the area were very effective from the perspective of the initiator.

Appropriateness of the Government, NGOs and Collective Action

As mentioned, many government policies are top-down oriented, which means that there is no room for participation and discussion on the priorities and expectations of the target group. According to Mitlin (2001), NGOs impose their agenda on their target group, which indicates that they are not open to the priorities of their target groups. As noted before, it is debatable whether a local organization always represents the whole local community, because it does not always make decisions by consensus, or by the principles of democratic and equity-oriented decision making.[45] Devas et al. (2001) mention that NGOs are not really interested in serving the poor, which means poor people are often not really benefitting from the former's work, and programmes are not designed to meet their needs and expectations. Devas et al. (2001) mention that many local organizations act to reinforce patterns of inequality and social exclusion, and are often dominated by men, particularly men of higher status and/or higher income,[46] which discourages the often crucial participation of women.

Regarding the selection of their neighbour in the new site, prior to their relocation, the relocatees were approached and their wishes were often carried out, which made many people quite content. In most other respects, however, no participation was possible in the formulation and implementation of the relocation process, and people were not happy with the outcome (although they appreciated parts of it like the future ownership and privacy of their house, and the provision of certain schemes like the Noon Meal Scheme and the PDS). Regarding the appropriateness of NGOs active in Ambedkar Nagar, the inhabitants felt that almost all the initiatives of the NGOs were not appropriate (with some exceptions like the savings group, but then the capacity was too small). Those who joined the collective initiatives in Ambedkar Nagar felt they were very appropriate, but it needs to be emphasized that some of the initiatives benefitted only the people who were financially better off and more powerful in the area. The poorest households were not allowed to join the chit funds, for instance, as they created a risk for the rest of the group.

7.5 Matching the Initiatives of the Poor with The Implementation of Formal Development Programmes by The Government and NGOs

Finally, we turn to the overall research question: whether initiatives and forms of collective organization of the urban poor can be matched with the implementation of formal development programmes, and if so, how this can be done more effectively.

The perception of academics, bankers, and other decision makers regarding the role of the government in developing countries from the 1950s until now has gradually shifted from that of provider to enabler. In terms of service provision, more room was to be left to the poor themselves, the private sector, NGOs or the development of partnerships. Also, the local community was to be enabled to participate in specific development programmes as they are undertaken at different levels (see Chapter 1).

If we turn to the provision of urban services, one can distinguish the following levels of participation or, one could say, the intensities of power sharing and participation starting at the highest level:[47] empowerment; the development of partnerships; enablement: the government creates appropriate legal, administrative, and planning frameworks to facilitate community organization, management, and action;[48] the government is neutral with regard to local initiatives, does not stimulate and organize the community or parts of it, but also does not pose any barrier and; disenablement: the government actively does not allow for community initiatives to occur.

In the above list, Arnstein (1969) refers only to the functioning of the government, but in this study, the list is also applied to the functioning of NGOs. We will discuss which levels of participation were found in Ambedkar Nagar, and their relative importance according to the sector under consideration. First, we will discuss them in relation to relocation and the provision of housing, then with regard to employment and basic services, and lastly from the point of view of social security provided by the government and NGOs.

In the relocation process, the government took all the initiative, greatly limiting community involvement. In the provision of housing a partnership between the government and an NGO came into being in the early years but frictions between the two partners led to the dissolution of the cooperation. Moreover, the government has been the only provider in terms of housing, sometimes allowing for limited community involvement. So if we return to the levels of participation as mentioned by Arnstein (1969) and Choguill (1996), we conclude that empowerment, enablement, and disenablement were not present; there was one partnership developed in the early years (level two), but the overall response of the government towards local initiatives was neutrality (level four).

In the provision of basic services, one partnership was developed between the government and a private company in the provision of water, which was not very effective for either of the partners involved nor for the inhabitants of the area. For all other matters, there was no other provider but the government and where the government was insufficient, local collective initiatives were developed. The local slum organization mediated in obtaining some basic services in the area and the local community organized the water provision and distribution. The role of the government was neutral towards these local collective initiatives; they did not stimulate them as they did not see their value, nor did they set any barriers. In the provision of social security, the government and the NGOs were the only actors and in some cases, partnerships were developed between the two. For instance, in the provision of vocational training and educational facilities, funds came from the government but the NGOs actually organized these facilities. On the basis of the figure of actors and agencies and their assumed relationships (presented in Chapter 2), we can conclude that what is missing in the partnership relations is a link between these partnerships and local initiatives. Also, no partnerships were found in the area between the community and the private sector. So if we return to the levels of participation as mentioned by Arnstein (1969), we conclude that empowerment, enablement and disenablement were not present in Ambedkar Nagar in this area either. Level two—the development of partnerships—was found as well as level four: governments neutrality towards the development of local initiatives.

Where there were gaps, the community took up collective initiatives like the organization of chit funds. Here, as in other aspects, the government and the NGOs were neutral. The lack of knowledge, appreciation, and estimation of the value of local initiatives is a major flaw in the work of both the government and NGOs. Had they been more aware of the existence of these initiatives and more open as to what was actually happening within the communities, they could have adjusted their programmes to the real needs within those communities and could have built on their knowledge and expertise.

Furthermore, active government support that reaches even the poorest within the community, such as the creation of employment, the provision of basic services and social security (the provision of loans, for example), should have been considered essential.

When these results are taken into account along with the scheme of actors and agencies, as shown in Figure 7.1, it becomes apparent that some links are much more important than others.

Let us now turn to the last issue regarding partnerships: the role of NGOs and that of the government. The World Bank and the IMF, amongst others, have suggested that the private sector would implement urban development policies more efficiently and effectively than the public sector.[49] This clearly is open to scrutiny and in our case, depended upon the nature and the

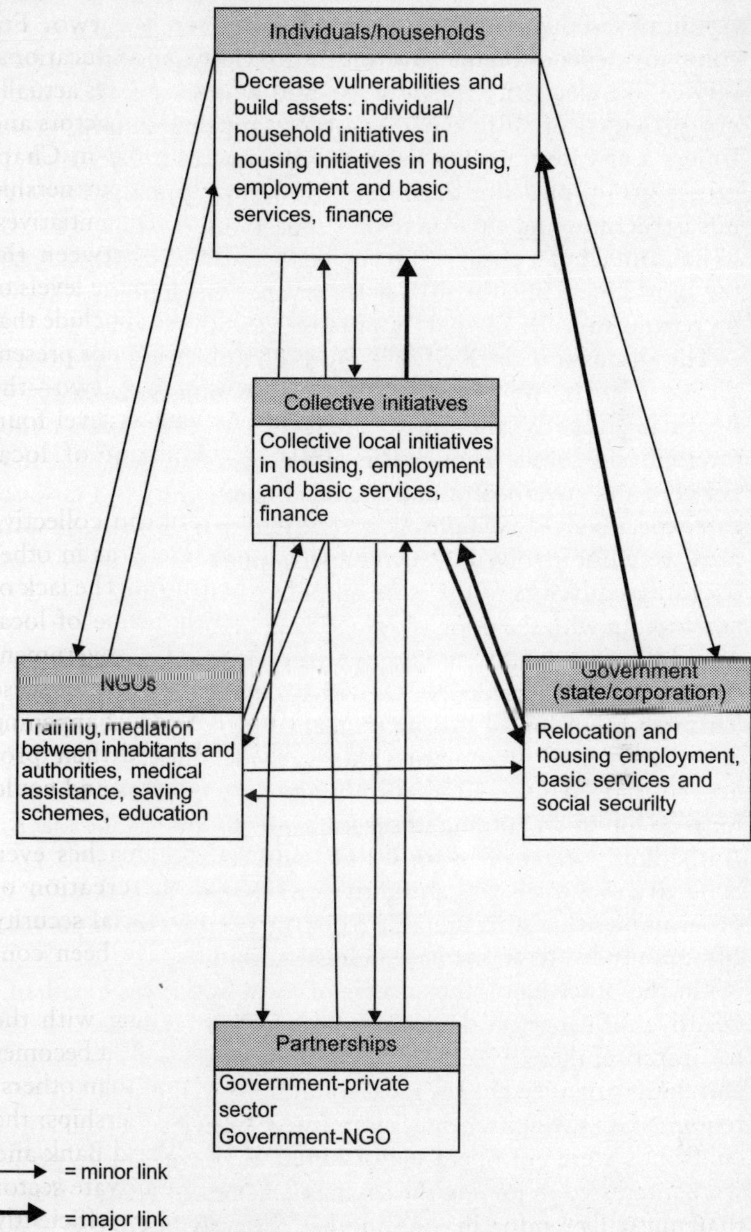

FIGURE 7.1: ACTORS, AGENCIES, AND RELATIONSHIPS IN AMBEDKAR NAGAR

conditions of the partnerships in the locality. Whenever a private company depends on the government for the provision of a basic service like electricity for instance, and whenever this service is not provided in sufficient measure, it appears simply wrong. Unless a private company properly investigates the needs of the target group and the local conditions like social structures, infrastructural and environmental conditions, it will not be able to have much of a positive impact. Also, it can be concluded that the World Bank and the IMF, in theory, put much more emphasis on partnerships than what, in practise, actually occurs.

The discussion on NGOs is more complex and operates at different levels. We have to make a distinction between NGOs operating locally and those operating at the national and international levels. Though it is often suggested that mediation between the government and the local community is a task one can expect NGOs will take on, it appeared that those in the study area were not involved in such undertakings. Also, they did not operate as advisors to the state on policy matters nor cooperate and link up with the poor and their local organizations. The link found between NGOs and the government was a financial one: the government provides NGOs with funds for their programmes. Through these funds, the government can influence the NGOs and the types of programmes they provide. Though it is often argued that NGOs could have a major role in empowering the local community, nothing of the kind was found to take place in Ambedkar Nagar. The only link between NGOs and local collective initiatives was a negative one in that the lack of NGO programmes that were suitable from the perspective of the local community led to an increase in local initiatives.

On the other hand, the success of local initiatives also had a negative influence on the success of NGO programmes. When, for instance, there were a sufficient number of well-functioning chit funds organized by the local community in the area, the need to join NGO savings schemes diminished. Conversely, when these chit funds were not operating or functioning well, more people were interested in joining the savings schemes of NGOs. Rather than mutually reinforcing one another, the activities of the NGOs in Ambedkar Nagar and the initiatives of the community proved mutually exclusive.

This study shows that although private companies, through the development of partnerships and NGOs, can provide certain services, in the end, the government, while not playing an empowering role, remains the most important provider of basic services and social security. The lack of provision of suitable services, employment opportunities, and social security is likely to lead to the development of collective initiatives, even without outside assistance from the private sector or NGOs.

This discussion, resulting from the scheme of actors and agencies as shown in Figure 7.1 leads to several conclusions. First, effective government provision of housing and basic services remains an important channel to carry out relocation in such a way that inhabitants can build up physical and social capital in the new area and obtain higher levels of tenure security than before. Collective action by households is a second important and independent and corollary in effective relocation. It is important in building up financial capital among households, although it tends to exclude the poorest. Local NGOs ignore the collective action undertaken by communities themselves, and remain more accountable to their financiers and their own perspectives than to local inhabitants. Partnerships, either government-private sector or government-NGO, remain fairly marginal. This strengthens the conclusion drawn earlier by Baud (2000) that their prevalence and strength may be much less than is generally suggested by the international agencies.

Matching Suggestions

The question remains as to how matching can be improved. Dia (1996) has suggested that in order to improve the matching between formal and informal institutions, a 'process of reconciliation' has to be taken up. He stated that there is a 'disconnect' between indigenous institutions and formal institutions. According to Dia, both types of institutions have specific drawbacks. The drawbacks of indigenous institutions are that they are inflexible and harbour dysfunctional practises. On the other hand, the strengths of these informal institutions are that they are anchored in local culture and values, and they can count on the sound pillars of legitimacy, accountability, and self-enforcement. They have a strong hold on people's commitment, dedication and sense of identity.[50] The formal institutions' drawbacks are that they are not rooted in local culture and generally fail to command society's loyalty or to trigger local ownership, both of which are important catalysts for sustainability.

In order to improve the matching between these actors, Dia (1996) has identified three requirements for what he calls 'successful implementation of the reconciliation paradigm'. The first is the need for a new, genuinely participatory process that focuses on building convergence between formal and informal institutions and on empowering beneficiaries and local communities. The second requirement is a new communications system that ensures access and voice for a larger number of beneficiaries and stakeholders who are quasi-illiterate. The third requirement is a stable institutional and political environment.[51] Dia (1996) proposed a six-phase plan leading to reconciliation between the informal and formal institutions. It is not applicable in our context because in his study, the formal institutions are 'transplanted' and therefore lack a link with the informal institutions. Given that this is not the case in the present study, a reconciliation process as suggested by Dia is not necessary.

It is clear that all the three major actors in this study have drawbacks, as well as advantages, raising the question as to how far Dia's recommendations are applicable in this context. The major drawbacks of local collective initiatives are that they normally are small and limited to class, kinship and caste (yet they emerge beyond local divisions whenever people identify strong common interests). The impact of local organizations is not always positive; they do not always assist in the reduction of poverty, do not allow the poorest people of the community to join, and they do not always promote the interest of the poorest within the community. Furthermore, they do not make decisions according to consensus. Moreover, the initiators are often the 'stronger' and relatively 'richer' people from the community. In contrast, the specific advantages of local initiatives are that, in addition to trying to achieve improved access to government facilities, they are also centred on building social capital. They are flexible, relatively easy to access, have clear targets, are rooted in local culture, and empower people. Target groups stated that the major drawback of the government and government policies is corruption: in order to get things done, people often have to pay. Service provision and maintenance is poor. It is difficult for the poor to get access to the government, due to the bureaucracy. Another important issue is the lack of information provision, which leaves people depending on those who do have the access, like the slum leaders. People have high expectations of the government as they feel the government should provide them with all the necessities, but they are also cynical regarding its functioning. Furthermore, local perceptions and expectations are not taken into account by the government. Another aspect, which was highlighted by Dia (1996) is that formal institutions are not rooted in local culture. Dia refers to them as 'transplanted institutions'. This situation is more typical of Africa than of India.

The major drawbacks of the NGOs are that their success depends on their local staff and not on their policy, which leads some to do well, others not so well. Overall, NGOs do not take the local perceptions and expectation into account, nor do they link up with local skills and abilities. Furthermore, they are too small, often do not cooperate with each other, and sometimes have preconceived negative ideas about their target group. Also, they fail to transform the local political power structure, but this is perhaps impossible to achieve.

Even though reconciliation in the way Dia suggests is not necessary, empowering the local communities is. An alternative specific to the Indian situation consists of improving or stimulating access. This includes, for instance, the access of local groups to formal institutions like banks. Chit funds can benefit by having access to bank accounts, and then specifically to flexible banks that are situated near their location and do not require elaborate procedures to access them. The same goes for other savings groups and temple festivals. These local initiatives are now very vulnerable and can become less so when they have access to formal institutions.

Dia's second point, namely that of improved communication, is relevant and important. Lack of awareness of government facilities is widespread, which leaves people depending on those who do have the information and the access to the government, namely the local leaders. To increase their independence and their access to government schemes, and so to empower them, communication should be improved. What the best methods might be for the urban Indian context should be studied; possibilities might include using local television channels, radio, local newspapers, cars (or cycles) carrying loudspeakers and driving through the area informing people on new schemes to which they can apply, through local NGOs, by setting up a local offices of the corporation and/or local government from where people are informed about schemes for which they can apply, or through a combination of methods. Furthermore, local community networks should be used to inform target groups.

On the other hand, the community should have easier access to the government. Bureaucratic procedures should be limited, and government schemes or names of schemes should not be changed each time another government comes into power. Target groups should be consulted before starting the design of another government or NGO programme. They should be actively involved in the formulation and implementation of new schemes. The right methods to achieve this should be studied more in detail.

The third point Dia raises, namely the requirement of a stable institutional and political environment is more problematic in the African context; in India it already exists to a large extent.

7.6 Further Research

The conclusions imply that future research should focus on analysing, in their own right, the activities of each actor involved in relocation. Such discussions should not be limited to the provision of housing and infrastructure, but should include the full gamut of activities that inhabitants undertake, such as employment, savings and credit systems, and so on. There should also be more recognition in such studies of the extent to which tenure security enables inhabitants to build up their physical and social capital in the new location.

It is also useful for our understanding to stimulate comparative case studies on relocation initiatives, in order to find out under what conditions NGOs can be more effective in supporting collective initiatives instead of ignoring them, and under what conditions local communities are interested in receiving support from them in order to build up their various types of assets.

Finally, research needs to focus more on the politics in the localities concerned. The undermining effects of political 'brokers' and criminal activities have not yet been fully analysed.

An interesting focus for further research could also be on the role of NGOs. Where and how do they act to stimulate collective initiatives? In which areas could they play a role of importance? Under what circumstances can one expect the local community to issue a real demand for support from them?

NOTES

1. Amongst others: Mitlin, 2001; Desai, 1995; Eckstein, 1990; Baud, 2000; World Bank, 2000.
2. Narayan et al., 1999: 220; Kumar et al., 1999: 38-9.
3. Kumar et al., 1999: 38-9.
4. Narayan et al., 2000: 282.
5. Moore, 1998; <www.worldbank.org/poverty/voice/listen-findings.h> [accessed in December 2001].
6. <www.worldbank.org/poverty/voice/listen-findings.h> [accessed in December 2001].
7. Overlaps with appropriateness in research question four.
8. Mengers, 1997: 12.
9. Berner, 2001: 3-5.
10. Pugh, 1997: 91-2.
11. Steinberg, 1996: xxix.
12. Pugh, 1997: 98.
13. UNCHS, 1991, as quoted by Cernea, 1993a: 17-18.
14. UNCHS, 1991: 44.
15. Hundsalz, 1994: 11; Davidson et al., 1993: 2.
16. Baken, 2000: 86.
17. Sundaram, 1993: 52.
18. Fernandes and Chatterji, 1995: 29-40.
19. CMWSSB, 1998: 13.
20. As put together by the author from: Cernea, 1993a: 22-4; 1997: 1575; 2000: 3363-7; Mertens, 1996: 89; Mathur, 1998; UNCHS, 1991: 40 and; Mahapatra and Mahapatra, 2000: 437.
21. Although the study includes only 19 respondents and is therefore not very representative, it may indicate a trend at some level.

22. Pugh, 1997: 91-2.
23. Steinberg, 1996: xxix.
24. Bennett et al., 1999: 3-4.
25. Kundu, 1996b: 220.
26. Kundu, 1996a: 199.
27. Mehta, 1999: 199-202.
28. Kundu, 1993: 163.
29. Vaidyanathan, 1995: 339.
30. Devas et al., 2001; Mitlin, 2001.
31. Desai, 1999: 248-57.
32. These concepts are defined as follows: *Accountability*: refers to holding the bearers of public office (and NGOs and local initiatives) responsible for their performance and the results of their decisions. The criteria set for determining whether an initiative of collective action or a government or NGO programme is accountable are: whether the target groups are informed and consulted, for instance, by the organization of meetings; the level of inclusiveness (meaning: for whom, leaders or the whole community); whether there actually was a choice to be made by the target group. *Effectiveness* of the activities: whether they produced a decided, decisive, or desired effect, from the perspective of the provider/initiator. *Appropriateness*: indicates the priority given to the activity by the target group itself.
33. Put, 1998: 372.
34. <www.worldbank.org/poverty/voice/listen-findings.h> [accessed in December 2001].
35. Verhagen, 1987: 22.
36. Leach et al., 1997b: 91.
37. If you don't set your targets too high, and don't integrate the opinion of the target group, the effectiveness is always very high.
38. Kundu, 1993: 163.
39. Put, 1998: 372.
40. Narayan et al., 2000: 282.
41. <www.worldbank.org/poverty/voice/listen-findings.h> [accessed in December 2001].
42. Mehta, 1999: 199-202.
43. Narayan et al., 1999: 220; Kumar et al., 1999: 38-9.
44. Baud, 2000: 10.
45. Leach et al., 1997b: 91.
46. Devas et al., 2001: 30.
47. Derived from Arnstein, 1969.
48. Helmsing, 1999, as quoted by Wils and Helmsing, 2001: 8.
49. Choguill, 1996; Arnstein, 1969.
50. Dia, 1996: 1.
51. Dia, 1996: 241.

APPENDIX I

Type of Job of Head of Household, and Second Earner

Type of Job hh	*Abs. Number*	*Rs*	*Type of Job se*	*Abs. Number*	*Rs*
MALES			MALES		
Daily wages:		A day:	Daily wages:		A day:
Coolie	31	72	Mechanic	3	90
Travels	4	50	Construction labourer	5	100
Construction labourer	21	90	Wastepicker	1	70
Carpenter	5	85	Electrician	1	70
Wood cutter	1	50	Petrol bunk	3	65
Painter	10	100	Coolie	1	80
Plumber	3	80	Baker	1	100
Welder	1	70	Driver	1	100
Shop/street seller	6	85	Auto driver	1	80
Biscuits seller	1	100	*Idli* business	1	50
Idli business	2	50	Plumber	1	80
Auto driver	10	100	Private business	1	150
Driver	4	70	Fishcart puller	1	60
Fishcart puller	1	75	Shoemaker	1	40
Cycle rikshaw driver	9	60	Tender coconut business	1	100
Private business	10	100	Tailor	2	60
Hotel	2	60	Ironing	1	60
Tailor	2	85			
Sweeper	1	50			
Wastepicker	2	80			
Shoemaker	1	70			
Mechanic	2	85			
Iron merchant	1	100			
Electrician	1	100			
Gardener	2	60			

Ironer	1	80			
Book binder	1	100			
Fisherman	1	60			
Monthly wages:		A month:	Monthly wages:		A month:
Government job	3	2,300	TV repair	1	600
Officer assistant	1	3,000	Private business	1	1,200
Milkman	1	1,000	Fishnet repairer	1	2,000
Marker	1	3,000	Dancer	1	5,000
Watchman	6	1,250	Watchman	1	200
Old age pension	1	150	Driver	2	1,350
No answer	2				
Unemployed	1				

Type of job hh1	*Abs. number*	*Rs*	*Type of job se*	*Abs. number*	*Rs*
FEMALES			FEMALES		
Daily wages:		A day:	Daily wages:		A day:
Idli business	3	50	Selling clothes	1	70
			Sweeper	1	70
			Construction labourer	2	70
			Private business	2	55
			Idli business	2	60
			Wastepicker	1	60
			Vendor of dry fish	1	45
Monthly wages:		A month:	Monthly wages:		A month:
Housemaid	2	300	Sweeper	1	500
Sweeper	1	1,000	Private business	1	800
			Housemaid	6	450
			Cook	3	500
			Chit fund organizer	2	100-1,000
			Export garments	1	1,000
			Old age pension	1	150
Total	158			58	

Note: * Shops/street vendor: vegetable/fruit vendor, teashop, pan-shop, meat-shop, tender coconut business, petty-shop.

APPENDIX II

Mariatta

A book on a scheduled caste woman called Viramma and who lives in a village near Pondicherry, Viramma tells the story of Mariamatta: 'Mariyamman came to earth one day when her husband Isvaran was furious and drove her out, covering her with twenty-one types of spots. He cursed her and said, "peuh! You're not worthy of my household! Get out of here! Sow the spots all around you and live on what people will give you to be cured!" Poor people like us saw this woman arriving all naked and covered in spots, and wondered who she was. Some launderers at the washhouse quickly soaked a white cloth in turmeric water and gave it to her to cover herself and treat her spots. Then she saw some cobblers. They prostrated themselves at her feet and gave her a pair of sandals so she could go round the world without hurting her feet. A bit further on, people from our caste [scheduled caste] were harvesting rice. They quickly picked a few ears, made flour out of them, offered it to the mother in an unpolluted coconut shell, and gave her *kuj* to drink. The mother carried on her way, granting good favour to everyone who offered her underskirts, saris, *kuj* and balls of flour. Afterwards, temples were built everywhere to honour her and that's why, when you have Mariatta, you go and get *gruel* from the launderer, and cooked rice from the cobbler.'*

*Viramma and Racine, 1997: 105-6.

Bibliography

Adams, W.M. (1992), 'Sustainable Development: A Solution to the Development Puzzle? Lecture held at the InDRA lecture series 1992/3, in *The Local and the Global: People's Participation in Development*, pp. 280-7. InDRA Reader Development Studies 1993/4.

Agarwal, A.N. and S. Narain (1997), *Dying Wisdom: Rise, Fall and Potential of India's Traditional Water Harvesting Systems*, New Delhi: Centre for Science and Environment.

Agrawal, A. (1993), 'Removing Ropes, Attaching Strings: Institutional Arrangements to Provide Water' [online], *IK Monitor* 1, 3. Available from: <http://www.nuffic.nl/ciran/ikdm/1-3/articles/agrawal.html> [accessed on 11 November 1999].

Aldrich, B.C. and R.S. Sandhu (1995), 'The Global Context of Housing Poverty', in: B.C. Aldrich and R.S. Sandhu, eds. *Housing the Urban Poor, Policy and Practise in Developing Countries*, pp. 17-33, New Delhi: Vistaar Publications.

Ali, S. (1990), *Slums Within Slums: A Study of Resettlement Colonies in Delhi*, New Delhi: Vikas Publishing House.

Arnstein, S.R. (1969), 'A Ladder of Citizen Participation', *Journal of the American Institute of Planners*, 35, 4: 216-24.

Arunachalam, M. (1980), *Festivals of Tamil Nadu: Peeps into Tamil Culture 3*, Tiruchitrambalam, Tanjavur District: Gandhi Vidyalayam.

Asian Development Bank (2001), *Handbook on Poverty and Social Analysis: A Working Document* [online]. Available from: <http:/// www.adb.org/Documents/Handbook/Poverty_social/default.a> [accessed in September 2001].

Asif, M. (2000), 'Why Displaced Persons Reject Project Resettlement Colonies', *Economic and Political Weekly*, XXXV, 24: 2005-8.

Auclair, C. (1998), *Ville à vendre: voie libérale et privatisation du secteur de l'habitat à Chennai (Inde)*, Pondichéry: Institut Français de Pondichéry.

Aziz, A. (1994), *Poverty Alleviation in India (Policies and Programmes)*, New Delhi: Ashish Publishing House.

Baken, R.J. (1990), 'The High Price of Cheap Plots: The Rising Threshold to Consolidation of Low Income Households in Karachi (1974-88)', *Urban Research Working Papers* 25, Amsterdam: Vrije Universiteit.

Baken, R.J. and U. Rao (1995), 'The Bhaskara Rao Peta Connection', *Urban Research Working Papers* 38, Amsterdam: Vrije Universiteit.

Baken, R.J. (2000), 'Plotting, Squatting, Public Purpose and Politics, Land Market Development, Low-income Housing and Public Intervention in Vijayawada and Visakhapatnam, India (1900-1993)', (Ph.D. thesis, Free University).

Banck, G. (1986), 'Poverty, Politics and the Shaping of Urban Space: A Brazilian Example, *International Journal of Urban and Regional Research,* 10, 4: 522-44.

Barrow, C. J. (1995), 'Sustainable Development, Concept, Value and Practise', *Third World Planning Review*, 17, 4: 369-86.

Batley, R. (1996), 'Public-Private Relationships and Performance in Service Provision', *Urban Studies*, 33, 4-5: 723-51.

Baud, I. (1989), 'Forms of Production and Women's Labour: Gender Aspects of Industrialization in India and Mexico' (Ph.D. Thesis, Technical University Eindhoven), Den Haag: Koninklijke Bibliotheek.

Baud, I., H. Schenk and M. Huysman (1994), *Final Report, New Approaches to Urban Solid Waste Management: Linkages between Formal and Informal Systems of Source Separation, Collection and Recycling in Indian Cities*, Amsterdam: University of Amsterdam.

Baud, I. and H. Schenk, eds. (1994), *Solid Waste Management: Modes, Assessments, Appraisals and Linkages in Bangalore*, New Delhi: Manohar.

Baud, I. (2000), *Collective Action, Enablement and Partnerships: Issues in Urban Development,* Inaugural Speech, Free University, Amsterdam.

Baud, I. and M. Hordijk (2000), 'City Hinterland: Reducing Environmental Impacts, Improving Sustainability in Cities and Hinterland, and Their Implications for Research', Paper Presented at Seminar on City-Hinterland Relationships, Utrecht, 28 January.

Baud, I., Grafakos, M. Hordijk and J. Post (2001), 'Quality of Life and Alliances in Solid Waste Management, Contributions to Urban Sustainable Development', *Cities*, 18, 1: 3-12.

Baud, I. and J. Post (2001), 'New Partnerships in Urban Solid Waste Management and Their Contribution to Sustainable Development: Experiences in Accra (Ghana) and Chennai (India)', in I. Baud, eds. *Re-aligning Government, Civil Society and the Market: Essays in Honour of G.A. de Bruijne*, AGIDS, University of Amsterdam, pp. 131-50.

Beall, J. and N. Kanji (1999), 'Households, Livelihoods and Urban Poverty', *Urban Governance, Partnership and Poverty Theme Paper 3*, London: Department of Social Policy and Administration, London School of Economics.

Beck, B.E.F. (1972), *Peasant Society in Konku: A Study of Right and Left Subcastes in South India*, Vancouver: University of British Colombia Press.

Behura, N.K. and P.K. Nayak (1993), 'Involuntary Displacement and the

Changing Frontiers of Kinship: A Study of Resettlement in Orissa', in M.M. Cernea and S.E. Guggenheim, eds. *Anthropological Approaches to Resettlement: Policy, Practice and Theory*, Boulder: Westview Press, pp. 283-305.

Behura, N.K. (1996), 'Environment, Displacement and Development: Case Study from Orissa', *Journal of the Indian Anthropological Society*, 31, 2: 149-59.

Bennett, E., P. Grohmann and B. Gentry (1999), 'Public-private Partnerships for the Urban Environment, Options and Issues,' *PPPUE Working Paper Series*, volume I, New York: UNDP and Yale University.

Berner, E. (2001), 'In the Absence of Practice: Three Decades of 'Enabling' Housing Policies', Paper presented at a SG3 seminar at the Institute of Social Studies, The Hague.

Besselink, S. (1997), 'Relocation, Suitable or Not? A Case Study of Gender-sensitivity in an EWS Scheme in Madras, India', Master's thesis, Faculty of Cultural Anthropology/Sociology of Non-Western Societies, Free University, Amsterdam.

Béteille, A. (1992), *The Backward Classes in Contemporary India*, New Delhi: Oxford University Press.

Bijl, J. et al. (1992), *Slum Eviction and Relocation in Bangkok: A Study Concerning the Eviction and Relocation of Slums, Resulting in Recommendations for Improvement of Slum Resettlement*, Delft: Center for International Cooperation and Appropriate Technology (CICAT).

Bijlani, H.U. (1998), 'Safe Water and Sanitation—The Future Outlook and Action', *Nagarlok*, XXX, 4: 68-82.

Blair, H. (2000), 'Participation and Accountability at the Periphery: Democratic Local Governance in Six Countries', *World Development*, 28, 1: 21-39.

Blunt, P. and D.M. Warren, eds. (1996), *Indigenous Organizations and Development*, London: Intermediate Technology Publications.

Brock, K. (1999), *It's Not Only Wealth That Matters, It's Peace of Mind Too: A Review of Participatory Work on Poverty and Illbeing*, Brighton: Institute of Development Studies.

Bruin, H.M. de (1996), 'Leprosy in South India: Stigma and Strategies of Coping', *Pondy Papers in Social Sciences*, no. 22, Pondichéry: Institut Français de Pondichéry.

Bunch, M. (1994), 'The Physical Ecology of Slums in Madras, India, 1986', Master of Arts thesis, Waterloo: Department of Geography, Faculty of Environmental Studies, University of Waterloo.

Bunch, M.J. (1996), 'The Physical Ecology of Slums in Madras: A GIS Analysis of the 1986 Survey of Slums', *The Indian Geographical Journal*, 71, 1: 12-32.

Burgwal, G. (1995), 'Struggle of the Poor: Neighborhood Organization and

Clientelist Practice in a Quito Squatter Settlement' (Ph.D. thesis, University of Amsterdam), Den Haag: Koninklijke Bibliotheek.

Castells, M. (1983), *The City and the Grassroots*, London: Edward Arnold Publishers Ltd.

—— (1997), *The Power of Identity, The Information Age: Economy, Society and Culture, Volume II*, Oxford: Blackwell Publishers Ltd.

Census of India (1991), *Tamil Nadu, part VII. Tables on Houses and Household Amenities*, Directorate of Census Operations, Tamil Nadu, in *Census of India*, series 23.

—— (1991), Paper 2 of 1993. Housing and Amenities: A Brief Analysis of the Housing Tables of 1991, in *Census of India*, series 1.

Cernea, M.M. and S.E. Guggenheim, eds. (1993), *Anthropological Approaches to Resettlement: Policy, Practise and Theory*, Boulder, Colorado: Westview Press.

Cernea, M.M. (1993a), 'The Urban Environment and Population Relocation,' in F. Davidson et al., eds. *Urban Relocation Policy and Practice: Proceedings of an Expert Meeting on Urban Relocation Held at IHS, Rotterdam, The Netherlands*, pp. 13-30. Rotterdam: Institute of Housing and Urban Development Studies.

—— (1993b), 'The Urban Environment and Population Relocation', *World Bank Discussion Papers*, no. 152.

—— (1997), 'The Risks and Reconstruction Model for Resettling Displaced Populations', in *World Development*, 25, 10: 1569-87.

—— (2000), 'Risks, Safeguards and Reconstruction: A Model for Population Displacement and Resettlement', *Economic and Political Weekly*, XXXV, 41: 3659-78.

Chambers, R. (1992), 'Rural Appraisal: Rapid, Relaxed and Participatory', *Discussion Paper*, no. 311, Brighton: Institute of Development Studies.

—— (1995a), 'Poverty and Livelihoods: Whose Reality Counts?' An Overview Paper Prepared for the Stockholm Roundtable on Global Change', 22–4 July 1994 and subsequently published, in *Environment and Urbanization*, 7, 1: 173-204.

—— (1995b), 'Poverty and Livelihoods: Whose Reality Counts?', *Discussion Paper*, no. 347, Brighton: Institute of Development Studies.

—— (1998), 'Foreword', in J. Holland and J. Blackburn, eds. *Whose Voice? Participatory Research and Policy Change*, pp. xv-xviii, London: Intermediate Technology.

—— (1998), 'General introduction', in J. Holland and J. Blackburn, eds., *Whose Voice?' Participatory Research and Policy Change*, London: Intermediate Technology, pp. 1-6.

Chaplin, S.E. (1999), 'Cities, Sewers and Poverty: India's Politics of Sanitation', *Environment and Urbanization*, 11, 1: 145-58.

Chathukulam, J. and V.K. Kurien (1995), 'Jawahar Rozgar Yojana: An Assessment?' *Economic and Political Weekly*, XXX, 6: 343-4.

Chennai Metropolitan Water Supply and Sewerage Board (1998), *Third Chennai Urban Water Supply and Sanitation Project: Resettlement Action Plan*, Chennai: CMWSSB.

Choguill, C.L. (1995), 'The Future of Planned Urban Development: New Directions', in B.S. Aldrich and R.S. Sandhu, eds., *Housing the Urban Poor, Policy and Practice in Developing Countries*, New Delhi: Vistaar Publications, pp. 404-17.

Choguill, M.B.G. (1996), 'A Ladder of Community Participation for Underdeveloped Countries, *Habitat International*, 20, 3: 431-44.

Clark, J. (1991), *Democratizing Development: The Role of Voluntary Agencies*, London: Earthscan Publications.

Coleman, J.S. (1990), *Foundations of Social Theory*, Cambridge: Belknap Press of Harvard University.

Crook, R. and J. Manor (1998), *Democracy and Decentralisation in South Asia and West Africa: Participation, Accountability and Performance*, Cambridge: Cambridge University Press.

Datta, A. and B. Chakravarty (1981), *Organizing Metropolitan Development*, New Delhi: Institute of Public Administration.

Datta, A. (1999), 'Institutional Aspects of Urban Governance', in O.P. Mathur, ed. *India: The Challenge of Urban Governance*, New Delhi: National Institute of Public Finance and Policy, pp. 87-106.

Dattatri, G. (1991), *Sustainable Cities Programme: City-Level Project: Madras*, Project Formulation Framework, 1st draft, UNCHS: Madras.

Dattatri, T.G. (s.a.), *Rehabilitation of Pavement Dwellers: The Velachery Experience*, Madras. TNSCB and Economist Group.

Davidson, F. and M. Peltenburg (1993), *Governments and NGOs/CBOs Working Together for Better Cities*, Rotterdam: IHS.

Davidson, F. (1993), *Urban Relocation Policy and Practice: Proceedings of an Expert Meeting on Urban Relocation Held at IHS, Rotterdam, The Netherlands*, Rotterdam: IHS.

De, Anuradha, et al. (1999), *Public Report on Basic Education in India*, New Delhi: Oxford University Press.

Deliége, R. (1997), 'At the Threshold of Untouchability: Pallars and Valaiyars in a Tamil Nadu Village', in C.J. Fuller, ed., *Caste Today*, New Delhi: Oxford University Press, pp. 65-93.

Della Porte, D. and M. Diani (1999), *Social Movements: An Introduction*, Oxford: Blackwell Publishers.

Desai, V. (1995), *Community Participation and Slum Housing: A Study of Bombay*, New Delhi: Sage Publications.

Desai, V. (1999), 'Anatomy of the Bombay NGO Sector', *Environment and Urbanization*, 11, 1: 247-65.

DeSouza A., ed. (1978), *The Indian City: Poverty, Ecology and Urban Development*, New Delhi: Manohar.

Devas, N. (1999), 'Who Runs Cities? The Relationship Between Urban

Governance, Service Delivery and Poverty', *Urban Governance, Partnership and Poverty Theme Paper 4*. Birmingham: International Development Department, School of Public Policy, University of Birmingham.

Devas, N. et al. (2001), 'Urban Governance and Poverty: Lessons from Ten Cities in the South', *Urban Governance, Partnerships and Poverty Research Working Papers*, DFID and University of Birmingham.

Dewit, M. and H. Schenk, eds. (1989), *Issues of Low Cost Housing*, New Delhi: Manohar.

DFID (1997), *Participatory Impact Assessment: Calcutta Slum Improvement Project Main Findings Report*, London: Department for International Development.

Dhanalaksmi, R. and S. Iyer (1999), *Solid Waste Management in Madras City—1994*, Chennai: Pudhuvazhvup Pathippagam.

Dia, M. (1996), *Africa's Management in the 1990s and Beyond: Reconciling Indigenous and Transplanted Institutions,* Washington DC: The World Bank.

Dietz, T. (1996), *Entitlements to Natural Resources: Contours of Political Environmental Geography*, Inaugural speech, University of Amsterdam, Utrecht: International Books.

Dillinger, W. (1994), *Decentralization and its Implications for Urban Service Delivery,* UNDP/UNCHS/World Bank: Urban Management Programme.

Directorate-General for International Cooperation of the Netherlands Ministry of Foreign Affairs (1992), *Policy plan for 1992-1995, India.*

Doss, A.A.R. (2001), 'Sustainable City Programme—Chennai', in UNCHS (Habitat) and Government of India, *Good Urban Governance Campaign: India Launch, Learning from One Another*, pp. 183-9, New Delhi: Human Settlement Management Institute.

Douglass, M. (1992), 'The Political Economy of Urban Poverty and Environmental Management in Asia: Access, Empowerment and Community Based Alternatives', *Environment and Urbanization*, 4, 2: 9-32.

——(1998), 'World City Formation on the Pacific Rim: Forms of Civil Society and Environmental Management', in M. Douglass and J. Friedman, eds. *Cities for Citizens: Planning and the Rise of Civil Society in a Global Age*, New York: Wiley and Sons, pp. 107-36.

Douglass, M. and M. Zoghlin (1994), 'Sustaining Cities at the Grassroots, Livelihood, Environment and Social Networks in Suan Phlu, Bangkok: *Third World Planning Review*, 16, 2: 172-200.

Dutta, B. and B. Ramaswamy (2001), 'Targeting and Efficiency in the Public Distribution System: Case of Andhra Pradesh and Maharashtra', *Economic and Political Weekly*, XXXVI, 18: 1524-32.

Eckstein, S. (1990), 'Poor People vs. the State and Capital: Anatomy of a

Successfull Community Mobilization for Housing in Mexico City', *International Journal of Urban and Regional Research*, 12, 2: 274-96.

Edwards, M. and D. Hulme, eds. (1992), *Making a Difference: NGOs and Development in a Changing World*, London: Earthscan Publications.

Eerd, M. van. (1995), 'Gender Related Labour Market Fragmentation in the Informal Recycling Sector: A Study in Bangalore, India', Master's thesis (unpublished), University of Amsterdam.

—— (1996), 'The Occupational Health Aspects of Waste Collection and Recycling: A Survey of the Literature', *UWEP Working Document* 4, part I, Gouda:WASTE.

—— (1997), 'The Occupational Health Aspects of Waste Collection and Recycling: An Inventory Study in India', *UWEP Working Document* 4, part II, Gouda: WASTE.

Ekens, P. (1992), *A New World Order: Grassroots Movements for Global Change*, London: Routledge.

Epstein, S., T.A.P. Suryanarayana and T. Thimmegowda (1998), *Village Voices: Forty Years of Rural Transformation in South India*, New Delhi: Sage.

Evans, P. (2000), 'Ecologies of Local Political Actors and the Struggle for Livability in Third World Countries', Paper presented for the International Conference on Democratic Decentralisation, Kerala State Planning Board, Thiruvananthapuram, May.

Fernandes, W., J.C. Das and S. Rao (1989), 'Displacement and Rehabilitation: An Estimate of Extent and Prospects', in W. Fernandes and E.G. Thukral, eds., *Development, Displacement and Rehabilitation*, New Delhi: Indian Social Institute.

Fernandes, W. (1991), 'Power and Powerlessness: Development Projects and Displacement of Tribals', *Social Action*, 41, 3: 243-70.

Fernandes, W. and S. Chatterji (1995), 'A Critique of the Draft National Policy', *Lokayan Bulletin*, 11, 5: 9-28.

Fisher, R. and J. Kling, eds. (1993), 'Mobilizing the Community: Local Politics in the Era of the Global City', *Urban Affairs Annual Reviews*, vol. 41, California: Sage.

Fisher, J. (1993), *The Road from Rio: Sustainable Development in the Non-Governmental Movement in the Third World*, Praeger.

Fox, W. (1994), *Strategic Options for Infrastructure Management*, UNDP/UNCHS/World Bank: Urban Management Programme.

Fuller, C.J. (1992), *The Camphor Flame: Popular Hinduism and Society in India*, Princeton: Princeton University Press.

Galjart, B. (2002), *Dreams and the Downtrodden: Essays in Development Sociology*, Leiden: Research School of Asian, African and Amerindian Studies (CNWS).

Galjart, B. and D. Buijs, eds. (1982), *Participation of the Poor in*

Development: Contributions to a Seminar, Leiden Development Studies 2. Leiden: Institute of Cultural and Social Studies, Leiden University.

Gangopadhyay, S., L.R. Jain and A. Dubey (1997), *Poverty Measures and Socio-economic Characteristics*. s.l.: s.n.

GEMS Foundation 1 (s.a.), *Information Bulletin*, Madras: Gems.

GEMS Foundation 2 (s.a.), *Velachery Rehabilitation Project and Role of Non-governmental Organization*, Madras: GEMS.

GEMS Foundation 3 (s.a.), *Velachery Rehabilitation Project and Role of Non-governmental Organization*, A paper presented by Mr. George of GEMS Foundation, Madras: GEMS.

Ghai, D. and J.M. Vivian, eds. (1992), *Grassroots Environmental Action, People's Participation in Sustainable Development*, London: Routledge.

Ghate, P. (1992), *Informal Finance: Some Findings from Asia*, Asian Development Bank: Oxford University Press.

Ghosh, A. (1995), 'Towards People's Initiatives and Grassroots Movements', in N. Candhoke and A. Ghosh, eds., *Grassroots Movements and Social Change*, Grassroots Politics Series 1, Developing Countries Research Centre, University of Delhi: Delhi University Press, pp. 1-17.

Gilbert, A. and J. Gugler (1992), *Cities, Poverty and Development: Urbanization in the Third World*, Oxford: Oxford University Press.

Gnaneshwar, V. (1995), 'Urban Policies in India—Paradoxes and Predicaments', *Habitat International*, 19, 3: 293-316.

Goebel, A. (1998), 'Process, Perception and Power: Notes from Participatory Research in a Zimbabwean Resettlement Area', *Development and Change*, 29: 277-305.

Golandaz, H.M. (1994), 'Urban Poverty Alleviation', *Nagarlok*, XXVI, 2: 29-39.

Gorman, R.F. (1984), *Private Voluntary Organizations as Agents of Development*, Boulder: Westview Press.

Goulet, D. (1995), 'Authentic Development: is it Sustainable?', in C. Thaddues, C. Trzyna and J.K. Osborn, eds., *A Sustainable World, Defining and Measuring Sustainable Development*, London: EarthScan Publications, pp. 44-59.

Gonzales, J., K. Lauder and B. Melles (2000), *Opting for Partnerships: Governance Innovations in South Eastern Asia*, Ottowa: Institute on Governance.

Government of India, Ministry of Urban Development (1992), *Nehru Rozgar Yojana—Main Features and Operational Guidelines*, New Delhi: Government of India.

——, Ministry of Urban Affairs and Employment(a). (s.a.). *Nehru Rozgar Yojana*, New Delhi: Government of India.

——, Ministry of Urban Affairs and Employment(b). (s.a.). *Swarna Jayanti Shahari Rojgar Yojana (SJSRY) Guidelines*, New Delhi: Government of India.

——, Planning Commission (1993), *Report of Expert Group of Estimation of Proportion and Number of Poor,* New Delhi: Government of India.

Government of Tamil Nadu, Evaluation and Applied Research Department (1995-6), *An Economic Appraisal 1995-96*, Madras: Government of Tamil Nadu.

——, Municipal Administration and Water Supply Department (1999-2000), *Policy Note on Corporation, Municipalities and Town Panchayats, Demand no. 49,* Chennai: Government of Tamil Nadu.

——, Housing and Urban Development Department (1995), *Note on Policy 1995-96, Demand no. 33, Urban Development Policy Note,* Madras: Government of Tamil Nadu.

——, Social Welfare and Nutritious Meal Programme Department (1998), *Demand no. 29, Social Welfare Policy Note 1998-99*, Chennai: Government of Tamil Nadu.

——, Social Welfare and Nutritious Meal Programme Department (1999a), *Citizen's Charter*, Chennai: Government of Tamil Nadu.

——, Social Welfare and Nutritious Meal Programme Department (1999b), *Demand no. 29, Social Welfare Policy Note 1999-2000,* Chennai: Government of Tamil Nadu.

——, Housing and Urban Development Department (1999c), *Demand no. 32, Housing, Note on Policy 1999-2000,* Chennai: Government of Tamil Nadu.

——, Municipal Administration and Water Supply Department (1999d), *Demand no. 49, Performance Budget 1998-1999*, Chennai: Government of Tamil Nadu.

Guhan, S. (1991), 'Reservations: The Tamilnadu Experience', *Manushi*, 63-64: 46-53.

Gupta, D.B. (1985), *Urban Housing in India,* World Bank Staff Working Papers number 730, Washington DC: The World Bank.

Haan, A. de. (1997), 'Rural-urban Migration and Poverty', *IDS Bulletin,* 28, 2: 35-47.

Haan, L. de. (2000), *Livelihood, Locality and Globalisation*, Inaugural Speech, Catholic University Nijmegen.

Haan, L. de. and P. Quarles van Ufford (2001), 'The Role of Livelihood: Social Capital, and Market Organization in Shaping Rural-urban Interactions', in I. Baud, et al. (eds.), *Re-aligning Government, Civil Society and the Market: Essays in Honour of G.A. de Bruijne*, AGIDS, University of Amsterdam, pp. 283-309.

Hardoy, J.E. and D. Satterthwaite (1989), *Squatter Citizen: Life in the Urban Third World*, London: Earthscan Publications.

Hardoy, J.E., D. Mitlin and D. Satterthwaite (1992), *Environmental Problems in Third World Cities,* London: Earthscan Publications.

Harriss, B. (1991), *Child Nutrition and Poverty in South India, Noon Meals in Tamil Nadu*, New Delhi: Concept Publishing Company.

Helmsing, A.H.J. (1999), *Community Perspectives on Government Enablement of Markets*, The Hague: ISS/Habitat.

Hof, R van der and F. Steinberg, eds. (1992), *Innovative Approaches to Urban Development,* Avebury: Aldershot.

Holland, J. and J. Blackburn, eds. (1998), *Whose Voice? Participatory Research and Policy Change*, London: Intermediate Technology.

Hordijk, M. (1999), 'A Dream of Green and Water: Community Based Formulation of a Local Agenda 21 in Peri-urban Lima,' *Environment and Urbanization,* 11, 2: 11-29.

—— (2000), 'Of Dreams and Deeds: the Role of Local Initiatives for Community Based Environmental Management in Lima, Peru' (Ph.D. thesis, University of Amsterdam), Amsterdam: Thela Thesis.

—— (2001), 'Combining Capitals: the Assets of Community Based Organizations and Local Government for Neighborhood Environmental Management in Lima', in I. Baud et al., eds., *Re-aligning Government, Civil Society and the Market: Essays in Honour of G.A. de Bruijne*, AGIDS, University of Amsterdam, pp. 109-31.

Hundsalz, M. (1993), 'Urban Relocation and the Global Shelter Strategy', in F. Davidson et al., *Urban Relocation Policy and Practice: Proceedings of an Expert Meeting on Urban Relocation held at IHS, Rotterdam, The Netherlands*, Rotterdam: Institute of Housing and Urban Development Studies, pp. 9-12.

Huysman, M. and J.S. Velu (1994), 'Solid Waste Management by the Bangalore Municipal Corporation', in I. Baud and H. Schenk, eds., *Solid Waste Management: Modes, Assessments, Appraisals and Linkages in Bangalore*, New Delhi: Manohar, pp. 24-45.

Huysman, M. (1994), 'The Position of Waste Pickers in Solid Waste Management in Bangalore', in I. Baud and H. Schenk, eds., *Solid waste Management: Modes, Assessments, Appraisals and Linkages in Bangalore*, New Delhi: Manohar, pp. 24-46.

Hyden, G. (1998), 'Building Civil Society at the Turn of the Millennium', in J. Burbidge, ed., *Beyond Prince and Merchant: Citizen Participation and the Rise of Civil Society*, New York: Pact Publications, pp. 17-46.

Indigenous Knowledge and Development Monitor (1998), 6, 2.

Jayal, N.G. (2001), 'Democracy and Social Capital in Central Himalaya: Tale of Two Villages', *Economic and Political Weekly*, XXXVI, 8: 655-64.

Jenkins, P. (2001), 'Relationships Between the State and Civil Society and their Importance for Sustainable Development', in M. Carley, P. Jenkins and H. Smith, eds., *Urban Development and Civil Society,* London: Earthscan Publications, pp. 178-91.

Jenkins, P. and H. Smith (2001), 'The State, the Market and Community: an Analytical Framework for Community Self-development', in M. Carley, P. Jenkins and H. Smith, eds., *Urban Development and Civil Society,* London: Earthscan Publications, pp. 16-30.

Johnson, S.M. and P. Hanumantha Rayappa (1994), 'Tamil Nadu Integrated Nutrition Project: an Appraisal', in Abdul Aziz, ed. *Poverty Alleviation in India (Policies and Programmes)*, New Delhi: Ashish Publishing House, pp. 57-90.

Johnson, S. and B. Rogaly (1997), *Micro-finance and Poverty Reduction*, London: Oxfam and ActionAid.

Kabra, K.N. and A.C. Ittyerah (1986), *The Public Distribution System: A Report on Target Group Orientation and the Viability of Retail Outlets*, New Delhi: Indian Insitute of Public Administration.

Kampen, M.H.A. (2000), 'Access to Development: A Study of Anti-poverty Policy and Popular Participation in Two Squatter Settlements in Pune, India', (Ph.D. thesis, Catholic University Nijmegen), Nijmegen Studies in Development and Cultural Change 30, Saarbrücken: Verlag.

Khan, A. (1995), 'Planning and Development: Policy Issues of Large Scale Resettlement Programme: A Case of Delhi Resettlement Colonies', *Nagarlok*, XXVII, 3: 60-79.

Korten, D.C. (1990), *Getting into the 21st Century: Voluntary Action and the Global Agenda*, West Hartford: Kumarian Press.

—— (1991), 'The Role of Non-governmental Organizations in Development: Changing Patterns and Perspectives', in S. Paul and A. Israel, eds., *Non-governmental Organizations and the World Bank: Cooperation for Development*, Washington DC: The World Bank, pp. 20-44.

Kothari, S. (1995a), 'Whose Nation is it? The Displaced as Victims of Development', *Lokayan Bulletin*, 11, 5: 1-8.

—— (1995b), 'Developmental Displacement and Official Policies: A Critical Review', *Lokayan Bulletin*, 11, 5: 9-28.

Kromhout, M.Y. (2000), 'Gedeelde Smart is Halve Smart: Hoe Vrouwen in Paramaribo Hun Bestaan Organiseren', (Ph.D. Thesis, University of Amsterdam), Amsterdam: Thela Thesis.

Kruse, B. (1997), 'Employment Generating Programmes in the Urban Context of India: The Nehru Rozgar Yojana', *IDS Bulletin*, 28, 2: 86-93.

Kumar, N.A. (1997), 'Nehru Rozgar Yojana: Some Observations', *Nagarlok*, XXIX, 2: 14-30.

Kumar, S. and PRAXIS Study Team (1999), *Consultations with the Poor: India 1999*, Patna, India: PRAXIS, Institute for Participatory Practises.

Kundu, A. (1993), *In the Name of the Urban Poor: Access to Basic Amenities*, New Delhi: Sage.

—— (1996a), 'Access of Urban Poor to Basic Services—the Changing Policy Perspective', in K. Singh and F. Steinberg, eds., *Urban India in Crisis*, New Delhi: New Age International, pp. 191-205.

—— (1996b), 'New Economic Policy and Urban Poverty in India', in C.H. Hanumantha Rao and H. Linnemann, eds., *Economic Reforms and*

Poverty Alleviation in India: Indo-Dutch Series on Development Alternatives no. 17, New Delhi: Sage, pp. 199-228.

Lal, D., R. Mohan and I. Natarajan (2001), 'Economic Reforms and Poverty Alleviation: A Tale of Two Surveys', *Economic and Political Weekly*, XXXVI: 1017-28.

Leach, M., R. Mearns and I. Scoones (1997a), 'Editorial: Community-based Sustainable Development: Consensus or Conflict?' *IDS Bulletin*, 28, 4: 1-3.

—— (1997b), 'Institutions, Consensus and Conflict: Implications for Policy and Practice', *IDS Bulletin*, 28, 4: 90-5.

—— (1997c), 'Challenges to Community-based Sustainable Development: Dynamics, Entitlements, Institutions', *IDS Bulletin*, 28, 4: 4-14.

Lee, Y.S.F. (1994), 'Community-based Urban Environmental Management: Local NGOs as Catalysts', *Regional Development Dialogue*, 15, 2: 158-79.

—— (1997), 'The Privatisation of Solid Waste Infrastructure and Services in Asia', *Third World Planning Review*, 19, 2: 139-62.

—— (1998), 'Intermediary Institutions, Community Organizations and Urban Environmental Management: The Case of Three Bangkok Slums', *World Development*, 26, 6: 993-1011.

Linden, J. van der (1994), 'Editorial, Where Do We Go From Here?' *Third World Planning Review*, 16, 4: 223-9.

—— (1997), 'On Popular Participation in a Culture of Patronage: Patrons and Grassroots Organization in a Sites and Services Project in Hyderabad, Pakistan', *Environment and Urbanization*, 9, 1: 81-90.

Lipton, M. and S. Maxwell (1992), 'The New Poverty Agenda : An Overview', *Discussion Paper 306*, Brighton: Institute of Development Studies.

Mahapatra, L. (1999), 'Testing the Risks and Reconstruction Model on India's Resettlement Experiences', in M. Cernea, ed., *The Economics of Involuntary Resettlement: Questions and Challenges*, Washington DC: The World Bank.

Mahapatra, L.K. and S. Mahapatra (2000), 'Social Re-àrticulation and Community Regeneration among Resettled Displacees', in M.M. Cernea and C. McDowell, eds., *Risks and Reconstruction: Experiences of Resettlers and Refugees*, Washington DC: The World Bank, pp. 431-44.

Mandal Commission (1991), *Report of the Backward Classes Commission, 1980: Reservations for Backward Classes*, Delhi: Akalank Publications.

Mathur, O.P. (1994), 'The State of India's Urban Poverty', *Asian Development Review, Studies of Asian and Pacific Economic Issues*, 12, 1: 32-67.

—— (1999), 'Governing Cities: Facing up to Challenges of Poverty and Globalization', in O.P. Mathur, ed., *India: The Challenge of Urban*

Governance, New Delhi: National Institute of Public Finance and Policy, pp. 3-51.

Matthews, C.M.E. (1979), *Health and Culture in a South Indian Village*, New Delhi: Sterling Publishers.

McLeod, R. (2001), *The Impact of Regulations and Procedures on the Livelihoods and Asset Base of the Urban Poor: A Financial Perspective*, Homeless International.

Mehta, D. and D. Mehta (1992), 'Privatization of Municipal Services', *Urban India*, 12: 1-24.

—— (1996), 'New Economic Policies and Urban Housing', in K. Singh and F. Steinberg, eds., *Urban India in Crisis*, New Delhi: New Age International, pp. 41-8.

Mehta, L. (1997), 'Social Difference and Water Resource Management, Insights from Kutch, India', *IDS Bulletin*, 28, 4: 79-89.

Mehta, M. (1999), 'Participation and Urban Governance', in O.P. Mathur, ed., *India: The Challenge of Urban Governance*, New Delhi: National Institute of Public Finance and policy.

Mengers, H.A. (1997), 'Urban Development in the State Karnataka, India: Policies, Actors and Outcome' (Ph.D. Thesis, Catholic University Nijmegen), Nijmegen Studies in Development and Cultural Change 27, Saarbrücken: Verlag.

Mertens, R. (1996), 'Forced Relocation of Slum Dwellers in Bangalore, India: Slum Dwellers, Landlords and the Government', *Urban Research Working Papers* 41, Amsterdam: Vrije Universiteit.

Mishra, G.K. and R. Gupota (1981), *Resettlement Policies in Delhi*, New Delhi: International Institute for Population Studies.

Mitlin, D. (2001), 'Civil Society and Urban Poverty: Examining Complexity', *Environment and Urbanization*, 13, 2: 151-73.

Moffatt, M. (1979), *An Untouchable Community in South India: Structure and Consensus*, Princeton, New Jersey: Princeton University Press.

Moore, M., M. Choudhary and N. Singh (1998), 'How Can We Know What They Want?' Understanding Local Perceptions of Poverty and Ill-being in Asia, *IDS Working Paper* 80, Brighton: Institute of Development Studies.

Morris, M. (1998), 'Social Capital and Poverty in India', *IDS Working Paper* 61, Brighton: Institute of Development Studies.

Moser, C.O.N. (1993), *Gender Planning and Development: Theory, Practise and Training*, New York: Routledge.

—— (1996), 'Confronting Crisis: A Comparative Study of Household Responses to Poverty and Vulnerability in Four Poor Urban Communities', *Environmentally Sustainable Development Studies and Monographs Series*, no. 8, Washington DC: The World Bank.

——(1998), 'The Asset Vulnerability Framework: Reassessing Urban Poverty Reduction Strategies', *World Development*, 26, 1: 1-19.

Mukhopadhyay, A. (1999), 'Politics and Bureaucracy in Urban Governance: the Indian Experience', in O.P. Mathur, ed., *India: The Challenge of Urban Governance,* New Delhi: National Institute of Public Finance and Policy, pp. 109-28.

Mukhija, V. (2001), 'Institutional Pluralism and Housing Delivery: A Case of Unforeseen Conflicts in Mumbai, India', *World Development*, 29, 12: 2043-57.

Munro, D.A. (1995), 'Sustainability, Rhetoric or Reality?', in C. Thaddues, ed. with the assistance of J.K. Osborn, *A Sustainable World: Defining and Measuring Sustainable Development,* London: Earthscan Publications.

Narayan, D. et al. (1999), *Voices of the Poor: Can Anyone Hear Us?* The World Bank: Oxford University Press.

—— (1999), 'Bonds and Bridges: Social Capital and Poverty', *Policy Research Working Paper*, no. 2167, Washington DC: The World Bank.

Narayan, D. et al. (2000), *Crying out for Change: Voices of the Poor*, Washington DC: The World Bank.

Nas, P.J.M. and P. Silvan, eds. (1999), *Modernization, Leadership and Participation: Theoretical Issues in Development Sociology: Essays in Honour of Benno Galjart,* Leiden: Leiden University Press.

Nath, V. (1991), 'Population Census: Some Facts and Policy Issues-II', *Economic and Political Weekly*, XXVI, 51: 2937-42.

National Institute of Urban Affairs (NIUA) (1994), *Power to the People: The 74th Constitutional Amendment and the Urban Basic Services Programme for the Urban Poor*, New Delhi: NIUA.

Neelakantan, M. (1994), 'Jawahar Rozgar Yojana: An Assessment Through Concurrent Evaluation', *Economic and Political Weekly*, XXIX, 49: 3091-97.

Nelson, N. and S. Wright, eds. (1995), *Power and Participatory Development: Theory and Practise*, London: Intermediate Technology Publications.

Oleson, A.K. (1984), 'A Study of Slums and Slum Improvement in Madras', Master's thesis, Planning Programme Institute of Development and Planning, University of Aalborg, Denmark.

Olson, Jr. M. (1965), *The Logic of Collective Action*, Cambridge: Cambridge University Press.

Ostrom, E. (1990), *Governing the Commons: The Evolution of Institutions for Collective Action*, Cambridge: Cambridge University Press.

—— (1996), 'Crossing the Great Divide: Co-production, Synergy and Development', *World Development*, 24, 2: 1073-87.

Ouden, J.H.D. den. (1975), *De onaanraakbaren van Konkunad* deel 1, Mededelingen Landbouwhogeschool Wageningen 75-11, Dissertatie.

Pai, S. (2001), 'Social Capital, Panchayats and Grassroots Democracy:

Politics of Dalit Assertion in Uttar Pradesh', *Economic and Political Weekly*, XXXVI, 8: 645-54.

Pandey, S.R. (1991), *Community Action for Social Justice: Grassroots Organizations in India*, New Delhi: Sage.

Pargal, S., M. Huq and D. Gilligan (1999), 'Social Capital in Solid Waste Management: Evidence from Dhaka, Bangladesh', *Social Capital Initiative Working Paper*, no. 16, Washington DC: The World Bank.

Parthasarathy, A. (1983), *The Symbolism of Hindu Gods and Rituals*, Bombay: Vedanta Life Institute.

Parikh, K.S., ed. (1997), *India Development Report 1997*, New Delhi: Oxford University Press.

Patel, S., C. d'Cruz and S. Burra (2002), 'Beyond Evictions in a Global City: People-managed Resettlement in Mumbai', *Environment and Urbanization*, 14, 1: 159-72.

Patu, V. (1994), *Celebrations: Festive Days of India*, Bombay: India Book House.

Piwari, P. (2000), 'Housing and Development Objectives in India', *Habitat International*, 25: 229-53.

Planning Commission (1992), *Report of the Working Group on Finance for Housing Sector*, New Delhi: Government of India.

Porio, E. (1997), 'State, Civil Society and Urban Governance in South-East Asia', in E. Porio, ed., *Urban Governance and Poverty Alleviation in Southeast Asia*, Manila: GURI/Department of Sociology and Anthropology, Atenea de Manila University.

Portes, A. (1998), 'Social Capital: Its Origin and Applications in Modern Sociology', *Annual Review of Sociology*, 22: 1-24.

Post, J. (1996), 'Space for Urban Livelihood and Urban Planning: Reflections on Urban Livelihood and Urban Planning in the Sudan' (Ph.D. thesis, University of Amsterdam), Amsterdam: Thesis Publishers.

Post, J. et al. (2001), 'Introduction', in *Re-aligning Government, Civil Society and the Market: Essays in Honour of G.A. de Bruijne*, Amsterdam: AGIDS, University of Amsterdam, pp. 1-22.

Prasad, K.V.E. (1995), 'Social Security for Destitute Widows in Tamil Nadu', *Economic and Political Weekly*, XXX, 15: 794-6.

Praxis (1999), *Consultations With the Poor India 1999*, A Study Commissioned by the World Bank to Inform World Development Report 2000-1.

Pugh, C. (1990), *Housing and Urbanization: A Study in India*, New Delhi: Sage.

——(1997), 'The Changing Roles of Self-help in Housing and Urban Policies, 1950-96', *Third World Planning Review*, 19, 1: 91-109.

Put, M. (1998), 'Innocent Farmers? A Comparative Evaluation into a Government and an NGO Project Located in Semi-arid Andhra

Pradesh (India), Meant to Induce Farmers to Adopt Innovations for Dryland Agriculture' (Ph.D. thesis, University of Amsterdam), Amsterdam: Thela Thesis.

Radhakrishnan, R. (1975), *Chit Funds*, Madras: Institute for Financial Management and Research.

Rajan, S.I. (2001), 'Social Assistance for Poor Elderly: How Effective?', *Economic and Political Weekly*, XXXVI, 8: 613-17.

Rakodi, C. (1993), 'Planning for Whom?', in N. Devas and C. Rakodi, eds., *Managing Fast Growing Cities: New Approaches to Urban Planning and Management in the Developing World*, Harlow: Longman.

—— (1995), 'Poverty Lines or Household Strategies? A Review of Conceptual Issues in the Study of Urban Poverty', *Habitat International*, 19, 4: 407-26.

—— (1999), 'A Capital Assets Framework for Analysing Household Livelihood Strategies: Implications for Policy', *Development Policy Review*, 17, 3: 315-42.

Ramani, R. (1985), 'Slums of Madras', *MIDS Interns Report*, no. 3, Madras: Madras Institute of Development Studies.

Rao, P.S.N. (1990), 'Private Sector Involvement in Water Supply Provision', *Nagarlok*, XXII, 4: 60-7.

Rao, M.N. and C.C. Nelson (1994), 'Housing for Urban Poor: A Case Study of Sites and Services and Slum Improvement Projects in Madras', in A. Aziz, ed., *Poverty Alleviation in India: Policies and Programmes*, New Delhi: Ashish Publishing House, pp. 147-73.

Ravaillon, M. (1992), 'Poverty Comparison: A Guide to Concepts and Methods', *Living Standards Measurement Study Working Paper 88*, Washington DC: World Bank.

Reddy, I.U.B. (1994), 'Poverty Alleviation Programmes: A Case of Self-Employment Programme for Urban Poor in Bombay', *Nagarlok*, XXVI, 2: 40-52.

—— (2000), 'Restoring Housing Under Urban Infrastructure Projects in India', in M.M. Cernea and C. McDowell, eds., *Risks and Re-Construction: Experiences of Resettlers and Refugees*, Washington DC: World Bank, pp. 167-83.

Robertson, C. (1984), *Sharing the Same Bowl: A Socio-economic History of Women and Class in Accra, Ghana*, Bloomington: Indiana University Press.

Roy, A. (1999), *The Greater Common Good*, Bombay: India Book Distributors.

Saberwal, S. (1995), *Wages of Segmentation: Comparative Historical Studies in Europe and India*, New Delhi: Orient Longman.

Samuel, M.J. and P. Hanumantha Rayappa (1994), 'Tamil Nadu Integrated

Nutrition Project: An Appraisal', in A. Aziz, ed., *Poverty Alleviation in India (policies and programmes)*, New Delhi: Ashish Publishing House, pp. 57-90.

Sanyal, B. and V. Mukhija (2001), 'Institutional Pluralism and Housing Delivery: A Case of Unforeseen Conflicts in Mumbai, India', *World Development*, 29, 12, pp. 2043-57.

Saschikonye, L. (1995), 'Democracy, Civil Society and Social Movements: An Analytical Framework', in L. Saschikonye, ed., *Democracy, Civil Society and the State: Social Movements in Southern Africa*, Harare: SAPES Books.

Satterthwaite, D. (1995), 'Viewpoint: The Underestimation of Urban Poverty and of its Health Consequences', *Third World Planning Review*, 17, 4, pp. iii-xii.

——. (1997), 'Urban Poverty: Reconsidering its Scale and Nature', *IDS Bulletin*, 25, 2: 9-23.

Schrijver, J. (1990), 'Changing Things from the Bottom Up: Grassroots Movements', in N. Schrijver and C.P. van den Tempel, eds., *Solidarity Against Poverty: A Socialist Program from Holland*, Amsterdam: Evert Vermeer Stichting, pp. 109-24.

Schenk, H. (1989), *Modernization, Accomodation and Dependency: Reflections on Housing and Planning in Madras,* Amsterdam: University of Amsterdam, werkstukken van het Planologisch en Demografisch Instituut.

Schübeler, P. (1996), *Participation and Partnership in Urban Infrastucture Management,* no. 19, Urban Management Programme, Washington DC: World Bank.

Schuurman, F. and T. van Naerssen, eds. (1989), *Urban Social Movements in the Third World*, London: Routledge.

Schuurman, F.J. (1989), 'Urban Social Movements: Between Regressive Utopia and Socialist Panacea', in F. Schuurman and T. van Naerssen, eds., *Urban Social Movements in the Third World*, London: Routledge, pp. 9-26.

Sen, A.K. (1997), 'Poor, Relatively Speaking', in S. Subramanian, ed., *Measurement of Inequality and Poverty*, New Delhi: Oxford University Press, pp. 159-79.

Shankar, K. (1994), 'Jawahar Rozgar Yojana: An Assessment in UP', *Economic and Political Weekly*, XXIX, 29: 1845-8.

Shivkumar (1979), *Stories from Panchatantra*, New Delhi: Children's Book Trust.

Singh, A.M. and A. de Souza (1980), *The Urban Poor: Slum and Pavement Dwellers in the Major Cities of India*, New Delhi: Manohar.

Singh, B.N. and S. Maitra (2001), 'Formation of ward committee: People's Participation in Urban Governance and Grassroot Level', in UNCHS

(Habitat) and Government of India, *Good Urban Governance Campaign: India Launch: Learning from One Another,* New Delhi: Human Settlement Management Institute, pp. 87-96.

Singh, K. (2001), 'Urban Governance in India', in UNCHS (Habitat) and Government of India, *Good Urban Governance Campaign: India Launch: Learning from One Another*, New Delhi: Human Settlement Management Institute, pp. 37-62.

Sinha, S. (1985), *Slum Eradication and Urban Renewal: Patna*, New Delhi: Inter-India Publications.

Smets, P. (1992), 'My Stomach is My Bishi: Savings and Credit Associations in Sangli, India', *Urban Research Working Papers* 30, Amsterdam: Vrije Universiteit.

—— (1996), 'Informal Housing Finance in Hyderabad, India', *Urban Research Working Papers* 40, Amsterdam: Vrije Universiteit.

—— (2002), 'Housing Finance and the Urban Poor: Building and Financing Low-income Housing in Hyderabad, India,' (Ph.D. thesis, Free University).

Sontheimer, S., eds. (1991), *Women and the Environment: A Reader: Crises and Development in the Third World*, London: Earthscan Publications.

Soto, H. de. (1992), 'Combatting Urban Poverty in Latin America: The Peruvian Case', in Netherlands Ministry of Foreign Affairs, *Urban Poverty Alleviation in Latin America*, The Hague: Development Cooperation Department, Ministry of Urban Affairs, pp. 31-8.

Srilatha, V.L. and P.K. Gopinathan (1996), 'Poverty Eradication: A Mission Not Impossible', in K. Singh and F. Steinberg, eds., *Urban India in Crisis*, New Delhi: New Age International Limited, pp. 207-12.

Srinivas, M.N. (1962), *Caste in Modern India and Other Essays*, Bombay: Media Promoters and Publishers.

State Planning Commission Tamil Nadu (1997), 'Report of the Expert Group on Estimate and Number of Poor', in *Ninth Five Year Plan, Tamil Nadu 1997-2002: An Outline*, Chennai: State Planning Commission.

Steinberg, F. (1996), 'Foreword', in F. Steinberg and K. Singh, eds., *Urban India in Crisis*, New Delhi: New Age International Limited, pp. xxix-lvii.

Subramanian, K.P. (1998), 'Devolution and Democratisation of Urban Management: A Case Study of Tamil Nadu', *Nagarlok*, XXX, 1: 56-64.

Sundaram, P.S.A. (1993), 'Relocation Experience in India', in F. Davidson et al. eds., *Urban Relocation Policy and Practice: Proceedings of an Expert Meeting on Urban Relocation Held at IHS, Rotterdam, The Netherlands*, Rotterdam: Institute of Housing and Urban Development Studies, pp. 51-9.

Sundaram, P.S.A. (1996), 'Evolution of Urban Development and Housing Policies', in Florian Steinberg and Kulwant Singh, eds., *Urban India in Crisis*, New Delhi: New Age International Limited, pp. 21-31.

Sustainable Chennai Project (1997), 'Towards Singara Chennai', *Newsletter of the Sustainable Chennai Project*, 1,1.

Swaminathan, M. (1995), 'Aspects of Urban Poverty in Bombay', *Environment and Urbanization*, 7, 1: 133-43.

Tendler, J. (1997), *Good Government in the Tropics*, Baltimore: John Hopkins University Press.

Thorbek, S. (1991), 'Gender in Two Slums Cultures', *Environment and Urbanization*, 3, 2: 71-81.

—— (1994), *Gender and Slum Culture in Urban Asia*, New Delhi: Vistaar Publications.

TNSCB (1990), *Performance and Prospects*, Madras: TNSCB.

—— (1997a), *Performances and Programmes* (booklet), Chennai: TNSCB.

—— (1997b), *Performances and Programmes* (paper), Chennai: TNSCB.

—— (s.a.), A *Note on Slums Along Water Courses*, Madras: TNSCB.

Todaro, M.P. (1994), *Economic Development*, England: Longman Group Limited.

Toye, J. (1999), Nationalising the Anti-poverty Agenda, *IDS Bulletin*, 30, 2: 6-12.

Triche, T. (1990), 'Private Participation in Water Supply,' *Nagarlok*, XXII, 4: 55-9.

Turner, J.F.C. (1988), 'Issues and conclusions', in B. Turner, ed., *Building Community: A Third World Case Book*, London: Habitat International Coalition.

Turner, J. (1976), *Housing by People*, London: Marion Boyars.

Ullewishewa, R. (1994), 'Women's Indigenous Knowledge of Water Management in Sri Lanka' [online], *IK Monitor*, 2, 3. Available from:<www.nuffic.nl/ciran/ikdm/2-3/articles/ulluwishewa.html> [accessed on 11 November 1999].

UNDP (1996), 'Poor Peoples Perspectives', in *The Report on Human Development in Bangladesh: A Pro-poor Agenda*, Dhaka: UNDP.

—— (1998), *Bangladesh Human Development Report, Monitoring Human Development*, Bangladesh: UNDP.

UNCHS (1991), 'Evaluation of Relocation Experience', Paper Prepared by F. Davidson, M. Peltenburg and M. Zaaier. Rotterdam: Institute of Housing and Urban Development Studies.

—— (1996), *An Urbanizing World: Global Report on Human Settlements*, Oxford University Press for UNCHS (HABITAT).

—— *Urban Statistics Handbook* [online] (2000), Available from: <http://www.niua.org/niuaorg/USH/index.html> [accessed in November 2001].

Vaidya, C. (1994), 'Urban Poor's Willingness to Pay for Water and Sanitation Services: A Case Study', *Nagarlok*, XXVII, 4, 60-71.

Vaidyanathan, A. (1995), 'The Political Economy of the Evolution of Anti-poverty Programmes', in T.V. Sathyamurthy, ed., *Social Change and Political Discourse in India: Structures of Power, Movements of Resistance, vol. 2: Industry and Agriculture in India Since Independence*, Oxford: Oxford University Press, pp. 329-47.

Vera-Sanso, P. (1997), 'Household Composition in Madras: Low-income Settlements', *Review of Development and Change*, 2, 1: 72-98.

Verba, S., N.H. Nie and J-O Kim (1978), *Participation and Political Equality: A Seven-nation Comparison*, Cambridge: Cambridge University Press.

Verhagen, K. (1987), *Self-help Promotion: A Challenge to the NGO Community*, Amsterdam: Koninkijk Instituut voor de Tropen.

Véron, R. (2001), 'The "New" Kerala Model: Lessons for Sustainable Development', *World Development*, 29, 2, 601-17.

Viramma, J.R. and J.L Racine (1997), *Viramma: Life of an Untouchable*, Paris: UNESCO Publishing.

Visweswaran, K. (1988), 'Illegal Slum Evictions in Madras City: The Case of Wallace Garden', *Economic and Political Weekly*, XXIII, 41: 2097-99.

Ward, P., ed. (1989), *Corruption, Development and Inequality: Soft Touch or Hard Graft?*, London: Routledge.

Werna, E. (2001), 'Shelter, Employment and the Informal City in the Context of the Present Economic Scene: Implications for Participatory Governance', *Habitat International*, 25: 209-27.

Wiebe, P.D. (1981), *Tenants and Trustees: A Study of the Poor in Madras*, New Delhi: Macmillan.

Wils, F. and A.H.J. Helmsing (2001), 'Enabling Communities and Markets: Meanings, Relationships and Options in Settlement Improvement', *Institute of Social Studies Working Papers*, no. 335, The Hague: ISS.

Wit, J. de (1989), 'Clientelism, Competition and Poverty: The Ineffectiveness of Local Organizations in a Madras Slum', in F. Schuurman and T. van Naerssen, eds., *Urban Social Movements in the Third World*, London: Routledge, pp. 63-90.

Wit, J.W. de (1993), 'Poverty, Policy and Politics in Madras Slums: Dynamics of Survival, Gender and Leadership' (Ph.D. thesis, Free University), Amsterdam: Centrale Huisdrukkerij Vrije Universiteit.

Wit, J.W. de and J.M. de Bruin (1994), *Grassroots Level Initiatives and Sustainable Development*, Indo Dutch Programme on Alternatives in Development Research Proposal.

Wit, J.W. de (1996), *Poverty, Policy and Politics in Madras Slums: Dynamics of Survival, Gender and Leadership*, New Delhi: Sage.

—— (1997), 'Decentralization, Empowerment and Poverty Alleviation in Urban India: Roles and Responses of Government, NGOs and Slum Communities', *Institute of Social Studies Working Paper*, no. 267, The Hague, ISS.

World Bank (1988), *World Development Report 1988*, The International Bank for Reconstruction and Development/The World Bank, Oxford University Press.

—— (1997), *Primary Education in India: World Bank II Series: Development in Practice*, Washington DC: The World Bank.

—— (1998), *Reducing Poverty in India: Options for More Effective Public Services*, A World Bank Country Study, Washington DC: The International Bank for Reconstruction and Development/The World Bank.

—— (1998/99), *World Development Report 1998/99*, The International Bank for Reconstruction and Development/The World Bank: Oxford University Press.

—— (2000), *World Development Report 2000/2001: Attacking Poverty*, Oxford University Press.

—— (2001), *Voices of the Poor: Listen to the Voices* [online], World Bank Poverty Net, Available from: <http://www.worldbank.org/poverty/voices/listen-findings.h> [accessed in December 2001].

Wratten, E. (1995), 'Conceptualizing Urban Poverty', *Environment and Urbanization*, 7, 1: 11-36.

Yap Kioe Sheng (1990), 'Community Participation in Low-income Housing Projects: Problems and Prospects', *Community Development Journal*, 25, 1: 56-65.

WEBSITES

<*http:*//www.tn.gov.in/tnassembly/ministers.ht> [accessed in February 2001].

<*http:*//www.geocities.com/Rainforest/vines/5740/14asbest.html> [accessed in March 2002].

<*http:*//www.unchs.org/scp/scphome.htm> [accessed in December 2001].

<*http:*//www.niua.org/USH/index.html> [accessed in November 2001].

<*http:*//www.cmdachennai.org> [accessed in February 2007].

Index